Advance Praise for *Got Social Mediology? Using Psychology to Master Social Media for Your Business Without Spending a Dime*

"In this eloquent and informative guide to social media, Jay Izso explains exactly how to make social media work for your business. Packed with practical ideas and applications for each of the major social media platforms, he doesn't just tell you what to do, he explains exactly why it will work. Anyone who is concerned that they might not be maximizing their company's online presence should read this book."

~**Philip Graves**, author of the Amazon Top Ten Best Business book, *Consumer.ology*

"In *Got Social Mediology?* Jay Izso explores the intersection of social media, psychology and business. Along the way, he describes what works and what doesn't in social media, details the unique culture of each social media platform, punctures a few myths, and makes a convincing case that social media, when used correctly, present some of the greatest marketing and business-growth opportunities in history. One of the most insightful, and somehow comforting, conclusions of this interesting, fun-to-read book is that despite how scary and overwhelming social media can be, they simply are a new manifestation of an age-old human reality: It's all about personal connections."

~**Steve Eisenstadt**, Eisenstadt Communications, High-Tech Communications Consultant & Former Senior PR Manager, External Relations, IBM

"While the majority of experts are satisfied to explain social media for business simply through its technology, Izso goes deeper, unveiling the intersection between user and technology: psychology! In a book packed with up-to-date research and illustrative stories, Izso artfully blends his expertise in *both* technology and psychology to provide the reader with a practical set of guidelines for turning customers on to your business through authentic interactions on social media."

~ **Alex Charfen**, CEO, Charfen Institute, an *Inc.* 500 Fastest Growing Companies

"Everyone wants to know how to effectively use social media for their business, which this book covers quite well. What Izso brings to the table in a way I've not seen or read before is the 'why'...why should you use one platform over another, why do people post, and why are some attempts at winning business through social media successful and others not so much. The 'how' is much easier when you are clear about the 'why,' and this book spells that out for readers in a way that's not only crystal clear, but a fun read to boot."

~ **Patrick Lilly,** The Patrick Lilly Real Estate Team
Wall Street Journal Top 100 Real Estate Teams in the United States

Got Social Mediology?

Got Social Mediology?

Using Psychology to Master Social Media for Your Business Without Spending a Dime

Jay Izso

First published by InterAction Press

First Edition

7300 Six Forks Road
Raleigh, NC 27615
Tel: 919-369-2121
www.interaction-press.com

Cover Design: Dunn+Associates, www.dunn-design.com
Cover Photography: David Williams, Pro Photographer & Cinematographer
Interior Design: Jerry Dorris, StyleMatters, www.style-matters.com

Library of Congress Control Number: 2014905880

ISBN 978-0-9915136-0-4 (hardback) – ISBN 978-0-9915136-1-1 (paperback) –
ISBN 978-0-9915136-2-8 (ebook)

Printed in the United States of America on acid-free paper
14 15 16 17 18 19 10 9 8 7 6 5 4 3 2 1

To the entrepreneur and small business owner,
who take risks without knowing what the future holds
and to my wife, Linda, whose faith in me makes me
feel like I can run through brick walls

Contents

Introduction

The term *social media marketing* begs plenty of questions. Can social media make money for your business? If you are an entrepreneur or business owner, that really is the first question, isn't it? The answer is simply "yes." The second question is, How do you use social media to make money for your business? The answer is found in the pages of this book. The final question you may be asking is how much social media is going to cost you. The answer is that it does not have to cost you one thin dime! The approach shared in this book shows you why.

So here we are in a social media world. You've seen the hype. You have been invited to attend the world's greatest social media marketing seminar, to pay for premium services on LinkedIn, or to advertise on Facebook. Chances are that you also have a profile on one or more of the social media platforms and that you've at least dabbled in them for your business; some of you may be using them regularly or paying someone to do so on your company's behalf. Regardless of which of these categories you fall into, the question for most of you is the same: Can social media really help your business? In this book, I show you that it can through the power of something I call *social mediology* (social media + psychology).

Let me explain. I am both a business consultant (the Internet Doctor) and a teacher of psychology. As I began to experiment with social media over the past decade as a business consultant while also teaching psychology, these two worlds started to merge. Everywhere I looked on social media, I saw yet another example of how psychology could explain what was going on with the people interacting there; it became clearer and clearer to me that psychology could provide insight into how people could behave on these platforms to increase their chances of business success. Thereby, social mediology was born.

Social mediology is a new term and so is much of the social media technology, but please don't be put off by that reality. Using social media to build your business is not nearly as complicated a process or even as new of an experience as many think it to be. In the end, the true power of social media comes from the way in which it can help you build relationships with people—people who can do business with you and who can tell others why they should do business with you too. It's not all that different from the way many businesses became successful over the past century. I only have to think back to my own parents, who were entrepreneurs in the mid-1950s to 1960s, to see how.

Mary Ann and Julius Izso were the proud owners of a "sweet shop" in Fords, New Jersey. That successful sweet shop on the corner of St. Georges Road and Clum Avenue sold sandwiches, ice cream, candy, baked goods, newspapers, and a few emergency grocery items. People came from nearby towns to eat, socialize, and simply have a place where they knew the owners and felt that they were getting good food at a fair price, whether they were partaking in the sixty-five-cent "Izso's Perkburger," a thirty-cent milkshake, or, my dad's favorite, the fifty-cent Royal Banana Split.

As business owners, the secret to my mom and dad's success was not advertising but building relationships. To support the people they knew, my mom and dad would show up at a kid's ballgame, a family birthday party, or a charitable event. My dad knocked on doors in the neighborhood to let folks know about the sweet shop and ended up having good conversation and a soda in people's kitchens. He also made friends with everyone at the local Liberty Tavern Restaurant. Before long, folks were telling others that they needed to check out Julius and Mary Ann's sweet shop for its great food and friendly owners. In cultivating these authentic relationships, my parents created a group of people who told others about their store. By building relationships, my mom and dad built a business.

Now move ahead some fifty years later, to a time when many people feel like the days of personal relationships are over. In fact, it may even feel to those of you who have been in business that technology is ruling the day. In reality, only part of that is true. Yes, technology can help your business, but you must remember that it is a tool, not the be-all, end-all, for success. More specifically, technology is there to help you conduct business, not to make the sales for your business. You have to turn your computer on and do something with it to achieve anything; the same goes for your tablet, laptop, phone system, computer software, any online tools you subscribe to, and, yes, social media. Technology may facilitate business, but technology, for the most part, does not win you business: Your interactions with other people do. It does not matter if your organization is B2B (business to business) or B2C (business to consumer); the fact of the matter is that everything is P2P (person to person), as word about your business naturally spreads from individual to individual through conversation.

In this book, I take you on a journey through social mediology that will remind you about the power relationships have to build your business. Together, we walk through the key psychological principles you can follow to turn your social media followers into purchasers and evangelizers of your products and services, not because you are manipulating them but because you are sharing an authentic piece of yourself and building strong personal and professional relationships with them via social media.

My parents gave me a great gift that I can pass along to you. The key to business success—creating relationships with your customers—really is not a secret. The way in which and the places where these relationships develop have changed; social media venues are virtual places to build authentic relationships with real people, who come to know you, like you, and—yes!—trust you and your business. So grab your cup of coffee or hot tea, pour yourself a glass of cold cranberry juice like I like to do on warm North Carolina days, or maybe have a glass of wine or your favorite beverage. Join me on this journey. I think you will learn to enjoy the world of social media, if you don't already, and the many ways that it will allow you to connect with others and truly benefit your business.

Stay successful, my friends!

Jay Izso, the Internet Doctor

How to Read This Book

I encourage you to read this book any way that you like—really! The first three chapters lay a nice foundation for the social media approach I am suggesting for business owners, but you can also get plenty out of the book by jumping ahead to those chapters that feel most relevant to you.

For example, if you care most about LinkedIn, feel free to focus on that chapter this month and then come back to the Facebook chapter six months from now when you are ready to direct more time and attention there. (If you bump into any terms you don't recognize while reading a later chapter, feel free to check out the index for a guide to where a term is first mentioned in the book.) You can also gather a quick snapshot of the material covered in each chapter by reading the Low-down summary provided at the end of the chapter.

For those of you interested in gleaning as much social media knowledge as you can from these pages, take your time and enjoy the process. You will find supplemental, grey call-out boxes (like this one) to augment what is being shared in the chapters, as well as hands-on exercises (denoted by a "Try This!" and light bulb graphic) to bridge the gap between the book and your real business life. Whatever approach you choose to use to read this book, enjoy the ride, and please feel free to send feedback to jay@socialmediology.com to let me know how this book has worked for you!

Why Are We Here?

> How can you squander even one more day not taking advantage of the greatest shifts of our generation? How dare you settle for less when the world has made it so easy for you to be remarkable?
>
> —Seth Godin

Likes, comments, shares, pins, tweets, updates, +1s, oh my! Whether you have been in business one day or fifty years, you cannot escape social media. Chances are you have a friend, business associate, or employee who talks about social media and raves about how great it is. If this is not enough, you have probably received an e-mail or six about including social media as part of your business marketing plan.

Everywhere you look, social media surrounds you. Turn on the news and it is there as the local newscaster and weather person have this @ symbol in front of their names with a little blue bird indicating that you can follow them on Twitter. Read your favorite newspaper or magazine and you will find a request to "Like us on Facebook" or "Follow us on Twitter," or you will be asked to take a picture of the QR code with your phone to automatically connect with its Facebook page or other social media account. Go to your local restaurant and you will see people with their phones taking pictures of their food and then typing with great fervor something to be sent out to who knows whom through some social media platform.

Is this state of affairs overwhelming? Yes. Is it confusing? It can be. Do you have some emotional reaction when you hear words like *Facebook, Twitter, LinkedIn, Google+,* or *Pinterest*? Sure you do. You may love it or detest it, but very few people feel absolutely neutral about social media.

Social Media Personalities

Whether you are an entrepreneur, social media manager, or techie, you may find yourself falling somewhere along the following spectrum of social media types, from using social media all the time to using social media rarely or in bursts, from loving social media to outright despising it. Here are the types I've observed.

- **Social Media Heartthrob:** You love social media; it is part of your day; and, as a matter of fact, it is hard not to think about it. You tweet or update your status regularly, and you thoroughly enjoy the updates of others. You retweet, like, and comment throughout the day. Social media is now a normal part of life, and it is hard to imagine living without it.

- **Social Media Traveler:** You like social media, but it is not your whole world. You will be social in spurts. Some days you are tremendously active, and other days you are not. You pay attention for the most part, but your usage is more sporadic. You are not really sure how to use it for business, but you are open to the potential.
- **Social Media Fly on the Wall:** Social media is okay. You do not really want to say much on social media and you are not necessarily a fan of the social media interaction, but you enjoy reading what people have to say and keeping up with the goings-on of your family and friends. When it comes to social media and business, the jury is still out.
- **Social Media Benchwarmer:** You have been on social media for quite a while, but you have been hesitant to get into the game because, quite frankly, you feel like you need more information before you get yourself fully involved. You are very open to the possibilities; you're just unsure of whether it's a real fit for your business and marketing routine.
- **Social Media Rookie:** You recently created a profile. You are not sure what you are doing, and you're hoping that someone will show you the right way to do this thing they call social media that will make a difference for your business. You think there is at least a chance that it can work for you.
- **Social Media Investor:** You look at social media as a means to an end. You spend money on it as far as advertising goes, but you are not going to tell someone that you had a great lunch or like the post about their

new puppy. For you, it is nothing but a necessary marketing evil.

- **Social Media Curmudgeon:** Social media be damned. You are not getting involved, and you are not even sure why you are reading this book. You see social media as having little to zero impact on your business. You shake your head at those who use it or tout its virtues. To you, it is a wasteland for nonsense and stupidity. Not only do you not see the possibilities, but you have already closed yourself off to considering them. Quite frankly, I am surprised you're still reading this book, but I am glad that you are hanging in there with me.

I am firmly convinced that there is something in this book for everyone. If you are a Social Media Heartthrob, you will find ways to interact with others on social media that you may have not considered before. Rookies and Benchwarmers, I give you practical ideas for getting into the social media world without having to worry if you did the right thing. I also simplify this whole process by giving you tips that can make your posts more interactive.

Travelers and Flies on the Wall, I give you a reason to stop and interact in these cultures in a safe way, teaching you to speak the language and understand the customs. Investors, I show you a different way—a way to glean benefits for you and your business that are free through your interactions, not acquired through payments.

Finally, Curmudgeon, because you are still reading, I may not change your mind, but I at least provide you with enough information to get this whole social media world to make sense. Furthermore, you won't have to use all of this information, but you may find that some of it can be especially useful and productive when you have a clearer understanding of how it can help you accomplish some of your professional goals.

Without Spending a Dime? Yep, Really

Like most people who are in business, when considering this world of social media, you probably have several questions. Perhaps one is, "What is social media?" Maybe another is, "Why social media?" However, there are two questions that I, as an expert in the field, am asked especially frequently. The first is, "Can social media make money for my business?" The second is related to the first: "How much is this going to cost?" I will answer them in order: "Yes" and "It doesn't have to cost you a physical dime." It may cost a little time (and not as much as you think) but, as we are about to see, to make social media work for your business, you do not have to increase your marketing budget by even a dollar to have a positive effect on your business bottom line.

At this point, you may be saying to yourself, "How is it possible?" First, as of today, you can sign up for all of these social media platforms for free. Second, I will show you that by understanding the psychology of the user and the culture of each platform, you can interact on these platforms in the right way, resulting in new customers bringing actual dollars to your business.

Social media represents a rare, free opportunity available to the entrepreneur and small business owner that can help create a brand, build rapport with a variety of people, establish credibility, demonstrate your knowledge, build trust, and create evangelists that lead to referrals. Today, a business can be built from nothing to successful through these free social media platforms. I am not talking about something that is all that foreign to business. When you are in business, it is not long before you hear the phrase, "You need to network." You probably have attended chamber of commerce events, shown up for a meet-up, or joined a local rotary or business club. Social media is very much the same concept, except you can network from your favorite chair via your computer or tablet or on the go with your smartphone. This amazing world of social media will allow you to connect with more people in a more personal way in less time than you can ever accomplish face-to-face, on the phone, or through an e-mail, with the bonus that you can do it in your pajamas.

What is more, many of these platforms also make available opportunities to keep up with the latest news from your area of expertise. In some cases, these social media platforms are like having free mini-conferences where you can learn how to improve the way you do business and increase your bottom line. However, what is even better, rather than just sitting in an audience of several hundred or a thousand where your voice or question may not be heard, you now have a platform from which you can have your questions answered. Or, perhaps even more powerful, you can establish yourself as the person that has the answers by responding to the questions of others, demonstrating your professional credibility in the view of large audiences. And you didn't even have to pull out your credit card.

What's in This Book for You?

Real questions surround social media. My goal is to answer these questions, in particular, to clarify the value of social media, educate you on how best to use social media for your business, reduce any social media–related stress, and make sense of the mess. How will I do this? First, I want to help you see that social media platforms are not merely tech tools but instead the home of living, breathing, human *cultures*. Each platform represents a group of people who have come together to create a unique culture with its own language and set of unwritten rules, norms, and expectations.

Second, I will help you understand that these social media platforms are a unique form of media and must be treated differently than traditional media of the past. Until this point in time, the vast majority of media has been unidirectional, going one way. For example, TV, radio, newspapers, and magazines are all forms of media that speak at you, without you being able to speak back. In contrast, social media is bidirectional, with people communicating and speaking to you and you speaking back. Social media is all about interaction, which makes it different from any form of media that has come before it.

Third, I am going to show you some invaluable psychological principles that will make you more effective in social media regardless of your industry, your work role, or your current social media expertise. It's what I call *social mediology*, the study of social media from the perspective of psychology. The term is further defined as follows:

> Social mediology is the study of social media from the perspective of psychology. The focus is on understanding the individuals and groups that make each social media platform a unique culture. Studying, researching, and understanding the behavior of the people that use and interact on these platforms can provide the primary key to success, both personally and commercially, on these platforms.[1]

Using the approach of social mediology, I will teach you that you only need to worry about one person: the user of the platform. If you understand how the user interacts on the platform—how the user typically likes to be approached and the best way to transform him or her from follower, connection, or friend to client—you will be further ahead of the many people who are trying to leverage social media through traditional marketing methods.

To this end, I will help you understand user motivations and how those motivations play a role in what you do. I will take you through a journey of discovery that will help you decipher fact from fiction and put you on the most beneficial and effective path when it comes to mixing social media with business.

Fourth, I will educate you, business owners and entrepreneurs, in a way that will enable you to ask the right questions and to challenge the "experts" and "gurus," so you cannot be duped into spending a great deal of money for a return that does not make your wallet any fatter. I am convinced that by the end of this book, you will have a clearer understanding of social media that will help you make better judgments when it comes to using it.

Finally, throughout this book, I will offer you practical and effective ways to interact on social media platforms—without spending a physical dollar—that will benefit you, your business, and those you interact with both personally and professionally. That's the fun of social media—you can grow your business, help others, and enjoy the ride along the way.

Does Social Media Really Matter?

Now that we know who this book is meant to support, let's explore the inevitable question, Does social media really matter? Well, it depends on whom you ask.

A key study conducted by IBM on the value of social media to business points in one direction.[2] In this study, IBM analyzed where the sales came from on one of the biggest shopping days of the year, Black Friday, in 2012. What IBM's researchers found may or may not surprise you. Of all of the online sales that were measured by the IBM Analytics BenchMark Social Summary, social media could be credited with *less than half of one percent* of sales! In other words, social media efforts by the businesses surveyed appeared to generate very little revenue.

Yet, a look at some of the small businesses around the country points in the other direction.

Jeff Snell, CEO of Enlign Business Brokers, credits winning a multimillion dollar account partly to his LinkedIn presence.

Jen Hankin of Joint Venture Jewelry gets positive feedback from customers who enjoy modeling new products and seeing their photos posted on social media. These same customers tell their friends to check out their photos online, which gets them looking at Joint Venture's products.

Realtor Linda Craft has sold homes to people who walked through her door and shared that they wanted to do business with her because of what she had posted on her personal Facebook page.

Although the IBM study seems pretty damning, it's hard to ignore stories like those recounted above, which remind us that social media can be a free way of creating brand awareness as well as garnering direct and referral business.

What is the truth? Is social media working for businesses today, or is it just a drain of time, energy, and money with very little return? From what I have seen with my clients over the years and in some of the research I explore in this book, it appears that social media can, in fact, be effective—very effective—for businesses. The problem is that many companies are using social media in the wrong ways, focusing on traditional marketing techniques rather than genuine interaction.[3] I have to wonder whether the companies analyzed in the Black Friday report by IBM were among this group that is focusing on doing things the way they always have done them rather than on understanding that social media provides entirely different, human-driven, bidirectional platforms that require marketers to use a different set of principles and to develop a different set of psychological skills.

What we're talking about here is a real problem within the social media marketing world with regard to what is measured and where marketing energy is focused. Likes, endorsements, followers, impressions, and click-throughs: It's not that any of these are bad. The question is, Are they enough? When someone likes your Facebook business page, follows you on Twitter, or endorses your profile on LinkedIn, what does that really mean for your business? Does a like or a follow really put one more dollar in your pocket? How would you know? Does it mean that these individuals are interacting with you or that they will in the future? Does it mean that they will eventually buy from you or tell all their friends about you? The answer is that likes, endorsements, and followers alone mean nothing. It is only when you are out there building on those pieces, creating a real connection with potential clients, that something powerful can happen for your business. That connection begins with having meaningful *conversation*. And not just a conversation: conversation that's friendly, personal, sometimes fun, and definitely genuine. Notice I did not say *promotional* or *self-promotional*. Promotion is part of the old way of marketing for other mediums, and it doesn't have the same positive benefit on social media.

A Radical Shift: From Promotional to Personal

Why does a personal approach work on social media, even for businesses, which are used to being both professional and promotional? We have to understand the reasons why people are on social media in the first place: to engage with others, to be validated for who they are, and to enjoy the resulting positive emotions that lead to a sense of validation. Social media will always be *social* first and *media* second.

What is more, if we think about what traditionally makes small business so successful, it is the personal connection that such businesses are able to establish one person at a time. Through that personal connection, individuals learn to know, like, and trust the person behind the business, typically the business owner, and the relationship transforms from a personal relationship to a business relationship. In fact, it almost appears as if they fall in love with the idea of doing business with that person behind the business, and their loyalty is such that they wouldn't dream of doing business with anyone else. They go from being a consumer, or even a customer, to a coveted *client*. What's the difference? Although these are not the strict business definitions of *consumer, customer,* and *client,* I differentiate them on the basis of my practical observations of the behavior of each. First, customers come and go; maybe they buy, perhaps they do not. Consumers are in the market to buy, but they do not always buy from you. Clients buy from you, return to buy more, and tell their friends to do the same. Jackpot!

Let's look at that "know, like, and trust" piece more, because it's a theme you're going to hear about throughout this book. Here's how it works: Clients become clients because they trust you and your business. To get their trust, you need those people to actually like you and your business. For people to like you and your business, they have to come to know you. To know you, you must have genuine conversations that move beyond business into the personal. When I trust you as a person, I am far more likely to trust your business. It is obvious, right? If it came down to a comparison of who you would want do business with—a person you trust or a person you do not trust—which one are you going to choose? I think we all know the answer. Trust, then, is at the very heart of the issue. Here is where social media has a tremendous benefit. There is no other place where you can reach more people in the shortest amount of time and develop real relationships than the world of social media.

Although the medium is new, the concept is not. We have been doing business this way for centuries. Our grandparents, great-grandparents, and past generations understood the basic concepts of "know," "like," and "trust." They understood the psychology of business relationships. They understood that to have a thriving business, they had to know things about the people around them. They knew their clients' children, and they knew many of the struggles and triumphs of the people that were doing business with them. Our long line of entrepreneurial relatives knew that if their grocery store, barbershop, dental office, or other such establishment was going to survive, they needed to have a personal relationship with others, because once people trust you, you have a customer for life and positive word of mouth. It was that important.

Now consider the situation today. What is the one advantage that social media can give a business? Social media now gives business owners the opportunity to build personal relationships that transform into business relationships, much as they did for our business forefathers. On social media, you, as a business owner, have the opportunity to develop relationships that focus on knowing people, having them like you, and building trust, so that the clients believe in you and the way you conduct business. What is more, these social media platforms, which have more than a billion people on them, can become an amazing vehicle for word-of-mouth marketing. And word of mouth is *free*.

As you develop these relationships on these platforms, you and your brand will start to extend way beyond your local store. You and your business will start to inhabit lands you never have considered or dreamed of, simply because friends have friends, followers have followers, and connections have connections. It is amazingly exciting! Social media provides many possibilities.

However, developing these relationships is not always easy. Furthermore, although they may be free monetarily, they do take time. But, in the end, your efforts are worth it for your financial success and your business future. You will discover, as many businesses (including my own!) have found, that these social media personal relationships developed one person at a time are critical to business success. The bottom line: People are on social media to connect with others, not to be sold to. If you respect that reality and play within its cultural norms and guidelines—as a genuine participant, not as a lurker or a promoter or a bloodsucker—you and your business will be rewarded with clients who will buy from you for a lifetime and tell everyone they know that you are someone worthy of doing business with.

Social Media's Secret Weapon: Converting Customers and Consumers to Clients

Many businesspeople would likely agree that at the heart of any marketing venture is the goal of turning business prospects into paying clients. We want to turn browsers into purchasers—to convert potential buyers into actual buyers. Social media is the ideal venue in which to help this conversion take place. With its relationship focus and the ease with which it allows for consistent connection and follow-up, social media will allow you to win clients, not just consumers or customers. Knowing the difference will help you attract the right kind of individuals to your business, as well as to appreciate how effective social media can be.[4]

The *customer* is the broadest of all categories. Anyone who walks through your business doors, calls you on a phone, texts you, or has an interaction with you (even if it is only to investigate or ask for information) is a customer. Customers are the most expensive to attract to the business because marketing dollars are spent to get their attention with no guarantee of return. The monetary investment represents a numbers game of getting enough clicks or a response to an advertisement to entice enough people through the door of your business so that perhaps one or a few will make a purchase. Customers may not buy, and if they do buy, they may not buy from you.

The *consumer* differs from the customer. The consumer consumes; we know consumers are going to make a purchase, and they regularly do. Their behavior is such that they have every intention of making a purchase; however, they are looking for the right place in which to make their purchase. The consumer is actually in the market, comparing the market, and ready to capitalize on the market when the right opportunity comes. Consumers can be expensive, because trying to develop a strategy that only attracts consumers is difficult. Consumers are far better than customers when it comes to sales, but they are difficult to identify up front and are typically expensive to entice for a business, because it requires enough marketing frequency and time to find the consumer among the customers.

The *client,* however, is unique. The client may have been a customer, but he or she does not have to be; the client is a consumer, but rather than doing any further comparisons within the market, the client is committed to the specific business where he or she makes purchases. Furthermore, the client returns for more from the business and influences his or her friends to use the same business because of the client's dedication and devotion to the business. Clients are the business's best friend, developed out of a continued relationship.

There is no doubt that the huge success of Apple is a direct result of its clients. Apple has created a client connection that has transformed into almost a religion, and its followers are willing to evangelize for Apple for free. If you watch any TV at all, you will see every Apple competitor outspend Apple on marketing and advertising. Apple doesn't have to spend those marketing dollars because their clients do their marketing for them. There is nothing more powerful than to have someone else tell another person about the virtues and values of your business. It is not intrusive, it is not self-serving, it is volunteered, and it costs you nothing as a business. For many businesses, client referrals are the number one source of business, and it is free!

How does this phenomenon occur? Well, certainly, you have to have a product or service that has value. Assuming that you have that value, then it becomes incumbent upon you to build, cultivate, fertilize, and provide a basis for maintaining those relationships. If social media does one thing better and faster than anything else businesses have had available up to this point, it provides a place in which to build relationships and connections. If you were looking for a way to find more clients for your business, social media may, in fact, be one of the most effective and efficient places to create and maintain clients, and without spending marketing dollars.

Got Social Mediology?

Perhaps you are noticing this is not going to be your typical "social media for business" book. This is my intention. Have you noticed my emphasis on psychology rather than technology? Have you detected my cynicism for the traditional ways of businesses operating on social media? In this book, we explore together the new field of social mediology, the study of social media through the psychology of how individuals and groups use the various social media platforms. Sometimes the psychology is similar across the platforms; sometimes it is unique. But one thing is for certain: To successfully grow your business via social media, you need to understand how people behave, create, and maintain a given social media culture, both as individuals and as groups. On our journey through this book and social mediology, we will explore some of the mental processes and behaviors of these individual users and groups on specific social media platforms as well as how these behaviors are similar and/or unique from platform to platform. The fact is, social media platforms are really about people. If no one used them, there would be no platforms, and the technology would no longer be useful or beneficial.

As Mark Zuckerberg, the founder of Facebook, stated,

> All of these problems at the end of the day are human problems... that's one of the core insights that we try to apply to developing Facebook. What [people are] really interested in is what's going on with the people they care about. It's all about giving people the tools and controls that they need to be comfortable sharing the information that they want. If you do that, you create a very valuable service. It's as much psychology and sociology as it is technology.[5]

There is very little I can add to his insightful observation. Psychology is needed to fully understand and make these social media platforms effective for small businesses.

Thus, in this book, we are going to look at effectively using social mediology to benefit your business. Technology may change and marketers may come up with new methods, but the psychology of how people behave and use social media is relatively stable. If you understand the psychology of the user, you will be able to move from simply trying to leverage these social media platforms to actually entering your consumers' world in a way that transforms them into clients that buy from your business, return for more, and refer their friends.

Why People Love Social Media

Psychology tells us a lot about social media, including why people are motivated to use it. For example, in 2011, Kennon Sheldon from the University of Missouri discovered that people who used Facebook more frequently felt more connected with other people.[6] This connectedness is extremely important. We all seem to look for a way to connect to others and stay connected. You may be from the school of "I make my friends the old-fashioned way, through face-to-face relationships," but the world has changed. Many relationships are being developed in a digital world, a place where I never have to see your face to feel a connection with you.

Other studies have demonstrated that social media may give people an ego boost, and others have found that—wait for it—there may be a narcissistic component to why people like social media. That is, we like talking about ourselves. Some psychologists have even suggested that narcissism and social media go hand in hand. Although society may see this as a negative, it actually helps us understand how to better interact with the users of these platforms, and that is extremely beneficial.

Social media can also become very addictive for people. A recent study conducted at Harvard University found through brain MRIs that self-disclosure on sites such as Facebook and Twitter provide people with stimulation similar to that experienced during sex.[7] The study went so far as to demonstrate that people would rather talk about themselves than receive money!

If you have ever viewed a Facebook or Twitter timeline, you know they are dominated by the little words *I* and *me.* It is no wonder that so many people are receiving diagnoses of what many are calling *social media addiction.* I can talk about me and not only get an intrinsic benefit from my brain, but if you like or comment on my post, I get an extrinsic reward. I get positive reinforcement for talking about me, from the inside of me and the outside of me. It is double reinforcement. It just doesn't get any better than that.

It is interesting that the same areas in the brain that light up when we have food, water, or sex or when we engage in addictions also light up when we are active on social media. In particular, we have a chemical in the brain known as dopamine. It is our happy chemical, and when we do or see things that we enjoy (e.g., talk about ourselves on social media), this chemical is released in these specific areas of the brain, which acts as reinforcement for that behavior. This makes us want to do the same or similar things again to produce this happy, almost euphoric feeling.

So whether it's sex or social media, we humans have a natural predisposition to go back for more. As a business owner, it might be folly to ignore a realm in which some of your potential clients will not just play once but predictably go back to time and again.

The fact remains that people use social media, like it, and don't want to give it up. These very same people are your potential clients. If people are in these social media worlds and getting so much from it, it only follows that when you become part of that world, you contribute to their emotional and mental well-being. In turn, they will grow to know, like, and trust you, opening up opportunities for you to do business together as well as with their friends.

In Sum: Social Media Can Benefit Your Business

Statistics and research studies are informative, yes. But I suspect that if you are a business owner or entrepreneur, in the end, you care most about the practical value of social media. Really, what's the point of spending your time there? Is it truly worth the time and effort? As I close this chapter, let's take a quick look at what some of the key benefits of social media are (with more to come on the benefits in Chapter 8) so you can get a better sense of whether and how this social media thing might be right for you and your business.

First, social media can help you develop credibility and influence in a relatively short amount of time. If you are an entrepreneur or small business owner and you have even a small number of followers, connections, and friends, you have the opportunity to demonstrate to these folks that you really are the expert in your industry. Through the words that you use and things that you post on social media, you can start to create credibility among your connections. Whether by posting a business-relevant link on Twitter, creating valuable content on Google+ that leads to higher search-engine optimization, or providing a useful answer to a question posed by someone in your LinkedIn group, you can position yourself as a thought leader to all those who know you in the social media sphere. What is more, you can become not just credible but an *influencer*—someone who affects other people's opinions, thoughts, beliefs, and even buying decisions.

When you influence others, they may, in turn, influence still others to follow you or even use your product or service. The key is to be able to interact with these influencers in a genuine and real way so they feel good not only about you but about what you represent, namely, your business. The bottom line here is that social media platforms are influential places. It is more and more commonplace for people to ask their friends on Facebook or Twitter where to shop, eat, buy insurance, or invest in real estate rather than do the research on a search platform. Search is not going away by any means, but if you want to make sure your business is a part of those friendly conversations on social media, you need to be part of it.

Second, social media can be a no-cost addition to your current marketing strategy. Regardless of what anyone else may tell you, the solutions and examples I am going to present to you for social media do not have to cost you actual marketing dollars to be effective, other than time spent. I do not advocate that you pay for ads or upgrade to a paid version of your social media account. As a matter of fact, if you are spending money on social media advertising as an entrepreneur or small business, you may be getting some potential business, but at a great cost, when there is a better way. The culture of social media is about real interaction, not business promotion, so paying for publicity can actually tarnish your image with clients rather than burnish it. In this book, I explore many of the ways to connect with others on social media for free that are more likely to grow your business than paying for ads ever will.

Finally, and most important, social media provides a way to truly interact with people like no other prior platforms have, helping businesses to generate and maintain clients. There is no other place where you can reach more people in as short an amount of time and develop real relationships than in the world of social media. Yes, the world of social media is virtual, but it is also very real. People visit each other on a daily basis and communicate regarding things they care about via social media. Now put that into the business context for a moment: Social media gives you a place to visit with your clients and potential clients on a regular basis and to communicate with them regarding things you and they are passionate about. It's a golden opportunity, and, aside from the time spent, it's completely free.

So whether you are using social media to influence your potential clients, create brand evangelists who tout your business, add a new no-cost marketing tool to your kit, or enjoy an easy way to stay in front of potential sales leads, there are a number of reasons why social media can truly impact your business for the better. As we begin our journey together, it is important that we understand that social media represents a ton of psychology at work. By looking through the lens of social mediology, we learn to understand how people act, react, and interact within the context of social media. We start to understand that each social media platform is unique, has its own culture, and has a different way for individuals to fit into the larger group.

There is so much to discuss, so much to discern. So make sure your tablet, phone, or other reading device is fully charged or you have some Band-Aids ready in case you get a paper cut from your book. Let our journey into social media begin!

The Lowdown

- People are on social media to connect with others, not to be sold to. If you respect that reality, you and your business will be rewarded.
- Paid marketing can be expensive and an unnecessary way to leverage social media for small business. Staying connected to clients, who are often your best source of referrals, is quite effective on social media and won't cost you a dime.
- People are motivated to use social media because it allows them to feel connected, gives them a place to talk about themselves, and makes them feel good.
- Social mediology is the study of social media from the perspective of psychology. By studying, researching, and understanding the behavior of the people that use and interact on these platforms, we can provide the primary key to both personal and commercial success on social media.
- Customers are individuals who may or may not buy, whereas consumers will purchase but may or may not buy from you. Clients are those who will only buy from you, will come back for more, and will refer their friends to you, and clients are who you want. Social media provides one of the best ways to develop and stay in touch with clients regularly while not being intrusive.
- Social media has value for you, the business owner, because it's free, lets you build credibility and influence others, and gives you a unique way to stay in front of your audience on a daily basis.

Debunking the Social Media Myths

Beware of false knowledge; it is more dangerous than ignorance.

—George Bernard Shaw

When it comes to social media and business, uninformed opinions and half-truths run wild. How often have you heard "I'm too old to use it," "No one ever got a client on social media," and, my personal favorite, "Social media is only for kids"? Many people are walking around with ironclad ideas on social media without ever questioning whether they are actually true. I hope to have you thinking twice the next time one of these beliefs comes up, because one of these notions may be the myth that stops you from getting the most out of social media. Do any of the following sound familiar?

- "Social media is just a passing fad, not a business tool."
- "Social media takes way too much time."
- "People with money aren't on social media."
- "My clients don't use social media so I don't need to play there."
- "My business is doing fine without it, so I don't need it."

Or, the opposite sentiment:

- "Social media is the total answer to success for any business."
- "To be successful, I have to use all of the social media platforms."

You've probably heard some of these strongly held if unsubstantiated beliefs, and chances are you may even hold one or more of them yourself. What each of these statements holds in common is an absolute view of the value of social media, in one direction or the other: Social media is either pointless or it's the best thing since sliced bread. Where does the truth lie? If you're going to get anywhere using social media for business, you'll have to sort through these myths to discern falsehood from reality.

MYTH 1: Social Media Is a Passing Fad, So My Business Does Not Need It

This may be the single most believed myth that people use to excuse themselves from using social media in their business. They argue that social media is just a pop culture trend, like wearing skinny jeans or doing the Macarena. They contend that social media will eventually fade away like leg warmers and fluorescent ski jackets did after the 1980s. Social media may be in today, these individuals say, but it will be gone tomorrow. It's certainly a tidy excuse for not engaging in social media. If the platforms are going to disappear anyway, then there's no reason to invest time or energy in using them.

Where does this passing-fad myth come from? It's generally based on current statistics that suggest that social media is not growing at the fast rate it did during its public inception. All I have to say to this is, "Of course it's not growing as fast—the more people who are on it, the fewer there are available to get on it!" That being said, every platform is experiencing consistent growth, not to mention the explosive growth of new platforms like Pinterest and Google+. Social media's current presence can hardly be ignored.

- Today, more than *one billion people* are using different social media platforms, and social media's presence is still growing.
- According to a Nielson InCite study of social media consumers released in December of 2012, social media continues to see a steady increase in users, brought on mostly by mobile and tablet use.[1]
- According to the same report, there has also been a 24% increase in the time spent on social networks over the same time period from 2011.

It is safe to say that social media is everywhere. The real question now is, is it here to stay? Is social media a case of skinny jeans, inevitably poised to be replaced with the next fashion fad, or is it more like past inventions like the television or the Internet, which have become fixtures of our personal and professional lives? Social media is going to become either cliché, unappealing, and out of date or integrated into the way we conduct our daily lives and run our businesses.

No one knows for sure what tomorrow will bring, but when it comes to social media, I see one very clear reason that points to its staying power: It offers huge personal, emotional, and psychological benefits to its users. In Chapter 1, we looked at some of these benefits, from experiencing pleasure akin to eating good food, having sex, or receiving an ego boost. Social media also offers a convenient place to connect and relate with other people. It enables us to be thousands of miles away from friends and family and yet have a feeling of personal connection.

Psychologists have talked about the importance of "weak ties" and "strong ties" when it comes to different types of relationships and how the strength of these ties influences the individuals in a relationship. Tie strength is simply the strength of the connections between people. Social media allows us to stay connected with those whom we already have strong ties—those we have a great deal in common with and that we trust. Just as important, social media gives us an opportunity to take a weak-tie relationship and, over the course of regular communication, develop it into a strong tie. Simply by being personally social, we have the potential to develop strong interpersonal relationships that create trust in who we are that can translate into trust of what we represent within our businesses.

In times past, this relationship development could have only been done via face-to-face contact; however, social media has certainly demonstrated that we can bridge that same gap without face-to-face communication. Clearly, this is one of the greatest benefits that social media gives us. What is more, we are now able to develop these stronger ties with more people nearly simultaneously. With all of these enticing benefits, social media is *reinforcing*. In other words, the more a person uses social media, the more he or she experiences its benefits; the more he or she experiences its benefits, the more he or she wants to use social media.

As a result of its reinforcing nature, people are unlikely to let their social media go. Sure, the platforms may change, but if anything was to be learned from the mass departure from MySpace, it's that people will migrate to some other social media platform to get their social connection (i.e., their reinforcement)—they won't drop social media altogether. When you get tired of shopping on a certain website, do you leave the Internet entirely? Doubtful. Most of us simply move to the latest and greatest online shopping platform. The fact is, like the Internet, social media is not going away. Even if Google+ overtakes Facebook or a new and exciting alternative social platform is born, the Pandora's box of social media has been opened, and users will likely keep going back for more.

"Fine," you may say, "social media may not be going anywhere, but that doesn't mean my business needs it." I've heard this before, and my answer may surprise you. Let me demonstrate with an actual story from a cocktail party at a local business owner's residence that I had the honor of attending with my wife, alongside a very exclusive list of highly successful business owners. As with most of these types of events, I started mingling with people; eventually, as the conversations continued, the inevitable question came out: "So, what do you do for a living?" Once I explained that I am the Internet Doctor and gave my thirty-second elevator pitch about how I help businesses both online and face-to-face, the emotional tone of the conversation changed.

One of the business owners in the small group I was conversing with raised his voice and said, "I have enough business! Social media isn't going to do a damn thing for me." This argument points to a corollary of Myth 1: "My business does not need social media because I already have plenty of customers."

Having heard this business owner's response quite often, I looked at him and said, "I understand. I wouldn't want you to use social media if you feel so strongly negative about it. There is nothing good that can come from it for you or your business if you choose to do something that you feel has no value." He gave me a puzzled look, as he was sure I was going to climb up on a social media soapbox to defend it to the end, but I didn't. Quite honestly, there is no reason to defend social media in that situation: I wouldn't want business owners to do something that they hated so much that they would use it negatively and undermine their own success.

That being said, the fact of the matter is this: Even if you are very successful today without social media, it's important to be ready for the future. You may have more business than you can handle now. Good for you! However, keep in mind that with every passing year, your next client is getting younger, he or she wants to be communicated with in a far different way, and this is a part of that ever-evolving business communication process. To completely ignore social media or suggest that it has no benefit for you, your business, or your future client is not in the best interest of your business's future. Even if you choose not to use it today, you should learn as much as you can about it, know how people use it, and understand how it interacts with business, because it is not only a part of our culture, but it is growing to be an important part of business. In fact, we are only seeing the beginning of the waves of change regarding how much of business is going to be done on social media: More and more businesses are finding ways to make social media a part of their business plan to connect with current clients, recruit future clients, gain referral business, and enlarge their brand.

Think about this: Did we think that we would eventually read a book on a small device such as a tablet or phone?[2] Did we ever think that Amazon.com, which at one time was simply an online bookseller that people were questioning in terms of profitability, would now be one of the first places that people go to purchase or compare prices for nearly anything? The world of business has been changing and continues to change. To believe in the myth that social media will eventually fade away or that your business does not need it is short-changing yourself and your business. At the very least, you need to know how it works and how it can be effectively used in business so that even if you do not use it today, you are prepared for tomorrow.

Get Real

Embracing the possibilities of social media will take you much further than holding on to any emotional negativity will. Although social media may not be perfect for your business today, it is changing the way much of business is happening. Having a better understanding of social media will clear any fear from your path and prepare you to adjust to trends to come.

MYTH 2: My Client Does Not Use Social Media

One of the biggest reasons I hear from business owners as to why they are not using social media is because they believe that their particular client base is not on social media. There is a sense among many of these folks that their clients are too rich, too busy, too educated, too old, too whatever to be on social media.

This is simply a myth based on something called *illusory correlation*. In psychology, illusory correlation occurs when we take note of specific instances, pair them with other instances, and then arrive at the conclusion that one instance is related to another when, in fact, it is not the case. It is like when you go wash your car and then, as soon as you're done washing it, it rains, and from then on you say, "Every time I wash my car, it rains." It's an overgeneralization about two entirely separate events.

The illusory correlation helps to explain why many people do not use social media as part of a business strategy. First, they may have a few clients who do not use social media, and perhaps these few clients have expressed negative attitudes toward social media. From this experience, the business owner begins to associate social media with the negative client. Next, the business owner concludes, "My clients do not use social media," and the illusory correlation—or myth—is born.

However, facts are facts. When we look at the hard data, we quickly discover that social media is represented by every culture, every age, and every spending profile. As of December 2013, PewInternet.org, an independent research company, reports that nearly 73% of all Internet users are actively using some sort of social media.[3] In addition, 71% of all Internet users use Facebook, and 42% of Internet users use multiple social media platforms.

If you were wondering about age groups, you would be correct in assuming that the highest percentage of social media user are young, with 90% of Internet users between the ages of 18 and 29 years being on social media. However, you may be surprised to know that 78% of 20- to 49-year-olds on the Internet are using social media, and 65% of 50- to 64-year-olds on the Internet are using social media. Oh, and those Baby Boomers 65 years and older? Well, about 46% of them are using social media.

If you are wondering what the financial status is of social media users, suffice it to say that regardless of income level, nearly 75% of every income range is represented, whether it is those making less than $30,000 per year or those making more than $75,000. The same is true across different education levels: Whether Internet users have a GED or PHD, about 75% of them are on social media. What conclusion can we draw from these studies? If your clients use the Internet, nearly three out of four of them are also using social media: male and female, all age groups, of varying education levels and incomes. As a result, you can't ignore social media. Not only is social media growing and expanding, but real buyers, real sellers, and real people with actual money are using it to connect with other people.

We do need to be cautious here, however, where there is some truth in the myth. Not every client is on social media, and some platforms may not have as many of our clients as others, which is why social media is not the only solution when it comes to growing your company. However, it bears repeating: If your clients use the Internet, almost three out of four are using social media. To ignore this or arrive at conclusions that keep you from using social media holds you back from interacting with many of your clients in a space where they are present.

Get Real

Whether you know it or not, many of your customers are, in fact, using social media. Not all of them may be there yet, but almost three quarters of them are on social media if they are already Internet users. This provides you with a prime arena in which to reach them—and in a new and genuine way that goes beyond marketing to creating authentic relationships.

MYTH 3: Social Media Takes Too Much Time

Another big complaint that I hear when people talk about why they don't use social media is "It takes too much time!" These folks have the notion that the people who are using social media are on it twenty-four hours a day, seven days a week; some may even think it is a twenty- to forty-hour-a-week job and that they have to come up with something to say several times a day or hire a full-time employee to manage the job. The faulty belief here is that a business has to post all the time to be successful on social media.

Although it is true that for social media to be effective, it will require you to take some time and to be consistent, that does not mean that you have to spend all or even the majority of your time using it. In fact, if you are spending all of your time on social media, you may be doing something wrong! The truth is that people can actually post too frequently. A study by Econsultancy.com found that the number one reason why people unfollow users on Twitter is because they post too frequently.[4] Additionally, in a study of why consumers subscribe and unsubscribe, ExactTarget found the number one reason why Facebook fans unliked a page was that the brand posted too frequently.[5] These are all signs that some brands and businesses may spend more time posting than they need to. It comes down to the old adage, "It's not how much you say, but what you have to say that is important."

So how much time should you spend on your social media? Great question. You can be effective with social media in two or three 15-minute segments per day for a total of thirty to forty-five minutes a day; depending on your skill level, you might even be able to get the segments down to ten minutes each for a total of twenty to thirty minutes a day. (As I explain later in the book, once a day is not as effective, because it does not give you a chance to respond to comments from others in a timely way.)

Keep in mind, too, that you can do a great deal of your social media exchanges while you are doing something else. There is nothing wrong with having a cup of coffee in the morning while spending fifteen minutes doing an update, commenting on a few posts, and liking several other posts. Then perhaps in the afternoon, when you're finishing up your lunch or you need a break from an intense work task, you can like the response to the post or posts you made earlier in the morning, make a few comments to keep the conversations going, make a few other likes and comments, and move on. Then, if you really fall in love with social media

(Social Media Heartthrobs, you know who you are), in the evening as you wind down, you can take ten to fifteen minutes to perhaps comment on a LinkedIn group discussion, retweet someone, like a few posts, or make comments where necessary. I'm out there using social media about three times a day, but if you are able to connect with it even two times a day, you can grow your connections, build your credibility, and see positive results. You do not have to be on social media *all* the time, or even *most* of the time; you just have to check in, connect, and check out. (See Ch. 9 for tips on how to effectively manage your time on social media.)

Get Real

Social media does not have to be all-consuming. Keep it simple, and remember that there is actually more of a danger of over-posting than under-posting. You also need to keep in mind that not every social network is the most appropriate for your business. True, you have to spend some time on social media for it to work for your business, but you can be extremely effective in 15-45 minute a day. What's more, over time you will become more efficient. Just remember the 3 C's: check in, connect, and check out.

MYTH 4: People with Money Do Not Use Social Media, So Why Bother?

Typically, this myth coincides with the myth that only young people use social media. The logic then follows, "Well, if only kids use it, certainly they have no money to purchase a product or service." Unfortunately, the logic is flawed, partially because I have already demonstrated that all age groups use social media. However, if we take it a step further and look at income levels, we find that not only do a significant portion of medium to upper income individuals use social media, but the very wealthy use social media as well. We shouldn't be surprised at this. When high-end companies like Tiffany & Co., Armani, Porsche, and Maybach have a presence on social media, we should probably pay some attention. These companies, as well as mega-corporations like Samsung, Microsoft, American Express, and L'Oreal, would not spend millions of dollars a year on social media (advertising, etc.) if they had not done their research to make sure that their target market was there as well.[6] Not that we need to simply trust these high-end brands. Let's look at the research.

In 2009, the Luxury Institute conducted a study of wealthy individuals and their social media habits.[7] In this study, the Luxury Institute found that approximately 33% of wealthy individuals used multiple social media platforms, with Facebook being the platform used most often by the most wealthy (assets exceeding one million dollars). What you may be surprised to find out is that many of the wealthy use social media in very much the same way most people do: They tweet, share pictures and video, talk with their friends, and play games on social media websites. I will wait for you to read that last one again. Maybe we do not understand the wealthy as much as we think we do!

If you are still one of the skeptics, you may be saying, "But Jay, that was 2009!" Okay, if the Luxury Institute's finding was not enough, bear in mind that in 2011, *The Wall Street Journal* reported that, according to Fidelity Investments, one third of millionaires were using social media, further emphasizing how the wealthy have a notable presence in the social media world.[8] What's more, *Forbes* magazine released data from a study conducted by the Spectrem Group that demonstrated not only the existence of high wealth users but the reality that this group of users has grown. Here are some of the highlights of that study, with a focus on Facebook use.[9]

- The percentage of Americans making between $100,000 and $1 million per year (the *mass affluent*) that use Facebook jumped from 29% in 2010 to 61% as of the second quarter of 2013.

- The millionaires (those with wealth between $1 million and $5 million) saw an increase in Facebook use from only 26% presence in 2010 to 55% in 2013.
- The super affluent (those with a net worth of $5 million to $25 million) also saw a jump in users from 27% in 2010 to 52% in 2013.

Increases on LinkedIn were also sizable for these groups.

The fact of the matter is that people with money do use social media, and the numbers are increasing. The wealthy and the well-off are connecting with people on social media, and they are getting referrals from their Facebook friends, their LinkedIn connections, and—yes—even their Twitter followers. They are becoming more comfortable with privacy issues and more a part of the online social world, where they are creating content and having real conversations with real people. Do you want to miss such a valuable opportunity to connect with this group? Remember, social media allows you to create relationships with people, not just peddle your product or service.

I certainly understand this particular myth from the business perspective. It comes from folks who mirror image their work ethic and combine that with their belief that real businesspeople or successful individuals do not have the time to play around with social media. I use the term *mirror imaging* because it is a common behavioral response that occurs when we make assumptions about others' behavior. If we believe that our success is a result of our hard work and our no-nonsense, strictly business attitude, then we will believe that others who share our success have the same attitude. When mirror imaging enters the social media and business world, we generally do not believe that people would use social media because, quite frankly, we do not. However, I would suggest to you to put your mirror away; you are not looking at yourself, and, in fact, the wealthy do use social media.

Before we wrap this myth, let's be sure to dispel one more related myth, which I mentioned at the start of this chapter. Just as many of us have this notion that wealthy people don't use social media, we may also have a companion notion that only young people use social media. I've certainly heard this complaint before: "I'm too old for social media." Well, not so fast, my friends! The statistics do not support your beliefs there either.

Try This!

Pause for a moment to think about your own reasons for avoiding social media in your personal or business life. How is your particular myth functioning in keeping you from investing more time in social media? If you let go of this myth, what is one thing you could do differently? Commit to doing that one thing for a week and see what happens. Have your beliefs changed?

Again, Pew Internet performed a study to find out how older adults use the Internet. They reported that from 2009 to 2011, social media use by people over 65 years of age grew 150% and that nearly a third of people over 65 years old use social media.[10] Older adults are using social media more and more every day to connect with old friends, new friends, and family; they are also there to connect with brands, to find discounts, and more. You (and your potential clients) are not too old for social media.

This myth about only young people being on social media might again relate to the problem of mirror imaging. If you are over the age of 35 years (a *digital immigrant*), social media may not be as second nature for you as it is for those under the age of 35 years (the *digital natives*). You don't like it, it feels stupid or awkward, and so you assume everyone else in your age cohort feels the same. Reality check: Just because you personally are uncomfortable on social media does not mean that everyone else your age is avoiding social media as well.

Now that we've gotten that uncomfortable truth out of the way, let me reassure you that these platforms are not designed to be complicated and that you can get over initial fears and hurdles. In fact, they have been designed to be user friendly and fairly intuitive. Once your profile has been set up (and you may need help with that piece), getting your thoughts out there is pretty simple. You simply write a short statement or phrase. True, you will need to connect with friends if you want anyone to see your posts, but all of the platforms make it very easy to search for people you know. You just start typing in someone's name and, voila, the person's name pops up; you send a friend request, follow them, or ask to connect with them; and you are well on your way. True, you will want to know some of the platform's cultural nuances (which I will be talking about later in this book—another benefit of reading it!), but soon you will be fitting in, joining in discussions, making comments, liking, sharing, posting, tweeting; heck, you may even find yourself using Instagram to post your photos to Facebook!

As foreign as social media may feel when you first get started, after a while, it will become very easy, even comfortable. Remember when you first learned to ride a bike? You saw other people do it. You knew you had to get one leg on one side and the other leg on the other, and you knew you had to do this peddling thing and stay balanced at the same time. It was a bit scary and intimidating. However, you got on and probably fell off a few times; you may have even become discouraged and wondered if it was worth the effort, the skinned elbows, and the scraped knees, but you got back on and tried it again. If you are like most of us who now take riding bikes for granted, it may even be hard to remember exactly what happened along the way, but the point is, after trying to balance on the bike over and over again, after mastering how to steer it, after becoming adept enough to go as fast as you could to keep up with your friends, you never thought again just how hard it was to learn to ride. Social media is very much the same way: You will try it, you may get discouraged, you may get frustrated, but keep getting back on. You have friends there, and they are waiting to connect and reconnect with you. What is more, you have opportunities there that you are missing. If you are not riding or writing, you will miss seeing the world from a different point of view.

Get Real

If you thought that social media was only for kids or people with no job and no money, think again. The wealthy are also using social media, and they are a growing segment of social media users. Certainly they are using LinkedIn. According to the previously mentioned Wall Street Journal article, 28% of wealthy people are using LinkedIn, but by far the most popular platform with the wealthy is Facebook. What was once believed about the wealthy being concerned about their privacy is clearly much less of a concern today. Those with money are using social media, they are connecting with people, and they are connecting with businesses. That individual and that business they are connecting with could be you and yours.

MYTH 5: Social Media Is the Silver Bullet for Successful Business

So far, I have examined some of the negative myths that stop people from using social media. But another kind of myth should be considered, too, and that is one that puts social media on a pedestal or that positions it as a sort of Holy Grail. A percentage of social media experts, gurus, and marketers have been bold enough to claim that social media will not only bring your business great riches but will also turn an ailing business around quickly. Unfortunately, when it comes to any business, there are no silver bullet solutions that will make it immediately more profitable, and I don't want you to fall prey to anyone who promises you that it can. Silver bullets do not exist. As a matter of fact, there are only two types of people who ever had use for a silver bullet: werewolf hunters and a fictional character called the Lone Ranger, and the Lone Ranger still had a horse named Silver and a sidekick called Tonto who bailed him out on many occasions. This is not to say that social is not beneficial; it can be very beneficial, but it is not a quick-fix solution for your business.

The key to social media for business is creating and cultivating relationships. Relationships take time; they require you to be intentional. Further, relationships are not easy. Relationship development via social media—which is certainly social media's strong suit—does require commitment and intention. There are a multitude of examples of successful businesses using social media, but their financial success did not happen overnight, and it certainly wasn't because they just created a profile on LinkedIn, Facebook, or Twitter. It resulted from intentional interaction. Joe Bunn, owner of Joe Bunn DJ Company (http://www.facebook.com/joebunndjcompany; @BunnDJco) in Raleigh, North Carolina, provides an example of the value of intentional interaction on social media. Social media was no silver bullet for Joe—he had to work hard to make it work for him and he developed his business in other ways, too—but he does credit social media with bringing on substantial business growth.

Joe Bunn has always loved music. From the time he was 15 years old, he was having parties and playing music for his friends in his mom's basement. While attending the University of North Carolina, Joe continued his passion by playing music for fraternity and sorority parties and in different clubs in Chapel Hill. Today, some 15 years later, Joe has his own DJ company, for which he hires DJ talent and provides DJ services for any type of event, from the small private gathering to wedding receptions to corporate parties. One of Joe's biggest and most effective marketing tools to find new clients and events is social media, with his primary platforms being Facebook, Twitter, YouTube, and Pinterest.

Joe started using social media five years ago, and it has helped him gain new events and clients and grow from a one-man show to now having seventeen DJs that he sends out to events all over North Carolina, South Carolina, and beyond. What is more, he doesn't spend one dollar on any social media advertising. He gains his business by having conversations with his past and current friends from his personal Facebook page and encouraging them to go to his Facebook business page, where he posts relevant content that people enjoy and are interested in. On YouTube, he posts videos about DJing; he pins pictures to Pinterest about weddings and wedding ideas that he finds interesting and unique; and he tweets, retweets, and has conversations about nearly any topic on Twitter.

As Joe pointed out to me, social media cannot be the only way a business is promoted, but it is a must-have part of any business strategy today. Although Joe continues to use traditional marketing methods (e.g., promotional flyers, magazine ads, and mailers), he is constantly amazed at how many of his clients have started as friends and followers and soon became clients and referrers for his company. "Social media is not something you can just occasionally do if you want to make it work for your business," Joe stated. "You have to be consistent, committed, and you have to be real with people, because if you are not real and are not there to make real relationships, it is just not going to work. You have to be a part of their conversation, not expecting people to just be a part of yours." Joe attributes much of his success and expansion to his regular use of social media. Did social media magically bring Joe exposure and referrals? No. It was only through time and consistent effort that social media helped Joe expand his business, and he also marketed in other ways too. But social media was certainly helpful.

Just in case you were wondering how much time per day Joe spends on his social media, he tells me that he spends, at most, one hour per day, divided into segments. He hinted that in reality it is probably a great deal less than that thanks to his mobile smartphone.

Get Real

Quite frankly, social media is not the key to a successful business. It is merely one part of an overall strategy that can contribute to success. The idea that it is the only thing or the first thing a business must do is a myth in and of itself. It is possible to build and maintain a business without social media, but it is also just as true that a small business can experience business success through social media. To have the ability to keep up with your potential clients, know what interests them, and be a part of their lives in a very real way is a business changer. However, you do have to spend some time there to create and maintain those relationships.

MYTH 6: To Be Successful, I Have to Use All of the Social Media Platforms

It is true that there are a great number of social media experts out there that strongly advocate for businesses using all of the social media platforms available. They always have a story about someone who has demonstrated success with every social media platform. When you start to read or hear all of this information, it can become very overwhelming to imagine that you have to be on three, four, or even six different platforms to be effective.

Clearly, it is not in the best interest of a social media platform to have large numbers of people say, "It doesn't work for my business." And, honestly, there is a media bias when it comes to social media effectiveness. Let's face it, we are not going to see or hear about the hundreds of people who have tried to use social media, attempted to measure the results, and deemed their efforts a failure. Beyond that, the social media marketing community wants you to be on every platform because they realize how nearly impossible it is for you as an individual owner to effectively use all of these platforms on your own; it only makes sense that they would tout the benefits of all the platforms so that you will hire them to manage your online image for you. Finally, and perhaps more psychologically honest, is that no one wants to admit they failed. To do so is publicly embarrassing and tremendously punishing. As most organisms will do when some sort of pain, physical or emotional, threatens, we will avoid it or attempt to escape it. Hence, it would be better to not say anything or demonstrate a small victory than to admit publicly that one platform or several are not working for your business.

Not every platform is going to work for everybody or every business. That is a fact. In addition, some of these platforms lend themselves better to some industries than others. There is no doubt that the retail industry has a distinct advantage over the service industry when it comes to measuring the effectiveness of social media. It is easier to track a product in the retail industry because customers can click and go right to the shopping cart from a social media ad versus the service industry, where customers may click the ad and then may or may not show up on the front door of the business. If customers do show up at your front door, you may never actually know it was due to social media, even if they tell you. This is because although social media may be the place they came from, it does not mean that other ways of marketing have not affected that final push to do business with you.

Let me say this again: *Not every platform is right for every business.* Some businesses, especially many business-to-business (B2B) businesses, are heavy LinkedIn users. They seem to do well there. In fact, for many, it is the only social media platform that they use. For other businesses, they find that a combination of LinkedIn and Facebook works for them. Yet, others find success in a combination of many different social media platforms, including YouTube, Pinterest, and Google+.

I have one basic rule: Make sure that your target market matches the demographic of the platform you are using. This is why you really must know who your target market is. Are they typically male or female? Is there a particular age range that is common to your target market? How about income level? One of the biggest mistakes that I see small business owners make is that they go to some social media seminar where someone is passionately explaining the virtues of a particular social media platform without considering whether that platform is really right for their business. All of the social media platforms have a place, but that does not mean that every platform is right for your business.

Which Social Media Platform Is Right for Your Business?

There are several factors at play when it comes to picking and choosing social media. First, do not start with the platform; start with your current database of clients. Find out which platforms they are using. This is an important first step, because if you find that the majority of your clients are using Facebook, then you will want to spend more of your time on Facebook. If you find that your clients are not using Pinterest, then there is less of a reason to use Pinterest. That does not necessarily mean that Pinterest doesn't have value, but pinning certainly is not the best use of your time.

Second, ask your current clients how they actually use the platform they are on. More specifically, do they use it every day? What do they post? What do they like looking at or reading? This can give you clues to how you should interact and what types of things you should post that can generate interactions. This is also where you should find out if they interact with business pages or keep things on a more personal level. In the end, it is our current clients who can lead the way in helping us find which social media platforms are right for our particular business.

LinkedIn makes great sense for B2B, but Pinterest may not be valuable at all. Facebook has many virtues for most businesses, but if you are selling a particular product that involves little to no personal interaction with the purchaser, it may not be the best fit.

This must-be-on-every-platform myth is one more reason why I believe people feel so overwhelmed by social media. This myth is just not true; dividing your time between all social media platforms is not the most effective way to use social media to benefit your business. As you learn more about social media—in this book and on your own—give yourself permission to focus on one platform first. Get familiar with what kinds of individuals tend to use each platform and start to identify which platform may best match your target market. In Chapters 4–7, I talk about the typical demographics of each particular social media platform so you can better assess which one or ones are right for you. One of the pros of social media is that you can customize it for your particular business—researching, picking, trying, and adjusting along the way.

Get Real

Whereas once there was just Facebook, Twitter, and LinkedIn, now Pinterest, Google+, and YouTube are available too. Whether it comes from reports from the media or buzz from colleagues and friends, it's easy to get the sense that you must be on every one of these social media platforms. Instead of feeling overwhelmed by the prospect of getting on all of them, focus on finding out where your potential clients play. If your target market shows up on that platform, think about using it; if not, give yourself permission to move on.

In Sum: The Myth Is in the Eye of the Beholder

Social media triggers both negative and positive emotions, especially when it comes to business. Some business owners are firmly emotionally invested in how social media can benefit their business. They believe in it. There is very little one can say to alter their entrenchment in social media as a marketing and business tool. However, sometimes this over-enthusiastic view is not justified. One must keep in mind that social media is just an additional tool, not the only tool, in the marketing toolbox.

Then there is the other end of the spectrum, made up of those who find that social media has no value whatsoever. At the most extreme end, some in this group are almost angered when someone tells them just how great social media can be for their business.

Last, there is one other person who exists at the middle of the spectrum when it comes to social media for business, and that is the person who is about to invest in it because he or she feels that it must be done. This person is in an emotional whirlwind. He or she vacillates from being ready to jump in with both feet, to running away from it as if it were a disease, to complete indecision.

Why such a variety of emotions when it comes to social media? Simply because there is such a mixture of success and failure out there, as well as a plethora of unfiltered information that can generate myths in the minds of business owners. Myths quite often represent an unrealistic view of the world, loosely based on a combination of fact and opinion. Although these myths are not fact, people are attracted to them.

Where do these myths come from? Some of them are created by the protestors who conveniently find excuses to avoid the use of social media: They are too old to learn it, too busy to use it, or too successful to need it. These beliefs are sometimes unconscious and not ill-intentioned; they just seem to be true. But if we stop to reflect on them a little more deeply, we may at least be able to see that—true or not—these beliefs are what's stopping us from using social media. If I say I'm too old to use social media, then I don't have to put in the effort to learn it. If my potential clients aren't on social media, then I am justified in not making the time to be present there. And if my business is already doing pretty well, then I don't have to come up with a plan for adding social media to the marketing mix.

If we are honest with ourselves, we will admit that quite frequently we can create a faulty story because of our reluctance to do something we do not want to do. Couple that with *confirmation bias* (the human tendency to search for only information that confirms our suspicions) and further add to that being around people who think and believe as we do, and it becomes quite easy to rationalize and make excuses not to do something, such as add social media to our business plan.

Sometimes these myths are not used as excuses; they are simply believed to be true. If that has been the case for you, then I hope this chapter has helped you start to see that perhaps it's time to rethink what is true about social media. There is very little to gain by holding on to these myths, and yet nothing to lose by letting them go. Please consider putting aside any beliefs that may be stopping you from getting the most out of social media.

Nothing is easy. We do many things in business we do not want to do. That being said, I don't want social media to be like eating brussels sprouts. If you use social media in the right way, you may just find that you will receive a tremendous amount of benefit, not only from a business standpoint but also from a personal standpoint. You might also enjoy using it!

The Low Down

- Social media is not a passing fad. As a matter of fact, thanks to mobile devices such as smartphones and tablets, there has been an increase in the number of people using it as well as how often people use it.
- People of every generation, culture, subculture, and socioeconomic status are using social media—including the wealthy. Your current clients are there, and so are your future clients.
- Social media does take some time; however, it does not have to take all of your time to pay dividends for business. Start with ten minutes a day and see where it takes you. Consistency is key: Check in, connect, and check out.
- Social media is not a silver bullet that will automatically make your business succeed. It does require consistency and commitment. However, social media has been demonstrated to help grow businesses and make them successful when implemented as part of a larger business strategy.
- You do not need to be on every social media platform. Instead, find out which platforms your clients use and what they like to post and do there, and you will have a playbook for where your company should be on social media.

Social Mediology 101: Using Psychology to Master Social Media

For the music business, social networking is brilliant. Just when you think it's doom and gloom and you have to spend millions of pounds on marketing and this and that, you have this amazing thing now called fan power.

—Simon Cowell

When it comes to social media, many of us are in search of the Holy Grail. What is the key to unlocking its power? Where is the magic potion or formula? How can we put social media to work without working too hard in the process? Some social media marketers will tell you that it's simply a matter of setting up the right paid advertising on these platforms. You pay these marketers to pay the social media platform to showcase your company on a piece of web real estate the size of a thumbnail, and the customers are supposed to start rolling in. Please don't be surprised, however, if the business leads generated fall far short of your expectations.

First, click-through rates on these kinds of ads are quite low, with the Facebook Ads Benchmark Study showing it at a mere 0.17% in the United States.[1] According to many social media marketers, a 2.5% click-through rate on your paid social media ad is considered high![2] As a business owner, I need better than a 2.5% click-through rate: If so few people were inspired to click on the ad, how many will actually be spurred to buy my products or services? Second, just because someone clicks on your paid ad does not mean that they are going to do business with you. They may have accidentally clicked on it, or they may poke around your site and then move on. Third, with paid ads, you may end up alienating many other potential clients as they get turned off by this approach (which is disruptive to the organic social media culture) and choose to take their business elsewhere. There must be a better way.

The New Order: People, Not Businesses, Make the Rules

Certainly, paid advertising does have value in some instances, and there is no doubt that unidirectional media can be effective when people are exposed to it frequently enough, which is why we continue to see and hear advertising on billboards, TV, and radio. Yet business owners would do well to realize that today we live in a bidirectional world: The media outputs while the consumer manages. Remote controls and DVR technology allow consumers to skip past or fast-forward through television commercials, or TV shows can be watched without commercials via online video streaming. Consumers can subscribe to ad-free radio for a few extra dollars a month, and wireless technologies make it easier than ever to listen to one's own music playlist and bypass radio altogether. The list of choices and power for the consumer goes on and on.

And yet advertising persists, with paid ads popping up on social media. Do not be fooled into assuming that these are effective. Laser eye studies have suggested that users are no longer looking at these ads and are instead highly focused on the news feeds (more details to follow). Yes, social media platforms have introduced advertisements in the news feed, but the consumer can still combat this by using third-party applications that do not allow the advertisements to come through. The point is this: Why would anyone allow themselves to be advertised to when ads can be avoided? The overwhelming majority of people are refusing to be part of the traditional marketing techniques on these platforms. They do not like it, will not respond to it, and may even get angry at businesses when they see it. What is the result? A less than 2.5% click-through rate.

In the good old days, when there was only radio and TV, we were told what we should buy, who we should buy from, and why we should buy it. We now use search engines to shop, compare, and get others' reviews before we make a purchase. With social media, we ask our Facebook friends, Twitter followers, and LinkedIn connections where we should go to purchase this product or service or what or who they would recommend for our next purchase. No longer is the consumer held hostage by the commercial; neither is the consumer bound by the sponsored search engine ads that show up at the top of the page or along the right side of our search results.

The truth is, as consumers, most of us do not trust these advertisements. We instead look for those searches that were not paid for but that show up in what we call the *organic search*. According to a study carried out by GroupMUK and Nielson as reported by Econsultancy.com, only 6% of users actually click on the paid search engine advertisements versus 94% for organic or natural search results.[3] This is a pretty good indication of just how savvy the Internet consumer has become and helps us begin to understand any consumer doubts and distrust of a business that uses paid-for advertising versus organic search engine placement. This is because the consumer understands that when a company shows up on the search engines organically or naturally, it is because that website has content with a better chance of being valuable to them. In contrast, businesses that show up in the search results because of paid advertising have no guarantee of quality or valuable content; their visibility only means that they paid to get their sponsored position. From the consumer perspective, clicking on businesses that paid for advertising is more of a roll of the dice in terms of whether searchers will find what they are looking for.

When it comes to social media paid advertising, we are seeing the same trends as with Internet search results. The social media user views these ads as nothing more than noise. For some users, these ads are even seen as distasteful or invasive. Can you imagine being out to dinner with friends and in the middle of a really good conversation saying, "Hold on—I need to read this really good advertisement"? It's the same on social media. People are there to connect, post, and converse, not to read about products and services—not via advertisements, anyway (product and services endorsements from connections they respect are a different ballgame.) In addition, now that Facebook has been watching what its users click and is trying to match advertising to search queries, social media users are noticing and are not happy about it. As several people have said to me along the way, "This is creepy" and "I don't like Big Brother watching."

There is also a psychological component to why paid ads on social media are not especially effective, and that is a phenomenon called *habituation*. Because of habituation, social media users quickly become familiar with where the sponsored ads are located on the page and automatically tune them out. Why? Human beings habituate or ignore stimuli that are constant. For example, have you ever been at a home where you can hear the sounds of heavy traffic when you are in the backyard, and as you stay out there for a long period of time and are continuously exposed to the noise, you no longer notice that it's there? Or perhaps you walk into a house with a turkey in the oven, and after being exposed to the smell of roasting turkey over a long period of time, you no longer notice it? We all have had sensory experiences like these. This is habituation. Why pay for social media advertising when the users of these platforms have habituated to the sidebar of advertisements, such that the vast majority of users no longer even notice them?

One of the areas of research on the Internet that I am especially interested in is the eye-tracking studies. These studies tell us how people look at web pages and websites and even how people view social media. In studies focused on Facebook, findings have been consistent across the board: Facebook users focus on the news feed; they rarely look over to the advertisements on the right side of the page.[4] One explanation for this behavior is habituation. We, in a sense, have classically conditioned ourselves to no longer pay attention to the ads. Yes, with a billion people using the platform, a number of people may click on an advertisement over time, but like the ever-present noise in the backyard or the constant odor of the cooking turkey, we eventually do not notice it any longer.

Using Social Media to Connect to and Create Clients in Modern Times

So if paid advertising isn't the way to go for businesses on social media, then what is? What I have discovered in recent years through professional observations and personal experience is that the real key when it comes to social media has to do with being able to *build authentic, genuine relationships* with people via these platforms. If you would like to get the most out of social media for your business, you have to use the platforms to connect with people, not to advertise to them. Let me share a real-life example, regarding my wife, Linda, of Linda Craft & Team, Realtors, a private real estate company that is consistently ranked among the very top real estate companies in the Research Triangle Park in Raleigh, North Carolina (www.facebook.com/lindacraftteam). When Linda wanted to start using social media as part of her business, she did what most small business owners do: created a personal Facebook profile, created a Facebook business page, and then tried to engage people from the business page. She was finding that her business page was meeting with very little to no success. She was becoming frustrated and sought advice from a traditional marketing company. She then tried some traditional advertising that increased the number of likes on her page, but the ads and likes did not generate any business that could be tracked.

In her concern for what perhaps she was doing wrong, Linda asked my opinion. I explained to her that people are not on social media to interact with Linda Craft & Team, Realtors, they are there to interact and have a relationship with Linda Craft the person. She said to me, "But I don't know what to do or say." I told her, "Just do what friends do and be a friend. Every day, first thing in the morning, go to your news feed and wish people happy birthday. Then read a few posts from your friends and perhaps "like" some posts, or make a comment if it is something that really strikes you. Don't overcomplicate it, and don't talk about business, just be friendly."

She said, "Okay," and set out to spend ten to fifteen minutes every morning wishing people happy birthday, liking posts, and making a few comments; she also started accepting friend requests. This went on for months. She eventually told me that she actually found it quite fun and that after setting up her Clients list, it was a great way to stay in touch with all her clients and know what was going on in their lives. The biggest takeaway for her was that she could stay in touch with so many people in such a short time; it would have taken her days to call the same number of clients that she was able to reach in a single morning with social media. Then another event occurred that made it all click.

Linda happens to be a corporate sponsor for the Carolina Hurricanes professional hockey team. She does a promotion for every game where there is a trivia question or other fun activity on the Jumbotron and she gives something away to the lucky winner. After one of these promotions, as she was walking through the main concourse back to her seat, a woman approached her and said, "Linda!" Linda stopped, not knowing who the person was, and said, "Hello." The woman continued, "I just wanted to say thank you for accepting my friend request on Facebook. I feel like I really know you. You are so nice and kind, I am a Linda Craft fan for life, and I am telling all my friends that if you are going to buy or sell a home you need to call my friend Linda." Linda walked back to her seat. She was in complete disbelief. It was right then that she understood the power of the personal. It had nothing to do with her business; it had to do with her. Since then, she has had more and more experiences similar to this one, but perhaps her most powerful story comes during the next phase in her social media experience.

In 2011, Linda's mom received a diagnosis of lung cancer. By 2012, the cancer had spread to her brain as well. Linda had been flying back and forth to Indiana to take care of her mom. Then, in the spring of 2012, her mom decided to come for a three-week visit. What none of us knew was that the three weeks were going to turn into several months. Linda asked me at the time if I felt it would be okay to post on her Facebook page the daily journey of dealing with cancer with her mom.

I said, "Absolutely! It makes you human, real, and touchable; besides, it would be very cathartic for you as well." So she used her Facebook page, taking pictures of herself and her mom as they journeyed to chemotherapy, met doctors, shopped, had lunch: Whatever they did, she posted. In August of 2012, Linda's mom passed away. Linda was glad that she took the pictures and had the posts because she now had a timeline of events with her mom that she still refers to, to this day, as a remembrance of their last days together. Wipe the tears, because here comes the amazing part.

Approximately one month later, a couple walked into Linda's office and said to her, "We would like you to sell our home." Linda asked, "How did you hear about me?" They said, "We have been following your journey with your mom and we had a similar journey with our parents. We were so touched by your journey that we knew immediately we would not do business with any other person than you." After the tears were shed, Linda understood the power of the personal. She saw that her story made her human, real, genuine, likeable, and trustworthy. More people started coming in, stating how they had been following Linda's story and knew they wanted to buy and sell homes through her because she was genuine and real. These people, by the way, were not one-time customers; they have become real friends who are also clients, who will do business with her again, and who refer their friends to her.

So what happened in this example, which shows that social media has changed the rules when it comes to business? Instead of trying to promote her real estate enterprise on social media, Linda simply focused on creating and maintaining genuine relationships by regularly connecting with her followers on social media—a comment here, a happy birthday there, a share there, and so on, but the most important element was her sharing about herself. These genuine relationships ultimately produced business for Linda, just as a good conversation on the street corner or at the checkout register created business for our grandparents and great-grandparents.

Another way of looking at it is like this: Linda's efforts were successful because instead of using social media to make a *call to action* ("Do business with me!"), she answered social media's call to interaction ("Let's talk, share, and connect!"). Linda was successful on social media because she knew, after just a little coaching and practice, how to use it the way it was supposed to be used: to converse and connect, not as a promotional billboard. The key to all of social media is to interact with the user in a way that builds trust and strong word of mouth, which then translates into real business.

Beware: You cannot fake these relationships. You cannot go into these relationships with the idea that you can manipulate your way to success. No, you must be a part of the conversation, both giving and taking, sharing and commenting, discussing what others wish to discuss, liking and being liked, but, more important, you need to be a real friend, follower, or connection who demonstrates goodwill toward others. You can certainly do that, as Linda did, and have some fun and connection—and maybe even catharsis—along the way.

I am not sure why, but here is where some businesspeople shake their heads and say that this kind of conversation is not worth their time. I have been told such things as "I don't have the time to talk to people about little things in their lives" or "That has nothing to do with my business" or "It is ridiculous to have to deal with people on this level." What I find so counterintuitive about these statements is that these very same businesspeople do the very same things in real life to make their business work (during phone calls, at meetings, at a client dinner, etc.) but they do not see that social media is, in fact, the same interaction, the only difference being that they are not face-to-face.

One of the biggest mind shifts that I hope you will make while reading this book is to understand that the conversation taking place on social media has a real purpose. It is not just banter but a legitimate opportunity to connect with potential clients. Remember that more and more, those potential clients will only hear you when you are engaging them person to person rather than as a business that is paying to get their attention.

The Psychology of Connection, Verification, and Social Media

I hope you are starting to see that social media is a place for not just conversation but connection. It is a world in which many people can stay connected in a short period of time. It is the perfect conversational scenario. Short posts, short comments, a quick like of a LinkedIn discussion, and we move on to the next person to do the same thing. It may seem to some of you that these are superficial relationships; however, they are far more significant than you may realize. These shortened conversations and clicks provide some very important psychological and social benefits.

For many people who use social media, the first and foremost benefit is being connected. As humans, we have a need for connection; we do not do well in isolation. Although social media does not provide physical connection, social media certainly provides some of the mental and emotional connection that we desire. Often, we just need to be heard, to know that someone out there is actually paying attention to what we are saying. Other times, we need to have a conversation that is not related to business where we can comfortably talk about what is going on in our lives. In other words, we need a little catharsis to just get some things out.

Social media also provides for many of us a place of self-verification (to use another psychological term). We all have beliefs about who we think we are; social media provides a place where we can be validated for the way we see ourselves. For example:

- I post a comment on Facebook that I'm writing a book on social media and I receive 23 likes and 10 encouraging comments. I feel verified and on track with my project.
- I tweet a link to a blog post I have written, someone retweets my tweet, and then several others do the same. I now feel that what I have to say has value and I have further verification that what I wrote has meaning to others.
- I join a discussion on a LinkedIn group and several people like what I have to say, comment on it, or write me privately that they want to talk to me more, further verifying my knowledge and expertise in my field.

Although social media can sometimes provide just an illusion of validation for some, many businesses have been created and ideas confirmed simply through others' verifying responses on social media.

Keep in mind the other side of this coin, too: It is extremely powerful when we verify others. When we verify others in the way that they see themselves, it instills confidence that extends through every aspect of their lives, both personally and professionally. It allows them to focus, for example. Hence, instead of spending time trying to become more comfortable in their own skin, this verification allows people to be concerned less with how others see them and to focus more on the business at hand. Never underestimate the powerful effects you can have on social media users simply by helping them verify themselves. It is here that we begin to understand just how powerful our influence is on others and how life changing it can be.

What is more, by being genuine and paying attention, you have started the journey of helping people to know you on a different emotional level and increasing your likeability, which also enhances our trust in you. Keep in mind that you must be genuine when you verify others; if you are just verifying others to get something later, they will quickly see through the disguise.

The key here in social media when transitioning from friend to client is to build genuine relationships and influence people in a positive direction that makes their lives better; when this happens within social media, both the receiver and the giver win in both personal and professional ways.

Where Relationships Rule, So Does Psychology

I am guessing that by now you are beginning to see the intersection of social media, psychology, and business (that sweet spot I call *social mediology*). You may still be reluctant at this point to use social media, but you are at least getting an understanding that there are psychological influences that can make these platforms effective for you personally and professionally (from avoiding the habituation of paid ads to getting involved in the conversation to helping to verify potential clients). The more we understand how people live and operate in a particular environment (including that of social media), the better we can be at providing people those things they need to thrive and survive in those environments (and help them develop a meaningful connection with us in the process). Much of what I am saying to you is that psychology has a tremendous impact and influence on our behavior, whether it be personal or professional, face-to-face, or online. Let's look at some specific psychological principles that can help you be more effective within the social media world and thereby transform your business. In other words, let's get familiar with the key tenets of social mediology.

Give and Take

The most simple principle for people to understand in social media is what is called *reciprocity*. This is the reality that if we give someone something small, that person is likely to return the favor (and many times in a larger way). In 1971, Dennis Regan performed a simple experiment in which he had students believe they were participating in an art appreciation experiment with a partner who was, in reality, part of the experiment (the *confederate*).[5] During the art appreciation event, the confederate left for two minutes and brought back a soda for the student. After the experiment was over, the confederate then asked the student if he or she would buy raffle tickets. Regan found that the students who were given the soda bought more raffle tickets than did those students who were not given a soda!

The experiment demonstrates how when a person gives without conditions, a person will give back—in many cases, over and above the cost of what was given. It is an automatic, unconscious reaction. This has more than likely happened to you on several occasions personally, when someone has unexpectedly given you a gift and you feel a sense of obligation to give back to them. Have you ever noticed that typically you will buy a gift for that person that has more value than the gift they gave you? That is the principle of reciprocity in action.

This principle is also seen in social media. Frequently people ask me, "What should I write (on Facebook, Twitter, LinkedIn, etc.)?" I usually tell them to worry less about what they will write and place greater emphasis on commenting on a person's post, retweeting a tweet, commenting on a discussion question, or simply liking a post or discussion. It is amazing when you do this how people will reciprocate (e.g., liking, commenting, or sharing your posts when you write them). As I talk later in the book about each particular social network, I discuss how to specifically apply the principle of reciprocity to that medium. But, for now, just remember that the more you give on social media, the more you will receive.

See and Be Seen

Another principle that can be effectively applied within the realm of social media is called the *mere exposure effect*.[6] This principle essentially operates like this: The more we are exposed to something (even if we initially have a negative emotional reaction to it), the more we come to develop a preference for it, whether it's the seemingly "dumpy" grocery store we pass regularly on our drive home and start to get comfortable with after a handful of visits or an unusual food dish that we try several times until we start to really like it.

This is the classic principle behind branding. We have all seen it: A company we have never heard of has an advertisement everywhere we look (think of GEICO car insurance, which was once a totally unknown player in the national insurance industry). At first, we are unsure of the company, but as the company continues to show its brand over and over again in a variety of different places and ways (remember GEICO's "so easy, a caveman could do it" slogan, and now think of their gecko character), we begin to develop more interest in and even a preference for the product or service. (Even if you are happy with your current car insurance company, you may just be tempted to check out Geico.)

Another good example of this is the company Nike. Although it's hard to even remember now, when Nike first entered the athletic shoe market, they were unknown. Companies like Puma, Converse, and Adidas were the major players at the time; then, in the mid to late 1980s, Nike began their campaign with slogans like "Just do it" and aired commercials with Michael Jordan. It was only a matter of time before their swoosh became famous and we all wanted to have one on our shoes. Today, when many of us see that swoosh, we experience a positive feeling about Nike. What is interesting is that Nike may not be the best shoe for everyone's feet, but because they have exposed the public to their products over and over again, they are at the top of athletic shoes sales.

Social media offers an incredible opportunity to develop a brand without spending a dollar, simply through exposure. Ask yourself, how often you are seen by the user on social media? The idea is to be seen regularly and in a variety of places (the psychological basis behind branding)—notice I did not say "constantly." As we interact consistently on social media with others, people, over time, do develop preference for us.[7]

There is no doubt that if you are not a regular communicator or consistent user of these platforms, your benefits will be limited. It is difficult to have confidence in a rarely seen person or brand. This is true on social media platforms as well. The person with the greatest advantage is the one who is consistently on these platforms and interacts on a regular basis. Little-known people and brands have been able to develop and promote themselves through social media by regularly contributing and interacting there, and this continuous usage creates exposure. Over time, that regular exposure creates preference. What is more, it creates a sense of trust.

The words that we use on social media, coupled with our personal presence, begin to create in others a preference for us individually. As we continue with our consistency within these platforms, we also become associated with what we do and what we represent; for the majority of us, that is our business. That leads us to the next valuable psychology principle.

Get Pavlovian

At the very heart of any success on social media is *associationism*. That is, the more frequently we associate one thing with another, the more that we learn that those two things go hand in hand. It is an old principle originally stated by Aristotle, but it was not until Pavlov and classical conditioning that people were actually able to see how a great deal of learning and preferences are developed. Most people probably know the story of Pavlov's dogs and how during his research on digestion, he noticed that the dogs would salivate as soon as the door to the laboratory opened and the researchers prepared an odorless food powder. Pavlov then went on to demonstrate that by pairing a tone with the presentation of the food, the dogs would salivate simply by hearing a tone. Later, John B. Watson, a psychologist at Johns Hopkins University, would leave academia to go into advertising, where he would demonstrate that by associating emotions with specific products, people would develop a preference for the product.

It is important to note here that people associate you with something, whether positive or negative. Very rarely is anyone considered neutral. Businesses are characterized by the people who own them. This is especially true for the sole proprietorship and the small business. You cannot escape it. You are not only the face of your business; you are how people view your business. Others are making an association between you and your business. Is that association a positive or negative one? What emotions are associated with you? How about your business?

Social media is perhaps one of the greatest ways to develop positive association, but certainly it can develop a negative association as well. What we post, what we say, and the pictures we submit create our image over time. If you post many things about politics, you will come to be seen as a political lightening rod. This may be positive for some but negative for others. If you post things with obnoxious language, you may be regarded as someone who has questionable taste or common sense.

In contrast, I post many things on Facebook about psychology, social media, and business philosophy. None of it is terribly polarizing; I am simply providing people with different concepts and topics to think about. Many times, these are things that are on my mind and that I want to get others' opinions on. I try to share my thoughts in a unique way and call them *Izsoisms*.

Typically, I receive a great response that creates some very entertaining dialogue. I recently was at a black tie event, where I ran into someone I had not seen in nearly a year. She came up to me and said, "I love your Izsoisms; they make me think and consider what I am doing." It confirmed for me that I was doing what I have intended to do all along: Always the college professor, the one thing I want to be known for is making people think and perhaps even creating change in them. I have had the same conversation I had at the black tie event with many other people. My intention has been to create for myself an image or persona of a thought leader in psychology and social media, and my efforts have worked. Inevitably, what you post will also affect how people see you within (and outside of) social media worlds.

Understand that the Izsoisms are not the only thing I post. I am also very human on social media. I post about things I am interested in, such as a recipe I may have attempted that turned out well or not so well. Perhaps I will talk about my experience trying to write this book and some of my frustrations. I will also post about my wife, my travels, my dogs, or an experience I had because, above all, beyond the thinking piece, I want to be known as human.

Also of note, I purposely and intentionally am careful about what I post in each different social media culture because I understand the language is different, the rules are different, and the expectations are different depending on the platform (e.g., Facebook vs. Twitter vs. LinkedIn). I also know that I want to be associated with specific areas in which I am confidently knowledgeable in. For example, on LinkedIn, which is a professional network, I want to be known for my knowledge and expertise within the world of psychology, social media, and business. In the discussion groups I am in, I make sure that whether I start a discussion or comment on a discussion, somehow my knowledge comes through. This develops my credibility and thought leadership within my professional field. Facebook is different: I understand that the culture is based on personal relationships and conversations, so I want to be associated with being human and at the same time with being a fun thought leader. Twitter is different: I want people to associate the @InternetDoctor with someone who does the research, makes practical connections, and is yet still a part of others' conversations. Google+ is a further extension of my scientific researcher, psychological, social-media self. I very rarely, if ever, deviate from these personas because I have created my online image by choosing how and what I associate myself with through my posts.

The point is that as humans, we are easily conditioned by association. It becomes extremely important that you, as the person behind the business, make sure you are not only fitting into the given social media culture but that you are being known in a way that you want to be known. As you are known, your business will also be known. Within social media, your business is simply an extension of who you are.

So what does your social media usage say about you? What associations are people making about the posts you write? Are these associations good? Bad? Are you posting things that would keep people from liking you? Are you posting things that make it difficult for people to know you? Then I would ask, is there anything that you have put in your social media, such as self-promotion or advertisement, that may inhibit others from ultimately trusting you?

How you and your business are perceived by others is largely up to you. It is imperative that you understand that you are your brand and that everything you do or say personally or professionally is a reflection of that brand. You create your value when you share yourself personally or professionally, authentically and appropriately, with others through the different social media channels. Over time, others will associate you with your company, and the two will become inseparably linked. And when the time comes that one of your friends, followers, or connections needs to make a purchase or perhaps hears of someone who may want to purchase your product or service, he or she will think of you.

Reinforcement: Bringing people back for more. Reinforcement is the act of doing something that increases the likelihood that a behavior will repeat itself in the future, for example, commenting on someone's Facebook post or sharing someone's YouTube video, such that the person will return to social media and post the same kind of comment or video once again. Here's an example. If you have been on social media for any time at all, you have probably seen some post that has said, "My girlfriend broke up with me. My life sucks." If you keep following this person on social media, it may seem to you that this is the only kind of comment that the person writes. Why? Have you seen the number of likes and especially comments this person gets when he writes this type of post? Things like, "I'm so sorry," "You will find someone better," and "I hated her anyway." Look at the attention he is getting! Pay attention further, and you may find that when this person writes something about being happy, no one says anything. What does this do to his behavior? It has now been modified so that he posts only sad posts, because the attention he gets is reinforcing that behavior.

Attention can be powerful as a reinforcer. As my longtime friend from graduate school Mike Longnecker said to me while talking about Facebook, "A lot of people feel the need to be noticed. It is like the beach-strutter bodybuilder who gets a kick out of people eyeing him. Or he'll take it to the extreme of exhibitionism—some people get off on being noticed. Sometimes you get a smile, a laugh, or a slap...sure, sometimes you get off on seeing the likes on your Facebook posts." I think Mike just explained why people take a selfie in their lingerie in the mirror in the bathroom. However, his point is well taken. People like attention; it is reinforcing. Perhaps the reinforcement is found in the emotions we experience when someone likes or comments on our post or makes it a favorite, retweets it, or shares it. Maybe the reinforcement consists of seeing people agree with us and watching our credibility increase as a result of something we posted. Whatever the reinforcer is, a billion people would not be using social media if there was not some reinforcing value to it, even if these people are completely unaware of exactly why they come back or don't understand why they posted the content they posted.

When it comes to what is reinforcing on social media, there are a number of factors. For some, it may simply be the ability to talk to old friends and family, see their pictures, and do it in nearly real time. Perhaps it is that relational connection that reinforces the behavior, enticing them to come back time and time again to social media. Then again, it could be something more general: Perhaps people are reinforced by simply receiving likes, comments, shares, +1s, retweets, and so on. Some are stimulated by the conversations on, say, LinkedIn or Google+; that intellectual interaction is reinforcing for them, so they continue those conversations or create those discussions. Some may be attracted to Twitter and continue to use it because it allows them to follow celebrities—to be privy to famous people's thoughts, ideas, and rants throughout the day, which they would not otherwise have any access to. The reinforcer may vary by platform and by person, but you can bet something draws social media users to come back again and again.

Social media offers you, the businessperson, a fantastic opportunity to reinforce your potential clients by giving them a fix of intellectual stimulation, emotional support, social validation, or whatever it is that they rely on social media for. People return again and again to social media to enjoy the good feeling of being reinforced. When others see you as the source of reinforcement, you increase the probability of people coming to you, evangelizing your business for you, and referring you. We all need some positive reinforcement in our lives. When we know where to get it, we go back for more.

Why will psychology help you be successful when implementing social media as part of your business strategy? It comes down to the fact that human beings are fairly automatic and instinctual creatures—especially when it comes to our behavioral responses to people.

This is important to note within social media because so many of the responses that are made within these platforms are automatic. As a simple example, a large percentage of people automatically follow, friend, and connect with other people they do not know simply because those people asked. It becomes even more likely that a friend request will be approved if there is a common connection. Neither person may know the other, but because they are connected in some way by a common person, they, in turn, connect.

I know there is resistance to the idea that consumers and users of social media act without thought. However, read a tweet, status update, or discussion, and you will quickly find that if people did use thought, they probably would not post half of the things that they post. What is more, you would find that many of the responses that are generated as a result of these posts are fairly automatic. I can hear the outcry as you are reading this; none of us want to be thought of as an automaton. And yet experts and researchers have seconded what I am expressing here. In his book *Consumer.ology: The Market Research Myth, the Truth about Consumers, and the Psychology of Shopping,* Philip Graves exposed how we as humans overestimate our very own behavior.

> Psychology and neuroscience have discovered that we're all rather bad at explaining our actions, as we are at predicting what we want or what we will do in the future.[8]

This is how David McRaney describes it in his book, *You Are Not So Smart*:

> The truth is, there is a growing body of work coming out of psychology and cognitive science that says you have no clue why you act the way you do, choose the things you choose, or think the thoughts you think. Instead, you create narratives, little stories to explain away why you gave up on that diet, why you prefer Apple over Microsoft, why you clearly remember it was Beth who told you the story about the clown with the peg leg made of soup cans when it was really Adam, and it wasn't a clown.[9]

What's of most practical importance here is that what we do within different environments changes that environment and, in turn, changes what people will do. As business owners and entrepreneurs on social media, we can affect others' automatic behavior. When you or I comment on or like something on a social media platform, we change the environment. Inevitably, another action will be taken. If we understand some basic principles of psychology and use them on social media in an ethical manner, we can create a positively winning environment for both our future clients and ourselves. We can use social mediology to grow our businesses and help them thrive long into the future.

In Sum: Psychology, Not Technology

When it comes to trying to conduct business on social media platforms, many of us have seriously miscalculated. First, much has been said, taught, and pushed on us to figure out how to leverage each social media platform rather than to really understand the people that visit these platforms. We do far better by focusing on the user versus the platform—why they are there and what motivates them.

Second, conversations are critical. If you are not generating conversations on social media, then you are not doing the right things. It may be because you are being self-promotional, acting polarizing, creating angst, or not paying attention. Or maybe you simply fell into the simple but ineffective trap of using paid advertising. The fact remains that if you want to see a transfer of the personal to the professional, you have to be a part of the conversation. This may mean that you stop posting and start interacting (e.g., commenting, liking, sharing). If you are still struggling with how to proceed, remember the principle of reciprocity: Give first before you expect to get anything in return. This also means that you need to demonstrate a genuine and honest desire to interact with others. Remember, people will see through your gestures very quickly if all you are trying to do is give to get. Give in earnest. Care with compassion. Laugh with someone. Genuinely emote with others. Walk with them in their shoes. The more genuine you are, the more people can trust you.

Third, if you want social media to work, you need to make sure you are seen and seen regularly. There is no substitute for the mere exposure effect. The more someone is seen, the more that person is preferred. This does not mean you have to be in these social media worlds twenty-four hours a day, seven days a week. It does mean that you need to be consistent.

Fourth, understand that social media users are being conditioned to associate you with what you say. Therefore, because you are the face of your business, what you say will be associated with your business. As a result, you must be careful that you are associating yourself with the right positive things. This also means that you need to pay specific attention to the unique social media cultures; interact using the right language; and follow the unwritten rules, norms, and expectations as established by the majority of the users. You need to be intentional on each platform. The best thing you can do is be associated with being real; being genuine; but, most of all, being human.

The Lowdown

- Beware of the paid-for ad. Too many consumers today are turned off by this kind of manipulative marketing and will respond far better to genuine opportunities to connect with you, the face of your business, through everyday social media conversations.
- When you give to others on social media—whether you retweet, like, comment, +1, endorse, or repin—they are likely to return the favor.
- Simply by being consistently present on social media, you will increase your followers' preference for you. It's called the mere exposure effect.
- People will learn to associate you and your business with what you post, so be sure to focus on sharing those unique ideas, photos, videos, and the like that will build your brand as you want it to be seen.

Putting LinkedIn to Work for Your Business

> Sometimes, idealistic people are put off by the whole business of networking as something tainted by flattery and the pursuit of selfish advantage. But virtue in obscurity is rewarded only in Heaven. To succeed in this world you have to be known to people.
>
> —Sonia Sotomayor

Most businesspeople who are online would say that LinkedIn is the true social media business platform. Although the other social media platforms certainly have great value for business, I would agree that LinkedIn has a more natural and familiar business culture. In fact, when you spend time on LinkedIn, it is much like going to a networking event or a business conference. People can join LinkedIn groups where ideas are exchanged (like virtual networking events), people's LinkedIn profiles look like extended resumes, and people write LinkedIn recommendations for each other and make endorsements. Resumes, networking, recommendations, and endorsements: Sound like some familiar props in the business world? As I demonstrate in this chapter, LinkedIn simply makes intuitive sense for business.

I especially like LinkedIn if a business owner is new to social media or perhaps a skeptic. If someone is new or reluctant to join social media and they immediately start on, say, Facebook or Twitter, it can be overwhelming and sometimes confusing to figure out how to leverage these platforms for business rather than just personal benefit. In contrast, LinkedIn is not tremendously interactive or busy (although you can make it busy if you so choose) and thus is not overwhelming to the social media newbie. For those who are sitting on the fence and want a taste of social media without so much of the noise, LinkedIn is a perfect place to start.

All of that being said, don't let the relative ease of using LinkedIn diminish its value. It is powerful! In a study cited in the *Harvard Business Review Blog*, 40% of the salespeople interviewed who used Linkedin on a daily basis stated that they had successfully generated revenue from their LinkedIn efforts.[1] *The Wall Street Journal* also conducted a survey of 835 business owners in early 2013. When the major social networks, including LinkedIn, Facebook, Twitter, YouTube, Pinterest, Google+, and others were compared, LinkedIn was by far the number one choice of business owners when it came to the most potential benefit for their company.[2]

Jeff Snell, CEO of ENLIGN Business Brokers in Raleigh, North Carolina, which matches privately held companies for sale with prospective corporate buyers, provides an example of LinkedIn's value on the ground.[3] Jeff credits his company's presence on LinkedIn with helping him and his client win a multimillion-dollar deal. Although the company Jeff represented for sale in this transaction was relatively small, the interested, large, corporate buyer took them seriously because of Enlign's online presence. As Jeff relayed, "There was no doubt that they checked me out *thoroughly* through my LinkedIn profile." Although the buyer was huge and powerful, Jeff believes that the playing field was leveled somewhat by the credible online reputation that Enlign could put forth on behalf of its client, showcased, in part, on LinkedIn via Enlign's business profile and recommendations. As Jeff explained, "It's really hard to promote yourself directly. But online there is a degree of separation while adding a layer of social and reputation management." Sometimes LinkedIn allows a small business to promote itself better than its principals or salespeople can.

The result? Jeff's client has gone under contract for purchase by the larger corporate suitor for an amount twenty-three times earnings, whereas three times earnings is the norm! As the broker, Jeff gets a hefty cut of that. And, yes, he is a believer in LinkedIn. Jeff analyzed the value of LinkedIn in this way: "LinkedIn and similar websites now effectively serve as a third-party endorsement with reviews, recommendations, likes, followers, et cetera, further strengthening prospects' confidence when making a purchasing decision. In our opinion, to ignore this marketing modality is business suicide."

It's also worth noting that Jeff's client—the one who hired him to represent them for sale—researched Jeff's personal and company credentials on LinkedIn before hiring Enlign. In other words, LinkedIn helped Jeff secure a new client simply by having a well-worded and complete profile that demonstrated his credibility and success. LinkedIn initiated the connection, Jeff's LinkedIn profile sold his value, and both he and his new client were able to reap positive financial benefits as a result. Are you ready to get your LinkedIn on? Keep reading.

Understanding How LinkedIn Really Works

To get the most out of LinkedIn, as with all of the social media platforms, you need to begin by understanding its culture. Culture? Yes, culture. In today's global world, we all know that cultural differences exist between countries and groups of people. The same is true for the different social media platforms. Throughout this book, as I introduce the different social media platforms, I will start by identifying each unique culture on the basis of its demographics and psychological and behavior user patterns. LinkedIn is not Facebook is not Twitter: Although LinkedIn has a traditional business culture, Facebook's culture is one of me, me, me (what I ate for breakfast or how I spent my time this morning), and Twitter is a culture of fame.

I am using the word *culture* in this context to refer to the behaviors, as well as to the unwritten norms, rules, and expectations, of a group. The importance of respecting the cultures of these platforms is no small issue: Break the cultural norms and rules and you will be seen as a foreigner: If you post what you ate for breakfast or a photo from your recent beach vacation on LinkedIn, people may think of you as unprofessional; conversely, if you are wearing a suit and tie in your profile picture on Facebook, people may see you as a stuffed shirt. Neither is a way to make meaningful connections for your business. *To be successful on social media, you must respect and follow the rules of the given platform.*

If you want to quickly get a sense of any social media culture, look at the term used when connecting with other people on that platform; that is, what are people called when they connect with each other? On LinkedIn, in the best business-networking tradition, they are called *connections*. When we see the word *connection* (as opposed to *friends* on Facebook), we know that we are not talking about personal culture; we are entering a professional culture.

Our next clue is how the profiles are constructed. Notice how on LinkedIn, the profile looks like an extended resumé. It is professionally laid out, it is not flooded with pictures, and the only allowable public interaction on the profile from others is through recommendations (which you can think of as references) and endorsements (which represent others' affirmation of your expertise in specific areas or regarding knowledge, skills, and abilities. LinkedIn, of course, has an e-mail function as well.

Overall, the language used on LinkedIn is predominantly professional—grammatically correct, intelligent, and business related. LinkedIn can also be described as promotional in the sense that your profile and what you say on LinkedIn are there to help others find you and understand more about what you do in your business life. People are relating to the work that you do, not your personal life (as would be the case for Facebook). Here are a few example excerpts from LinkedIn to show the nature of the language:

- "My goal is to deliver high-quality training to healthcare organizations." (profile)
- "Jane Doe has been working in the financial industry for the past 15 years." (profile)
- "Strive for excellence, not perfection." (post)
- "Could this be relevant to your business team?" (post sharing a link)

In addition to looking at the typical language used on LinkedIn, we can also look at demographic data to give us some indicators of the LinkedIn culture. According to Quantcast, a statistical and data-gathering web platform, LinkedIn users tend to be more educated than those on the other social media platforms, with approximately 74% of LinkedIn users having a college or graduate school education.[4] LinkedIn users, on average, are also wealthier than those on any of the other social media platforms, with one third of users making $100,000 per year or more. As for the gender breakdown, 54% of the people on LinkedIn are men compared to 46% women.[5] Finally, LinkedIn is largely made up of older users, according to Quantcast, as almost two thirds are 35 years of age or older. These statistics reveal that on LinkedIn, you can connect to well-educated, financially successful, and well-established people. Knowing this may further define your language on LinkedIn, how you approach others, and your understanding of how you are expected to behave within the culture. For example, you may share an interesting link to a *Harvard Business Review* or *The New York Times* article, not the latest celebrity news from TMZ or The Hollywood Gossip. If you are looking for a place to talk about the latest sporting event or movie, LinkedIn is not the place.

The subculture of groups on LinkedIn wields the greatest power.

Groups on LinkedIn are collections of LinkedIn users who have a special interest in or connection to a particular topic, industry, profession, or organization, such as social media marketing or technology, electrical engineers, human resource professionals, or the American Medical Association. It could also be people associated with a specific group or company, such as an alumni association or a business group. These professional groups are where you will find the most interaction on LinkedIn.

It's important to know that not every LinkedIn group is structured in the same way; for example, some groups take their professionalism to higher levels than others. You will also find that certain groups allow some self-promotion. Other groups do not tolerate self-promotional discussions and are only interested in generating ideas, educating each other, and providing valuable resources to help the members of the group. Depending on the group, you will find a vast array of both positive and negative experiences. I discuss how to use the groups for your greatest success later in the chapter.

So, LinkedIn is different from the other social media platforms and yet it is quite "business-y" and thus familiar. It is a great place to get started on social media. It is your resumé, it is your profession, and it is your credibility. Keep in mind that while you are looking to make those amazing connections that can help you grow, there are also people out there searching on LinkedIn for people like you to help them as well. This is why, when it comes to your LinkedIn profile, not only can you make yourself available to those whom you already know, but you can also be found by new connections who are looking to do business with those in your field. BAM!

What's the Point? Why Should You Use LinkedIn?

For the business owner, there are a number of practical advantages to LinkedIn.

Get Ranked on the Search Engines

One of the most important and overlooked advantages of LinkedIn is the search engine optimization (SEO) power that LinkedIn provides when people search for either you or your company. Your name or company name will likely show up in the first couple of pages of the search results if you are present on LinkedIn. What is more, this SEO is organic, meaning that you do not have to pay for it: LinkedIn's credibility when you build a profile will simply push your name and your business right to the front page of the search engines when someone searches for you by name, company name, and sometimes specialty. How's that for publicity?

Establish Your Credibility

This leads to the second key benefit of LinkedIn, and that is how quickly you can develop your professional credibility there. One of the biggest frustrations of small business owners and entrepreneurs is finding an audience to whom you can demonstrate your knowledge. On LinkedIn, you have ready access to special interest groups; if you really know your profession, you can build your credibility quickly by simply joining the discussions within these groups. However, there is a caveat: If you do not add value to the conversation, your commentary can have a negative effect on your credibility. So it is important to really know what you are talking about when you decide to post and get involved.

Find and Be Found: Making Important Relationships

Also of value, LinkedIn is searchable, meaning that people can search for you or your business right there on the platform. This is why it is important that you have complete profiles for both yourself and your business. This will help to make sure that if people are looking for someone like you or a business like yours, they can find you.

LinkedIn is also powerful for finding the right employees for your business. If you are looking for people with particular qualifications and experience, you can easily locate them by searching for those specific types of people. Once you locate them through a search, you can then peruse their profiles and learn a great deal about the potential employees prior to ever conducting the interview.

Possibly the most unique feature of LinkedIn is the ability to connect with true leaders and influencers from around the world. I have found that when you have a complete professional profile, people you may not normally be able to get close to on a face-to-face basis are willing to connect and communicate with you on LinkedIn. As I stated earlier, some very affluent and highly educated people use LinkedIn, which means that you may also gain access to a very desirable set of folks for your own business growth. As you develop relationships with these individuals, whether through groups or LinkedIn e-mail, it may quickly become apparent that creating that dialogue and opening those lines of communication has tremendous business benefit, whether through the expertise that these individuals can offer you, interest they may have in using your products or services, or any movement on their part to bring others to you by sharing what you say or by making direct referrals.

For the B2B business owner, LinkedIn has tremendous value in terms of getting your foot in the door. Whereas in the past, you might have made a cold call to gain an audience with someone at a company only to have that call end with a quick "no," you can now introduce yourself via LinkedIn or ask a related connection of yours for an introduction. In addition to getting connected to individuals at your company of interest, you can also follow that company on LinkedIn. As a follower, you now have the ability to comment on posts by that company and forge a relationship in that way as well. Think of LinkedIn as an easy way to see how all of the people whom you know are related to each other and to quickly zero in on how you can get connected to new companies. It's as if the gatekeepers are gone and the once-secret contact information is now out in the open.

Why LinkedIn?

LinkedIn is the simplest of all the platforms, has great SEO, and does not require daily interaction. Think of LinkedIn as your social media anchor. It is the safest place for you to learn about interacting on social media, and yet you can worry less about the frequency with which you interact.

It is also a great place to start because it has most of the aspects of the other social media platforms. I find that it is the most natural fit for most business owners, because it has a similar feel to a chamber of commerce networking event. Instead of exchanging business cards, you are exchanging business profiles, and, similar to attending a webinar or business group in person, you can join LinkedIn groups and enter discussions that pertain to your business or that peripherally connect with your business.

Of course, to be effective, it's important that you use LinkedIn and commit to it. Like any other skill you develop, you'll need to practice your interactions there. In sum, LinkedIn is a great place to get started on social media, and it's a nice staple of any social media program, whether you are a newbie or a seasoned pro.

Your Business Rx: Getting the Most Out of LinkedIn

If you'd like to get the most out of your LinkedIn presence, you need to properly set up your profile (including selecting the right photo), compile strong LinkedIn recommendations, and participate in appropriate groups. Here is some guidance on how to do each of these most effectively.

Creating a Polished Personal Profile

Regardless of whether you are a B2C or B2B company, if you are going to really make LinkedIn work for you and your business, the place to start is with creating and/or completing your profile. Your profile is a complete summary of who you are professionally. It should include what you do presently, what you did in the past, your education, and your expertise. If you are going to make the right connections with the right people, then you need to be very intentional about how your profile looks, what it says about you and your business, what exactly it is you do, and the value you provide.

There are two profiles available to you on LinkedIn: The first is the personal professional profile, which focuses on you. Think of it as your professional resumé. The other profile is the business profile, which is more of a business listing where your business can be found. Although the business listing has value for small businesses because of its SEO benefits, the personal profile has far greater value because of the capacity to personally interact and connect with other people via this profile.

The right photo. When it comes to building an eye-catching and impressive personal profile, start with your profile picture, because it is extremely important. Many people do not understand just how important profile pictures are, but a great deal of psychological research shows how people judge others on the basis of a picture. In less than a second, humans will look at someone and decide if they are attractive, trustworthy, aggressive, and so on. This has been called the *halo effect* or the *halo error,* in which people make personality judgments on the basis of what they see in a face. If people like what they see in a person's face, they attribute positive personality characteristics to that person (or, as it was thought early on, a person is seen as having a halo over his or her head). It does fit in quite neatly with the attractiveness stereotype: The more attractive someone is, the more positive qualities are attributed to the person. The opposite is also true: If someone is seen as unattractive, negative qualities are attributed to him or her. Although you may not be able to do much about your genetics, the fact is that the more attractive your picture, the higher the probability that someone will connect with you.

Like it or not, the halo effect is an automatic human response; this built-in mechanism in your brain is there for a number of reasons, such as sensing danger and selecting a mate. I am not saying that having a great LinkedIn photo will land you a mate, but, then again, you never know. The fact is, your LinkedIn personal profile picture is critically important. A nice picture of you creates the halo, whereas a bad picture can destroy it. If the halo is destroyed, you either will not attract people or may attract the wrong people.

Some people have chosen not to include a picture on LinkedIn, but there is a tremendous danger here as well: If you are not willing to be transparent with something as simple as a picture, you may give the impression that people cannot trust you when it comes to business. You have possibly provided viewers with the perception that you are hiding something. It may not be your intention, but your perception is our reality. A missing photo might also imply that you are not technically savvy, that you don't pay attention to details, or that you just don't care enough to include one. Whatever the reason, we will believe what we see or, in this case, what we do not see, and the impression will not be a good one.

So what should your picture look like? First of all, make sure it is professional looking. This does not mean that you have to necessarily hire a professional to take the picture. Just make sure that your picture is of professional quality. It should be clear. You should be easy to see. If your picture is fuzzy, lacks quality, or perhaps is too playful, many people will not connect with you on LinkedIn simply on the basis of your picture. Remember, the goal is to do everything in your power to keep people from eliminating you from their consideration for any reason, especially people that would be potential clients. You'll also want to make sure that the background is neutral (in terms of symbolic meaning). I once ran across a profile where a person took his picture in front of a Confederate battle flag. Although that may have little meaning for some, it is quite offensive to others. Why eliminate potentially great clients because of something you have hanging in the background?

Of course, you'll also want to make sure that you are well dressed and professional looking in your photo. Nothing says "Don't trust me" like wearing sunglasses and a t-shirt that says "Bang!" next to a headline reading "Owner of ABC123 Financial Planning" in a supposedly professional photo. Cicero has been quoted as saying, "The countenance is the portrait of the soul, and the eyes mark its intentions."[6] This is so true. Flash those baby blues, stellar grays, or beautiful browns. Doing so will attract potential clients and invite them to connect with you on LinkedIn.

After you have your great photo, it is important that you have a complete profile. When it comes to your profile, it is important to take the time to really think through what your profile is going to say and to fill in as many elements of the profile as possible. Why? The more complete and accurate your profile is, the more likely you are to be found when people search for the kind of products and services that you offer. As mentioned earlier, LinkedIn has tremendous credibility when it comes to search engines for your name and your business. That, my friends, is free SEO for both you and your business. This makes it all the more important that you pay close attention to how your profile looks and reads.

A headline that draws interest. Next, consider your professional headline, which appears beneath your name, to the right of your fabulous photo. The headline is a very important piece of your LinkedIn profile, so you need to be intentional about what you say in it. When people search for you on the web and your LinkedIn profile shows up in the listings, your headline will be what they see. When people visit you on LinkedIn, the headline is the second line of text that they will see. And when people search for a specific industry, expertise, or knowledge on LinkedIn, it's your headline (with your name and photo) that is going to be seen first. Is it any surprise that you should take some time thinking about what your headline should say?

When it comes to how best to formulate your headline, there are many theories. Some have said you should be creative, some say you should simply state what you do, and a vast array of other opinions hang in between. I recommend that you focus on creating a straightforward headline that very consciously uses the keywords you expect people to use when searching for a business like yours. So, if you want to attract people in search of physical therapy, your headline might read Physical Therapist. Taking it one step further, if you want those seeking a therapist who specializes in athlete rehabilitation to get connected with you, you might put Sports Physical Therapist or Athlete Physical Therapist in your headline. Consider including industry-specific terms in your headline so that your future client can actually find and connect with you on LinkedIn. Here are a few effective sample headlines to give you an idea of how these can look.

- New York Condominium Real Estate Specialist
- Experienced Book Editor Nonfiction
- Owner Cleopatra's Women's Fashion Boutique

As you can see, there's nothing fancy in there, but these headlines are well thought out, are clearly targeted to the desired audience of potential clients, and can draw interest because of what the profiled professional specifically does. The goal here is to describe yourself using the keywords that people will likely use when searching for businesses like yours. Often we make the mistake of using a headline that describes how we want to be known rather than what people are actually searching for on the web or LinkedIn. Many times, the two can be the same; however, this is not necessarily the case. So be conscious about creating a headline that has simple search terms people are likely to use.

Try This!

Take ten to fifteen minutes to construct or update your LinkedIn headline. Be sure to consider your target market and how these individuals may search for you within LinkedIn. If you are in a specific niche, include specific terminology in your headline that your future client would know. If you need inspiration, search for your industry or vocation on LinkedIn and see what headlines other people have used. Do any strike you as particularly clear, relevant, and useful? There is no magic or science to finding the right keywords for your profession or industry, so use your best logic and be willing to experiment. Try something for ninety days and see if you are getting more visits to your profile.

Now it's time to complete the rest of your LinkedIn profile, which covers topics such as past work history, professional summary, education, projects, and (with a little help from others) recommendations and endorsements. When filling in this information, plan to be as concise as possible. You may be a chatty Kathy or Ken when it comes to conversation, but being too wordy on your LinkedIn profile may overwhelm readers and turn them away. In today's world, most people read far less and look at pictures and video far more, so be selective about the words you use.

As with the headline, while completing your profile, also keep in mind what terms people will use when searching for businesses like yours on LinkedIn or the web. This is because what you put on your LinkedIn profile is indexed by LinkedIn. If people are searching for someone on LinkedIn, they will enter specific keywords that will help them find the right person who is doing exactly what they are looking for. You want to be sure to have in your profile the words that your potential client will be using when searching for your products or services.

In addition, keep in mind that the most effective profiles on LinkedIn for business are going to be those in which the focus is on fulfilling a want or a need rather than pumping up how great we are or how impressive we can make our LinkedIn resumé and profile look or sound. For example, it would be better to tell people about what you can do for them rather than list your amazing qualities.

If you are unsure of what you should say or how you should say it, LinkedIn has a link under each section of the profile where you can find examples. Use these examples as a guide to help you develop your profile in the right way.

Curating Recommendations

So you've got your LinkedIn profile built, and your professional and compelling photo is on display. Now what? One of the exciting elements of the LinkedIn profile that people tend to overlook is the Recommendations section. (Do not confuse this with the Endorsements section, which sounds similar but is actually quite different and is discussed a bit later in this chapter.)

The value of recommendations. Think of the Recommendations section as a library of testimonials from past clients that future clients can review as they consider reaching out to you or hiring you. Remember that rather bland "References available upon request" line at the end of most resumes? Well, LinkedIn provides you with a dynamic means of providing those references up front so potential clients can check you out right away. It's a win–win situation for everyone as

- your references write one recommendation for you and you never have to bother them again
- you get to choose which recommendations are viewable
- your potential client receives early reassurance that you are trustworthy and good at what you do by hearing from others about the quality of your work
- your potential client can be wowed by the sheer number of people who think highly of you, which creates very compelling social proof

Recommendations are a simple way for people to see what others say about you, to build your credibility, and to publicly certify your expertise and knowledge.

There are several reasons why the recommendation from others can be so powerful. First is the issue of social proof; that is, people have a tendency to do things that they see other people doing. When potential clients see a recommendation of you from others, that increases the probability of others wanting to see what it is that you do and what you are about. This can be especially powerful if the recommendation is made by someone who has legitimate or perceived authority. The psychological research continues to demonstrate that people with even only perceived authority can get groups of people to do many things that they themselves never would believe they would do. When someone whom others perceive as having authority writes a recommendation, those others will want to interact with you.

Second, keep in mind that there is more power in the recommendation of an everyday person versus one from some professional reviewer (e.g., an institution or media outlet). In a series of studies, Weber Shandwick and KRC Research found that consumers will pay attention to fellow consumer reviews over professional reviews by more than a three to one margin.[7] What this study begins to indicate is just how powerful the fellow consumer review is. Although authority is important, when people similar to your potential clients purchase your product or service and write about them or you, they can have a tremendous influence over these potential clients' purchase decisions.

Tips on getting recommendations. There are some practical things you can do to help make recommendations work for your business. First, give recommendations before you ask for them. Recall the principle of reciprocity? If you give first, you will have a much greater likelihood of receiving recommendations back. Second, do ask for recommendations, but make sure that they are from people who truly know you, your work, your knowledge, or your expertise. This leads to the third point of recommendations: When you ask for a recommendation, please be specific about the desired focus of the recommendation. There are a couple of reasons for asking for specifics. First, general recommendations are nothing more than fluff and have little meaning for your prospective client. If someone says, "Jay is a nice person and I enjoyed working with him," that offers little insight or value for a future client. However, when someone says, "I have been through Jay's social media for marketing presentations and was quite impressed with his understanding of the media and his ability to connect its use to the bottom line," now there is something that people can specifically relate to and find value in. When I desire a recommendation, I ask people to recount specific ways my work benefited them. If I am speaking, I may ask for someone to comment on my speaking ability so that I can be hired in the future. If I am focusing on business consulting, I will ask someone to recommend me for my knowledge and expertise in that area. The point is, when you ask, be specific.

Second, when you ask for something specific, it actually takes the pressure off the person who is writing the recommendation. I get requests to make recommendations regularly. Most of the people just send me the standard recommendation default e-mail that says, "I'm sending this to ask you for a brief recommendation of my work that I can include in my LinkedIn profile. If you have any questions, let me know. Thanks in advance for helping me out." This is not helpful. I struggle to figure out what I should say. Should I just say, "I recommend their work" or "I am recommending this person so that they can put this on their LinkedIn profile"? When you ask for a recommendation from one of your LinkedIn connections, edit the generic e-mail with specifics. A better thing to say is something along the lines of the following:

> Hi Jane,
>
> You were recently at the ABC conference where I was speaking. I would like to ask if you are comfortable writing a recommendation of my speaking ability.
>
> Thank you in advance,
>
> Jay Izso, Internet Doctor

Or,

> Hi John,
>
> I appreciate your hiring me to help with your business social media strategy. If you are comfortable, would you write me a recommendation concerning my knowledge and expertise on social

media and how I have helped your business?

Thank you.

Jay Izso, Internet Doctor

This makes it so much easier for the person undertaking the recommendation to write it. They now have a clear outline of what to write, and, what is more, you are inviting specific information that now increases your credibility and highlights your knowledge, expertise, and skills.

Something else should be pointed out here. In my examples, notice I use the phrase "if you are comfortable." I believe that it is extremely important to give a person a way out of writing a recommendation, without pressure. It is important that we never demand a recommendation or even make the person feel emotionally shamed if they do not. I have found that people appreciate the gesture and have personally said to me how it made them feel as if our relationship would remain intact even if they did not recommend me. I have also discovered that many times the recommendation shows up weeks—even months—later, because the person writing the recommendation wanted to put together something really spectacular for me when they had the time. These people were able to do so because they felt no pressure to write the recommendation immediately. Always give people a way out! A phrase as simple as "if you are comfortable" can go a long way in helping you gather better and more recommendations.

This leads us, then, to the interesting question of, Can you have too many recommendations? My answer is no, because the more people that recommend you, the stronger the social proof to others that you have great value. LinkedIn only posts a few of your recommendations (you can select which ones), and if people want to dig deeper, they can certainly read through them all. This may be especially important if you have a number of recommendations from a previous career that may not be as relevant today as they were prior. You may want to pick and choose just a few of those recommendations that are more relevant to what you are doing in your current business. This will help the reader to develop an understanding of your historic track record; how you came to the business you now own; and how your previous knowledge, skills, and expertise were developed. Bottom line: When asking for recommendations, be specific about what you want recommended.

What to do with endorsements. Now, what about the Endorsements feature of LinkedIn? Does it have value? Why is it there? The Endorsement feature was introduced by LinkedIn at the end of 2012. Endorsements are one-click ways for people to endorse or credit you for the knowledge, skills, and abilities that you possess. LinkedIn defines them as follows:

> Skill endorsements are a great way to recognize your 1st-degree connections' skills and expertise with one click. They also let your connections validate the strengths found on your own profile. Skill endorsements are a simple and effective way of building your professional brand and engaging your network.[8]

Their purpose is to help readers get a quick overview of your skills, knowledge, and expertise. LinkedIn allows you to be endorsed in up to 50 different areas. If you have not specifically chosen the maximum number of areas to be endorsed, people can endorse you for other things. Do not worry: You can hide or delete categories that you do not want to be endorsed for, such as those competencies that are not readily associated with your current business.

Do endorsements have value? Maybe. It is not clear how LinkedIn uses these endorsements, if they use them at all, or if they will have some future purpose. Some people have surmised that perhaps LinkedIn uses them as part of their search algorithms (affecting whose LinkedIn profile gets posted first in response to a keyword search). I can neither confirm nor deny that is true, and LinkedIn has not publicly stated as much. If endorsements are part of the search algorithm, they are certainly important, although I do not currently know if that is the case.

For sure, endorsements have some importance because they give the reader a quick view of you. Is the view accurate? Well, because anyone can endorse you with the simple click of a button and there is no way to monitor whether this person really knows your level of skill in this area, the view created by endorsements may or may not be accurate. But if you had a choice, would you rather your potential clients go to your profile and see twenty endorsements or zero endorsements? Fifty endorsements or ten endorsements? If given the choice, most of us would want to have more endorsements on our profile than fewer. This is because of the *numerosity heuristic,* that is, larger numbers have greater meaning, especially if they are directly compared with a smaller number.

People tend to be attracted, right or wrong, to larger numbers. They influence us. When you see someone with over ninety-nine endorsements for social networking versus someone with ten endorsements, take a guess at who you are more likely to consider credible? Sure, the one with ninety-nine-plus endorsements. If a person looks at your profile and scans your endorsements, they will come to conclusions about your skill and popularity as a businessperson, right or wrong, on the basis of their plentitude. Of course, if you do not have many endorsements, this does not mean you are not competent in your business. By the same token, if someone has a huge number of endorsements, this does not qualify them as an expert.

The quickest and easiest way to get endorsements? Start endorsing people. The psychological power of reciprocity is amazing in this instance. When you start endorsing people, the number of endorsements for you is sure to rise. Now, I know that this sounds like you are gaming the system, but it's just the reality of how the feature interacts with human psychology. I am not one who believes in manipulating the system for gain; instead, I believe that one needs to use this feature as it was intended, and that is to endorse only people that you know well and to endorse them for things that you know they do well. As of the writing of this book, over 200 million endorsements have been given on LinkedIn, and it does not seem likely that they will go away.

LinkedIn has now enabled you to add videos, documents, pictures, and links to your profile. I encourage you to take advantage of these opportunities where you can. Remember, people love pictures and video. If you can give people a sense of you and your business, it will serve you well to do so. My only caution here is to keep it simple. It is possible to fill your profile with so much information, pictures, and video that the profile can get overwhelming. Periodically, I ask people to review my LinkedIn profile and provide feedback. This has been an invaluable source of information over the years in my continuing effort to improve it.

Although LinkedIn is probably the most static of the major platforms, changes are sometimes made. It is helpful to stay on top of these changes and respond, whether that be to adjust your profile accordingly to enhance how you can be found by your future clients and how you are seen by others or to start trying out a new feature so you keep up with the rest of the LinkedIn community. In general, these changes are not all that frequent, and they typically are enhancements to the profile itself, such as endorsements. I would not get overly concerned about these changes, because at the end of the day, the most important feature of LinkedIn is being able to connect and interact with the people that use it. It is simply a good practice to stay in the LinkedIn loop so your profile does not become outdated over time.

Creating Your Business Profile

LinkedIn also offers you the ability to build a business page for your business for free. It is a place where you can allow the members of your company to attach themselves, talk about the mission of your company, and add a company description. It also allows you to give updates similar to a blog for your company. Like your personal profile, you can also ask for and receive recommendations for your company from your current and past clients, which I recommend that you do so that if people should happen to visit your business profile, they can immediately get a feel for your company and its credibility. I believe there is some value to the LinkedIn business page, but not nearly the value that you will gain from your personal profile.

You should build a business profile for you company if for no other reason than to build your brand and give your company some extra SEO power on both LinkedIn and the search engines. However, I question the value of the LinkedIn business page for the solopreneur, entrepreneur, and small businessperson. Most people who use LinkedIn are connecting with people individually; that is, they do most of their searches for people who are connected to the business and not the business itself. What's more, I have yet to see any empirical data that would suggest that spending time on your business page has more value than spending time improving your personal profile page or being active in discussions. Keep in mind, too, that LinkedIn is the least conversational and interactive of all of the social media platforms, and this is even more true in relation to the LinkedIn business page. This detail is important, because the business page can easily become just one more thing for you to manage as the business owner, in spite of the fact that you may not have all that many opportunities to interact with people via this page. In the end, although some professionals may eventually end up on your business page after doing some research, most are going to rely on your personal LinkedIn profile. Thus, although it's a good idea to have a respectable business page with a completed profile, I still encourage you to spend more of your LinkedIn time nurturing your personal profile, where you may get more return on your efforts.

The Real Power of LinkedIn: Groups

Now that LinkedIn has been around for several years, I suspect that many of you have done your best to jump onto the LinkedIn train. You have likely created an account and a profile, posted a picture, and maybe even started garnering recommendations and endorsements. When people of interest send you an invitation to get connected, you probably accept, and yet you still may not have become truly active on LinkedIn. It's as if your account is a glorified online Rolodex where you are collecting contacts. Although LinkedIn is certainly a good way to keep track of people you meet in professional settings or to stay linked to business connections from the past, its real power is in the ability to regularly connect to other groups of people who are having active discussions on LinkedIn on a daily, weekly, or monthly basis.

In my view, LinkedIn's value lies in the ability to join and interact in these groups. As I have mentioned, groups are the subcultures (or, sociologically speaking, the *collectives*) of LinkedIn, and they exist (or can be formed) for nearly every industry. These groups allow you to develop and enhance your professional credibility, demonstrate your knowledge, and share your expertise. I am often surprised at how few people participate in groups, given these benefits.

You can join many groups on LinkedIn, with the maximum number you can join being limited to fifty. For the life of me, I am not sure why someone would want to be in that many groups—the sheer number of notifications from each group and the overall number of discussions generated would overwhelm you, not to mention consume the majority of your time. In my view, there are four basic group types you should be a part of on LinkedIn. I like to think of the groups as being a little like a trampoline. For a trampoline to be stable and safe, you need four legs. The four group types I recommend that you join are the legs of your trampoline, providing a place where you can bounce ideas around and thereby become more of an expert in your field.

Groups like you. The first type of group you should join is one in which people are doing what you do and are similar to you. This is important for four reasons. First, it gives you the opportunity to stay on top of the latest information relevant to your business. Second, it allows you to relate to the struggles and successes of others. Third, you can get solutions from people who do what you are doing. Finally, it is the place where you can demonstrate that you are a thought leader in your industry. There is something very powerful about people within your own industry seeing you as a leader. Quite often, when your peers see you as a leader, this leads to referrals and public opportunities you would not otherwise have available to you.

Local business groups. The second leg of the group trampoline you should join is a local business group. These groups are particularly beneficial at providing updates of how businesses are being affected by current goings-on in your local community. I also find that they notify members of networking events that they may want to participate in. However, the biggest reason you should join local groups is that quite often within these groups, people rely on the group members for referrals for specific businesses and specialties. There is nothing wrong with volunteering yourself, your business, or another business you know in those particular situations when you can truly help the person who has a need. Again, the discussions are important within this group. If you find an opportunity to demonstrate your knowledge, then you should take advantage of it. Keep in mind that people within these professional groups are going to associate you with your business. As you demonstrate your knowledge, you are also gaining more credibility within your own local community.

National and international groups. The third group I recommend you join is a national or international group related to your business. This group is especially important because, quite typically, you will come across topics and information that you may not get from a local group or a smaller industry-specific group. This also allows you to interact with people from other places that you may have not considered before. These types of groups are great for learning unique ideas and gaining more industry knowledge. As with the previous two groups mentioned, it can be a place to increase your credibility, but, beyond that, now you have a national or international platform from which to demonstrate that credibility.

Target market group. Finally, the last type of group I encourage you to join is what I refer to as your *target market group*. This is a group where people in your target market talk and interact regarding issues and information that affect them. So if you are a private consultant to small business, you would perhaps join a small business group. Chances are that members of your target market are going to be there. Remember that these are professional groups, so they are going to be bringing up issues that affect their group. This group will deliver to your doorstep your target market's issues at hand. In addition, these groups may help you uncover the things you need to change in your business to make it more appealing to your target market. This is also an excellent place to play superhero when appropriate. Many times within this group, they will have discussions you can step into and provide answers for because you are the supplier for that target market. This does not mean you should advertise; it does mean you can empower them by providing education and understanding. Whenever you have the opportunity to help your target market understand and learn about your area of expertise, and you do this for free, you have put yourself in the best position to be their answer when they need someone to supply what they want and need. These groups are powerful and can give you and your business a tremendous boost.

When deciding which groups to join, scroll through the Discussions section of the groups to see how interactive the group is. If the group's discussions are consistently generating comments, it is a fair indicator that the group is active and one to consider joining. Also, read the group's rules, if they have them. Not all groups have rules; however, I find that those that frown on self-promotion are far more effective. Last, some groups can be categorized as "open," meaning that as soon as you click the *Join* button, you are in the group. Other groups admit members who submit their requests to the manager(s) of the group, who must approve a person's entrance into the group. I have found both open and by-permission groups to be valuable and useful. I have also come to the conclusion that the rules of the group and the manager(s) truly dictate how productive the group will be.

Here is a personal story that demonstrates how LinkedIn groups can provide a platform for building one's credibility. A few years ago, I joined a group called the Psychological Marketing Network because it was made up of people like me who were interested in psychology and marketing and contained a great blend of consultants for business, consumer psychologists, psychology professionals, and marketers. I commented on specific discussions where I believed I could provide valuable knowledge and expertise. I was commenting (and still do) about every couple of weeks when the manager of the group, Mike Lovas (who with his wife, Pam, is the founder of the company About People, http://www.aboutpeople.com, a business psychology company out of Spokane, Washington), wrote me an e-mail after reading many of my comments.* In this e-mail, he said that my comments demonstrated thought leadership and that I truly enhanced the group with my knowledge and expertise. He then asked me, "Would you be interested in managing the group with me?" I immediately replied, "Absolutely!" even though I never had the intention of trying to step into this role.

This invitation was not only flattering but also gave me immediate credibility in this group, which currently has more than 2,000 members, as I was now a comanager. For the manager of the group to ask me to help and for him to inform all of the members of the group that I was a comanager boosted my credibility tremendously. It would be very difficult for me to develop this kind of credibility so quickly outside of social media; LinkedIn provided me with a chance to not only rub shoulders with 1,500 other peers on a regular basis but to facilitate the discussions among these folks! I am grateful to Mike; we developed a great professional relationship and, more important, an enduring personal relationship that extended far beyond the group. I learned an incredibly valuable social media lesson from this experience: If you have knowledge and expertise and can translate that into value for others, LinkedIn groups are a powerful way to achieve immediate credibility.

I am often asked how frequently a person needs to participate in these groups. In fact, I do not believe that LinkedIn groups are entirely about frequency; instead, participating in groups is about the quality of your comments and the discussions you put out there. My personal rule of thumb is to read through the discussions once a week. Perhaps make a comment every two weeks and create a discussion approximately once a month. Also, note that you can and should manage your groups so that you get what is referred to as *digest format notifications*. Therefore, instead of seeing every single discussion that may come through your groups, you will get a digest of the discussions for the group maybe once a week. This will help you to

---

* Mike recently passed away before he could read this book. This only shows just how fragile life is. Although I never met Mike face-to-face, it was through LinkedIn and our communication with each other that he became more than a colleague: He was a real friend.

decide what discussions you want to participate in, read, or simply ignore. If you choose to manage LinkedIn in this way, you can control the flow of information and it will not be nearly as time consuming.

Try This!

Schedule thirty minutes on your calendar this week to explore and join four different LinkedIn groups. Consider the four kinds of groups I suggest—one related to your field or industry, one local group, one national or international group, and one group that matches your target market—then tailor your groups to your needs. After you have joined the groups, adjust your settings to receive a weekly group digest, schedule time on your calendar in the coming week to read that digest, and make a thoughtful comment within each of these groups.

Repeat for another week or two until you get comfortable reading and commenting and it starts to feel like second nature. What do you think? If needed, use your calendar to set reminders to stay engaged on the group discussions going forward. Give it time and watch how your credibility can grow on LinkedIn and how the referrals may start to flow in.

In Sum: LinkedIn as Credibility Generator

LinkedIn can provide great benefits for you and your company without taking too much of your time. What may stand out the most about LinkedIn is that it has amazing SEO value for you and your business. However, there is no doubt that LinkedIn's value for you also includes the opportunity to build your credibility by demonstrating your knowledge, skills, and abilities and to have them further verified by others through recommendations and endorsements.

LinkedIn, although it may be the most static and least conversational of the platforms, has tremendous value for you professionally and for your business. It will take some time to work on profiles for you and your business, and you will need to periodically update them. In addition, if you are going to get the most of LinkedIn, you will need to be active in groups. Keep in mind that you do not have to belong to dozens of groups; you only need to be in the right groups. And if you are unhappy with a group you are in, there is nothing wrong with leaving the group and finding a place where you can demonstrate just how credible you are in your industry and how you can help others: This is how you will be able to gain not only clients but also great referrals. Ultimately, LinkedIn is a comfortable fit for many business owners and entrepreneurs. It's a great place to start on social media, and it can give you access to individuals that you otherwise might not be able to connect to or converse with outside of the social media realm. Add to that its ability to give you a platform to distinguish you and your business from others out there, and you are on your way!

The Lowdown

- Save posts on what you ate for breakfast and photos of you at the beach for Facebook. LinkedIn is a professional culture, which means you should talk and act like a businessperson there.
- Call human beings superficial, but they will judge you by your photo. Make sure that your LinkedIn photo is professional looking, has a neutral background (no Confederate flags!), and shows your eyes.
- Don't be a quitter: Make sure that your LinkedIn profile is complete. It tells people viewing your profile that you complete the task at hand and you have nothing to hide.
- LinkedIn has tremendous Google search strength. Your Linked profile will often show up on the search results ahead of your website. It's free, so be on it!
- Make sure you ask for recommendations on LinkedIn and be specific about what you want. Recommendations are a way for people to see how others have responded to the quality of what you do and for others to emphasize your knowledge, skills, and expertise.
- Join groups, but be selective. Look for groups that do what you do, local groups, national and international groups, and groups in your target market.

Facebook: Friends that Know You, Like You, and Trust You and Your Business

> You can have everything in life you want if you'll just help enough other people get what they want.
>
> —Zig Ziglar

When it comes to social media, Facebook is a titan. Facebook has self-reported to have over 1 billion users worldwide, with over 160 million of those users in the United States.[1] Although these numbers are a bit suspect (as many people have multiple profiles, which add to this number), there is no doubt that Facebook is currently the largest of any of the social networks. Certainly, in the United States, it is the most popular.

More than likely, your target market is on Facebook. Let's test this theory out by looking at the demographics. It has been estimated that 50% of Facebook users are over the age of 25 years, with 58% of Facebook users being women and 42% of them men.[2,3] Sixty-two percent have an annual income of $100,000 or greater per year, which makes the user base rather affluent (this may come as a surprise). Additionally, 53% of Facebook users are in college or have had a college or graduate school education. The conclusion? If you are interested in connecting to those who are older than 25 years, affluent, and educated, you can find them on Facebook. This social media site, once used only by college students, is now representative of a cross-section of the general public and is thus more than likely relevant to you and your business.

This does not make Facebook the perfect business social networking platform. It is not. In fact, Facebook might even be described as a problem for business, the social media marketer as well. This is because Facebook was not initially created for use by businesses; it was created for people to interact and connect personally. Eventually, Facebook allowed businesses to have a presence on Facebook with "business fan" pages. Although many businesses rushed to get a page, people were not joining Facebook so they could have a relationship with a business. They were (and still are) joining Facebook because they have friends and family using it, and it is a convenient place to connect relationally, on a personal level.

In the beginning, these business pages worked very much like the personal page. If you "liked" a page, you would get to see what that the business was up to, very much like you would see what your friends were doing. Some of us who were liking business pages quickly realized that businesses were clogging up our timelines with business stuff, so many of us started "unliking" pages to reduce the noise.

Something else soon changed for businesses on Facebook as well, and it was called *EdgeRank*. EdgeRank was and is Facebook's robot program that determines just who and how many people who "like" your page will actually see your posts from the business page—meaning that if you have one thousand people who like your business page, only a very small percentage of those people will actually see your business page posts on their news feed. If you want more people to see your posts, you have to spend money through Facebook to promote your posts to the rest of your opted-in fans and others. (In the last quarter of 2013, Facebook further reduced the percentage of people who will see your business posts on their news feed.) It was a clever piece of bait and switch on Facebook's part: Give the business a free page, but set it up so that very few people who like the page will actually see the posts, so the business is now forced to pay to be seen—not just once, but over and over again for each post it wants to promote. Many business owners and managers have felt duped by Facebook, especially the small and microbusiness owners, who have far less cash to spend on marketing than the bigger entities do. Today, more and more small businesses are opting out and abandoning their Facebook business page for other alternatives.

This is why I am attempting to educate you on free ways to use these places. Although Facebook may be trying to force businesses to spend, if the psychology of the user is understood, we, as business owners, do not have to spend money on Facebook: We can earn our business the old-fashioned way, by cultivating and developing relationships that lead customers to know, like, and trust us.

The truth is that I do not consider the Facebook business page to be the best way for small businesses to get business via Facebook, especially those of you who are in sales or the service industries. If you have a product, perhaps there is some value, but if you are in real estate, insurance, financial services, or a B2B industry, your business page may be a waste of time and money. In contrast, your personal profile has tremendous value; what is more, it is free! Other social media marketers will not talk about this, though; as a matter of fact, they probably do not even understand the power of your personal profile for both B2C or B2B businesses. Even business owners themselves do not understand the power of the personal page. This is because they are so focused on traditional marketing methods that they forget about the most powerful and free marketing available: the power of personal relationships and word of mouth.

I cannot say it better than Dan Zarrella, who wrote,

> Old-school marketers just waking up to this reality (Facebook Marketing Power) have been quick to jump on the advertising bandwagon and flood Facebook with mounds of ads with low click-through rates (CTRs). Although the targeting functionality of Facebook's self-service platform is quite powerful, advertising should be a distant second in the Facebook marketing priority list.[4]

There are marketers who will attempt to justify these expenditures with numbers. However, they are, in the end, only marketing to a minority of people, while losing the majority, perhaps forever. As a small business owner or manager, you can ill afford these losses or being associated with the resentment that users experience when it comes to Facebook advertising.

What the social media marketer and businessperson appear to have neglected within Facebook is the psychology of why users are on Facebook (i.e., their motivation): People on Facebook are there to connect with friends, family, and others, such as new acquaintances and friends of friends. They are not there to connect with businesses. It only follows that between Facebook's algorithms to keep businesses from showing on news feeds and the fact that people are not motivated to interact with businesses, the business page is not where things are happening. Instead, the most value for your business lies on the personal page. The keys are to understand the culture of Facebook and the personal motivations of the user (enter social mediology!) so that you can get the most out of Facebook without having to spend a marketing dollar.

Understanding How Facebook Really Works

As a culture, Facebook is easy to define: It is all about personal relationships. The key to this culture, like any social media culture, is in the connection name. Whereas for LinkedIn, we connect as *connections,* on Facebook, we connect as *friends.* This is consistent with the motivations of people connecting on Facebook. In a study conducted by Pew Internet & American Life Project, the number one reason people reported for using Facebook was to connect with family and friends in a personal way.[5] In particular, the three major reasons why people connect, according to the survey, are to stay in touch with friends, stay in touch with family, and reconnect with old friends.

Why is this important? It reminds us that the overwhelming majority of users are not on Facebook to connect with businesses. Keep this in mind. Whereas LinkedIn is a natural culture in which to connect as a business, Facebook is not. In fact, as a business on Facebook, you are more than likely seen as an unwanted stranger; an interrupter; an annoyance; and, at times, just plain evil in the eyes of users. Business motivation is to sell and make money; Facebook culture is to connect and make friends. The two motivations are like oil and water: They do not mix. This can be a challenge for small businesses, which have to use a different strategy to be successful without ticking off their Facebook friends. A little later in the chapter, I describe practical ways to do so effectively, but, for now, let's deconstruct the Facebook culture so you have a true sense of how best to interact there.

It's Personal, Not Business

Facebook is a playground for the personal. Just look at what is being communicated there. The fact that when someone makes a personal status update, the update box asks "What's on your mind?" encourages users to post something personal. It could be a photo, a video, a feeling, or anything the user is thinking or doing. The vast majority of posts are personal in nature; the conversations are personal. When it comes to Facebook and business, there is no overt selling. What is more, the majority of users see advertisements and marketing as noise that interferes with their personal conversations and the ability to keep up with their friends. This is an important part of the culture and one that is difficult—although essential—for most businesses to understand. *It is not a natural part of the Facebook culture to simply connect with a business.*

True, Facebook has business pages, but you will find that, unless you are a major brand, growing these pages in an organic way is difficult to do. For example, although Facebook is a culture of personal conversation, it is quite difficult to cultivate conversation on a business page. This is because the very roots of the culture are founded in the person-to-person connection, not the person-to-business connection. You don't see a lot of conversation on most business pages. Unfortunately, most social media marketers will have you focusing on your Facebook business page. However, as I show in this chapter, for the entrepreneur and small business, your personal Facebook page may be the most effective tool that you have simply because of the role that certain principles of psychology can play in relating your business to who you are personally and what you say as a human being rather than as a business entity. The following section may make this reasoning more clear.

Selling You, Not Your Business

If you have ever been invited to a casual dinner party or wedding reception, then you already know why you and everyone else shouldn't be directly promoting your businesses on Facebook. Let me explain. At a social event, you have been invited not to do business or treat it as a networking event; instead, you are there simply because you are you, and the host of the party believes your presence would make a contribution to the party's success. It's the same on Facebook.

There are fundamental unwritten rules, norms, and expectations when you go to these parties. One is that you are not going to take advantage of the other guests by trying to sell them your product or service. You know how these events are supposed to work. You show up to the party and thank the host for inviting you; he or she ushers you toward the appetizers and other culinary delights and tells you where the drinks are. Then you are on your own. If you happen to know someone, social entrée is easy; he or she may know someone you do not and you get introduced. Otherwise, you will probably eat and drink and listen in on some conversations. Some of them are extremely personal, some are general in nature, and some have a generic business edge to them, but they are between people who are in the same industry or perhaps know each other. You, though, are the outsider.

Like most businesspeople in this situation, you have probably brought a handful of cards with you, and you have your one-minute elevator speech well practiced and ready to go. However, you know that it would be rude to launch right into your business pitch. So what do you do? What you know you should. You make small talk and create conversations; find commonalities; talk sports, movies, TV shows, the latest best buys—whatever it takes to be a part of a conversation.

What does that have to do with business? Nothing and everything. Nothing, because there is no business conversation. Everything, because nearly every successful businessperson knows that having a personal conversation that creates a connection provides an opportunity. Can you imagine if you violated these unwritten norms, rules, and expectations at this party by standing on a chair and announcing, "Hello, everyone, I know most of you do not know who I am, but I own ABC Company and we sell real estate. If you are looking for a house or know someone that is, I'm here! I have my cards with me. Stop by before you leave the party and pick one up! I can't wait to talk to you about how I help people with all their real estate needs! We are fantastic! Actually, number one in the city!" Oh my. Everyone would look at you as if you had dropped in off a distant planet. In fact, you would be lucky if the host didn't say to you, "Get out." Furthermore, you wouldn't be able to count on being invited to any other parties, either.

It does not matter if you are at a wedding reception, at your kid's sporting event, at a national conference, at a casual dinner party, or on Facebook. Personal relationships have always been the most powerful way to create business. Therein lies the power of Facebook: its ability to allow you to build a personal relationship with others by having conversations and revealing the authentic, likable you (not your business) via your personal page.

What's the Point: Why Should You Use Facebook?

The point I am trying to make here is that Facebook is powerful because it allows you to create personal connections through regular conversations that can eventually lead to business wins, referrals, and clients that last a lifetime. Here are some of the specific benefits you can expect if you use Facebook in the ways I am recommending in this chapter.

Personal Interactions that Lead to Professional Relationships

Facebook allows you to express your personal side to potential clients. Building authentic relationships by sharing small talk, expressing humor, congratulating others on milestones, and commenting on their posts lays the groundwork for business transactions. This is how our grandparents did business, and it's how most of us still do business.

This approach is especially significant to the small business owner or entrepreneur who is the face, heart, and soul of his or her business. Unlike major corporations, the small business truly reflects on its owner. If you want people to have a sense of your integrity, character, honesty, or personality, there is no better way to demonstrate it than to interact on a personal level. To that end, Facebook is a powerful tool for showing your Facebook friends what a fantastic person you would be to do business with, without ever directly promoting your services.

Some people have used Facebook as what I like to call a "brag book." You have probably seen these posts before, something like, "I just sold 400 widgets today." A few close friends and family members may congratulate you, but most will probably just ignore the post and move on. That doesn't mean that people shouldn't know occasionally what you are doing, but there is a better way of saying it. For example, if you are concerned that people do not know what you do (although you shouldn't be too concerned because most of us click on the About section of your profile to find out where you live, what you do, etc.), you could say something like, "Had a great conversation with my new client and new friend Tom Jones.

It's great to work with people who know what they want." "Hold on, Jay," you may say, "you said nothing about what the person does for a living!" You're right, but isn't your curiosity piqued? It's almost like creating a story where people have to go to your profile to read the "what you do for a living" ending. Keep in mind, Facebook is about relationships and being personal, so be creative in the way you talk about your business. There is certainly nothing wrong if you want to talk about how your team or place of business helped in the local food shelter and how amazing your experience was. You could also talk about what you experience with your business in a fun and personal way, such as, "Finally home after a long day of negotiating contracts, I am so grateful and at the same time a bit tired." The point here is that you are letting people know about your work without bragging or promoting while trying to be relational at the same time. You are not telling people to do business with you; you are taking them on a journey through the places where your business and personal feelings overlap.

However, do not think for a moment that we can manipulate the people around us on Facebook. Facebook is about being authentic, investing in people and their lives, and intentionally working on relationships. The more genuine we are on this platform, the more we can develop relationships that affect us personally and, as a positive consequence, professionally.

Building Authority, Gaining Influence

Another reason that Facebook is potentially valuable for your business is that it is a perfect place for you to build your authority and gain influence. Influence is important for businesses for several reasons, but two directions of influence on Facebook are most relevant here. The first is *your influence on others*. Do not underestimate just how much authority you have and how influential you are within this platform. You should not be surprised if, when you post a picture of a restaurant that you enjoy, people will quickly respond with "I have been there" or "I need to try it," and then sometime later you will find out that as a result of your picture of the restaurant, five of your friends went to that restaurant.

You can use that same influence to get the word out regarding your business. You just have to be authentic, like you would with real friends, not sales-y or promotional. For example, if you write a book, there may come a time that you want to tell your Facebook friends that your book is about to be put into print, just as you might tell your friends when you saw them at a party. "It has been a long journey; thank you for your support and encouragement. This book is going into print—very exciting!" If you owned a grocery store chain, you might tell your Facebook friends about a 5K race that your organization is sponsoring this weekend and invite friends to join you at the finish line, where you'll be giving out free lemonade. Will your friends buy your book? Will they come get some free lemonade and cheer on local runners? Not all of them, but if you have some influence and you're authentic and human in your posts—not promotional—they just might.

The second channel of influence is *the influence others have to encourage their friends and family to use your business*, simply because they have come to know you, like you, and consequently trust you. You may not believe that this is a true statement, but nearly every one of us has been influenced to go to a restaurant, hair salon, health care provider, auto shop, insurance agency, realtor, photographer, or retail store simply because our friends have told us how great of an experience they had there. If we, in fact, like these friends, we can be easily influenced by them to use products or services that they recommend. This potential for influence is seen on Facebook as much as it is seen in the real world. If you spend any time there, you will see friends extol the virtues of their favorite restaurant; post pictures of products they love; and share joy about their new car, new shoes, or new deck furniture. If those individuals are liked and respected, they may well influence the purchasing decisions of others.

In his book *Influence: The Psychology of Persuasion*, Arizona State University psychology professor and researcher Robert Cialdini, PhD, exposes the realities of how easily humans are influenced and the role that liking takes in that potential for influence.[6] For example, as Dr. Cialdini pointed out, if a salesperson uses the name of someone you like, you have a greater likelihood of purchasing the product or service he or she is selling simply because you like the name-dropped person. When we are liked by others, an amazing amount of trust is associated with that liking.

Facebook Is Follow-up

Last, Facebook is a great follow-up tool to use with potential and existing clients. Although most of us have the time to call or e-mail only a handful of people a day for sales or business development while we are balancing our other business responsibilities, on Facebook, you can stay connected with ten, twenty, even thirty individuals a day with the simple click of the *Like* button, a quick post of "happy birthday," or a relevant comment on someone's status.

If there is one thing that Facebook does better than any other platform, it's enabling people to maintain relationships. We know whose birthday it is, when they get engaged, when they got married, when they have a baby, and so on. We can also create custom lists of people from the different areas in which we are involved. Local friends, distant friends—heck, Facebook even makes recommendations on which list a new friend would possibly be a best fit for (e.g., those from your same high school, college, or city). As for you, the business owner, by regularly participating on Facebook, you are able to show your clients and potential clients that you care about how they are doing while also staying "top of mind" for them, making it easy for them to hire you, promote you, refer you, or hire you again. Think of it as building your brand from the inside out.

I suggest that you create lists that you can easily remember. For instance, you could have a list that's called Current Clients and put any of your current clients that are using Facebook on that list when you friend them. Then you can simply go to the left side of your Facebook news feed, go down to the Friends section, move your mouse over until you see "More," and click on it, which will pull up all of the Friends lists you have created. Simply find the Current Client list and click on it to bring all of the posts that your current clients have posted up on your news feed so you can comment, like, or share them. To go back to the general news feed, just click on the Facebook *f* in the top left corner. Lastly, it's helpful to know too that when you write a post or add a comment, you can call someone out specifically by adding an @ symbol in front of that person's name. This further allows you to create that back-and-forth conversation that helps in building relationships.

This, in a nutshell, is the point of Facebook for the businessperson: to use the platform to get to know others, stay connected, and let them get to know you in a personal, safe, and fun environment that may lead to business and business referrals over time. In fact, if you do nothing more than use Facebook for follow-ups, I believe it can be the biggest revenue generator of all of the social media platforms because it allows you to stay in touch so easily with your previous and current clients—your best referral source of all.

The Psychology of Being Liked

Facebook provides a great way to share parts of your life with others so they can begin to know, like, and trust you (see Chapter 1 for the value of knowing, liking, and trusting). Here are some tidbits from psychology on why people tend to like us and how you can use this understanding to connect most effectively with others on Facebook.

People like those they see as attractive. As human beings, we are drawn to attractive people; even infants will turn their head to a picture of an attractive person versus an unattractive person.[7] Reports of a study in Canada conducted during federal elections also found that attractive candidates received more than twice as many votes as did less attractive candidates. As humans, we find more attractive people more intelligent, more friendly, and certainly more likeable. There is nothing we can do about our physical attractiveness; however, you should know that this is why it is so critical to have a good picture of you on your personal Facebook page: to make you as attractive as possible.

People like those who give them compliments. You may have heard the saying, "Flattery will get you nowhere." That is not true. Research has shown that compliments create liking. What!? It sounds so simple, and it is true. When people compliment us, especially in public, our affinity for them grows. On Facebook, the compliment you give can be as simple as liking someone's new profile picture, sharing a post (especially one you know will be of particular interest to someone), or making a comment on the post. If you are genuine and intentional, these relationships will pay off repeatedly, both personally and professionally.

People like those they see as being similar to them. Psychology also tells us that we like people who are like us, agree with us, and share similarities with us. By the way, even the smallest similarity can be very powerful. Facebook has done a very good job of understanding this. Have you ever wondered why Facebook asks for TV shows you like, books you read, and so on? It is because they are looking for friends that may share common interests with you so you can grow your friend family. It is a very interesting reason why Facebook works. It allows you to find mutual friends and common interests, and it recommends these friends to you. Although that may seem a bit disturbing (ask anyone whose ex has popped up in the "people you may know" list), the fact is that it can be a good thing for you because you can have a built-in group of people that you can build relationships with that can help you and your business grow.

People like those they are familiar with. The last reason I will go into why people like us relates to frequency. Earlier in the book, I talked about the mere exposure effect by Zajonc, which posits that the more people see us, the more they develop a preference for us. I have a classic high school story to tell that illustrates this effect. It's about the girl who sits next to a guy in biology lab to whom she is not attracted. However, by the end of the semester, she develops an attraction toward him.

I know this one well; it is how I lured—or maybe it's better characterized as wore down—my wife. She will tell you that initially she was not attracted to me, but there was a point at which she realized that we were frequenting the same events due to similar interests. Over time, yep, she found me attractive. As fate would have it, she married me. Sometimes simple frequency and repetition causes preference. Zajonc called it the mere exposure effect, whereas in marketing, we think of it as branding. Whatever you choose to call it, the fact is, the more we see something, the more we develop a preference for it. If Facebook doesn't offer you a natural platform to be regularly seen by your potential clients, then I don't know what does. It's a place where you can post status updates daily and get in front of people in a fun and welcome way.

Your Business Rx: Getting the Most Out of Your Personal Page

It is time we take a serious look at your personal profile so you can design it effectively and be well set up to connect with others, following the cultural norms of Facebook. There are, in fact, some very simple things that you can do right in your profile to become a relationship builder.

Creating a Friendly Profile

Your photo. First, your profile picture (the photo that is seen when you post) is extremely important, because it creates people's first impression of you. I see two frequent mistakes that business owners make with their Facebook profile picture. The first one is that they use their business picture. Unfortunately, there is nothing that says "I am here for business purposes and not relationships" more than people posting their business card pictures. Remember that Facebook is a friend culture, so make sure your picture is fun, casual, or interesting (not a business headshot); in this way, people will know you are there for the right reasons, not ulterior business motives. Let them see in your picture the casual, nonbusiness side of you, whether it be you playing an instrument, striking a yoga pose, or hiking in the woods.

The second mistake I see people make with their personal profile picture is to have a picture of their dog or cat or something other than themselves. Beware! Users are often put off by people who do not have a personal profile picture of themselves, whether because they seem disengaged, not real, or as if they are hiding something. We don't want to talk to your cat or dog, we want to talk to a person, and although we may think your kids are cute, they are still not you and don't let us know who you are and what you look like. The truth is that we need to see you; in fact, we rely on your picture to help us form an understanding of who you are.[8] Regardless of a person's reasons for not including a picture of oneself, the absence of a picture can put the user on high alert or lead to a sense of distrust. Your photo is one of the simplest ways to warm up your Facebook profile, allowing you to come alive on the computer or smartphone screen and become a real person and relationship maker; it's important to share it.

These days, your personal photo is not the only photo on your profile. You also have a cover photo. This is the large photo that sits at the top of your personal Facebook page, serving as the main backdrop. Consider a couple of things when choosing this particular photo. First, keep in mind that this is your personal page, so, again, avoid a business look. To date, not much research has been done on the cover photo; however, I would strongly suggest that you make it either fun or interesting and, most of all, representative of you as a person, not your business. For example, if you have a picture of your family that you like, put it up. Perhaps it is a picture of your favorite vacation, or maybe it is something funny. The key here is to tell people more about what makes you tick and avoid being an advertisement.

One last word about profile and cover photos: Do not be afraid to change them to signify a special event or to simply update your picture. Remember, the most commented and liked status updates on Facebook are photos. I am consistently amazed, when someone changes either their profile picture or their cover photo, how many people make comments or simply like it. As always, listen to your friends here: They have subtle and sometimes not-so-subtle ways of telling you what they like and don't like. When it comes to others not liking your photo, rarely will they say anything, meaning that people will not want to publicly say, "Well, that photo sucks!" They are more than likely not going to say anything. I personally use this as a default value for the success and failure of photos. If I get some comments and likes, then the photo probably has touched someone in a positive way. However, when no one says anything, I will change it. Keep in mind that people generally like pictures, so there is nothing wrong with changing your pictures just to generate some commentary and interaction. If you cannot think of something to say on Facebook, change your profile and cover pictures out and see what happens.

Your profile name. The next thing to consider is your Facebook profile domain name. One of my least favorites is when a business uses their company name as their personal Facebook name, as in "Jane Smith Insurance." What the person did, in this case, is sign up for Facebook as if "Insurance" were her last name. I shake my head and simply say, "Why?" We all know what you are doing. We know that you are trying to promote yourself. We are also suspicious of your motivations. Why is your last name "Insurance"? Because your motivation is to sell us insurance. Well, Ms. Insurance, we want to talk with Jane without Jane talking about insurance. Just use your real name, please.

Facebook does give you the option of creating your own domain name. For example, although I signed up as "Jay Izso" and am searchable as "Jay Izso" on Facebook, my domain name is http://www.facebook.com/internetdoctor for my personal page. I think this is where there is a slight exception to the suggestion that we avoid use of our business name. First, I am the Internet Doctor, and I have found that my brand name is easier for people to spell than my last name. You would not think so, my surname being only four letters, but the combinations that people use to spell it are creative, for whatever reason. If my name were simpler to spell, I certainly would have used it. However, if you read my actual personal page, it does not say Internet Doctor, it only says Jay Izso. I do not sell anything, I stay friendly, and my interactions with people are as Jay Izso and nothing more than that. I think this is where you really need to be careful. If you are in sales, stay away from a sales-y profile domain name.

With your Facebook profile picture, cover photo, and domain name set up, you are well on your way. You can complete your profile by entering information regarding your interests; your relationships; your birthday; past travel; and even your favorite movies, books, and quotations. Although you certainly don't need to provide information for every profile prompt offered by Facebook, I encourage you to provide enough of a sense of who you are so that your profile starts to bring your personality to life. This is also a great opportunity to include your work and educational background as well as a company website—an easy way to let people know within the natural context of Facebook a little about what you do.

Making Friends

With your profile built, you are ready to launch into the world of making Facebook friends: It's time to start inviting people to become part of your Facebook community. First, start with people you know—friends, family members, neighbors, book club acquaintances, those on your bowling league or softball team, and so on. Then, as you go about your daily life, you will likely meet and perhaps have a good conversation with people who may ask if you are on Facebook. In situations like these, I friend them and recommend that you do the same. This is also a good opportunity for you to ask others that you meet to become friends on Facebook.

Some people are not so keen on the idea of this type of friendship on Facebook. Many people believe that Facebook is only for their close friends and family and would never friend a colleague or acquaintance. Well, that's fine if you are just using Facebook for fun, but if you are using it for your business, then turning down these opportunities just doesn't make sense. Think about it: Word of mouth is still the most powerful free tool available when it comes to marketing. Word of mouth is both personal and professional. When it comes to the small business owner, your personal page is the best way for people to get to know you, and, let's face it, you are the business. If people come to know you as a person and come to like you because of the way you interact on Facebook, they will come to trust you and, more important, trust your business and be willing to refer you to others. Let me give an example.

Nancy Nguyen is a fun and savvy thirty-year-old author and entrepreneur. One of her businesses is a hair salon called Sweet T Salon that is located in Raleigh, North Carolina. Nancy is a strong Facebook user. Although she does have a business page (http://www.facebook.com/SweetTSalon), it is her personal page that truly connects her with Facebook users, many of whom are also her clients (http://www.facebook.com/NancyNguyenUSA). When I interviewed her, Nancy explained to me that it is her personal side that people connect with and trust. She doesn't have to talk business on Facebook; she is just friendly and supportive of others. She understands that as she supports other people and what they do, they, in turn, will support her endeavors as well. As I sat in the Sweet T Salon and observed the clients coming and going, I was blown away by the way in which everyone seemed to have a real and personal relationship with Nancy, even if she wasn't the one who was going to cut the client's hair. Hugs, hellos, and "how are you's?" to Nancy were the norm. "I saw on Facebook that you were in Chicago. How'd it go?" a customer might ask Nancy. It didn't matter if the client was a young college woman or a burly 50-something man, everyone seemed to feel comfortable giving Nancy a hug. It was knowing, liking, and trusting in action.

Although Nancy is unable to pinpoint just how many clients Facebook has helped her generate and maintain, it is clear that she understands how to use Facebook to create relationships and goodwill. Perhaps it is because Nancy grew up around her family's hair salon or because she has her MBA, but Nancy understands business. She smartly told me, "Who does not want referrals? We all do, and my Facebook friends are some of my best referral sources. It all starts with just doing what Facebook is designed for, being a friend and doing what friends do."

I often wonder if people have forgotten the importance of referrals. I also am curious if people have forgotten that personal connections are a major part of why referrals even occur. I have worked in several industries, including real estate. The one thing successful real estate agents do very well is to refer business to each other. Why they refer one agent over another is quite interesting. First, the agent being referred has to be qualified, that is, he or she must have the skills. However, the key factor that I consistently find when it comes to giving referrals is that the person referring and the person being referred have developed, in a very short time, some personal connection. Typically, it happened at a conference where a small group of agents had a spontaneous lunch or dinner, or perhaps shared drinks at the hotel bar. In interviews, these agents reported that they get a ton of business cards during a conference; however, the cards that they pay attention to most frequently and use for referrals were from those agents that they spent some personal time with, having personal conversations.

Recently, I talked to a number of real estate agents. Those who were using Facebook said that staying in touch with other real estate agents personally via Facebook has made a huge impact on their referral business. Why? As one agent pointed out to me, "My personal Facebook page lets me keep up personally with my colleagues, interact personally, and develop a real relationship that keeps me 'top of mind.'" There it is: the mere exposure effect and personal influence all wrapped into one. With Facebook, more than any of the other social media platforms, you can develop and maintain personal relationships that transfer over to real, professional, bottom-line business.

Launching a Business Via Facebook

Perhaps one of the most compelling examples of Facebook's power for business can be seen in the story of Travis Brodeen, cofounder of Digital Grove (http://www.facebook.com/digitalgrove), a start-up IT consulting company out of Austin, Texas, that was founded in the fall of 2013. When Travis first started his company, like most entrepreneurs, he was trying to find a way to get his message out. Candidly, he said, "I made a mistake at first. I decided that I would try to announce my new venture using e-mail, but it did not generate clients." Travis, who is very relational on Facebook, made a decision. For months prior to launch, he had been sharing with his Facebook friends his goals and passion for his new adventure of starting a new business. He then decided that he would ask his friends for support in making his business venture a success by writing the following on his personal Facebook page:

> Need a part time CTO? Have a software development project or integration need? Want to improve your company's performance on either a technical or a managerial level? No? Do you know someone who does? I'm taking new clients and providing free consultations and health checks.

Travis shared that when he wrote this inquiry to his Facebook friends, he felt fear and trepidation. His thought was that perhaps he was being too sales-like. However, what happened next changed all of those fear-filled emotions: Travis immediately received three text messages that all turned into paying clients. In one case, Travis remarked to me, "One of my friends texted me and told me he was going to talk to his boss, after all, it was free, they had nothing to lose." He landed the account. In fact, not only did Travis land all three jobs that were texted to him, he also found his first two employees through the same post! He told me that they were not really looking for jobs; they just wanted to help him out.

Several things are important to note here. First, Travis did not continue to hammer his Facebook friends with his business requests. Second, he had set this up by first creating solid relationships with his Facebook friends, taking them along his new career path and journey of starting a new business. As Travis shared with me, "We have all seen the posts of people using Facebook as a billboard. I didn't want to be that guy or business. I did want to be authentic and genuine about my passion. My Facebook friends knew that I was preparing to start a new company and I was on an adventure. I felt that I could take them on my journey without begging for business." Third, he offered something for free without obligation. Finally and most important, it was Travis's great relationships with his Facebook friends that created amazing evangelists for his start-up.

As it turned out for Travis and Digital Grove, this was the only post he needed to make to get his business off the ground. Those first three jobs turned into additional work, and his business grew organically from there, with each contract running in the thousands of dollars and his client base now having extended into Europe. Thank you, Facebook!

I am not saying this will happen to you, but it certainly demonstrates the potential your Facebook relationships can have. Let's keep in mind too that this is a B2B company. We often forget that behind every B2B company are real people who make decisions and have tremendous influence that can create, maintain, and grow a business. It all starts and ends with the relationships you cultivate on Facebook. If you take Travis's approach of developing those relationships, the potential to count on those people to grow your business may just be exponential.

What to Post

We now move to the question, What should you post on your personal page and how should you use your personal page? Here is my simple answer, in the form of another question: "What do you talk about with a group of friends face-to-face?" Facebook is not that complicated and, what is more, it shouldn't be. You don't have to be clever, be overly creative, or have some exuberant personality characteristic. You just have to be able to talk to people like you would personally in real life. What things do you talk about with your friends—well, that you can make public? Do you talk about restaurants, a movie, a TV show, your children, or something you found interesting? Post it.

I believe that the reason why so many people, especially businesspeople, are reluctant to use Facebook regularly once they are on it is because they believe that there is some trick to it. There isn't. It is just people having everyday conversations, and there are many conversations going on at the same time. Pick and choose which conversations you want to be a part of and be a part of them. All that's happening on Facebook is the casual conversation that we have every day with ordinary people, like what we cooked for dinner or how we spent the weekend, which gives them insight into who we really are as people.

I know that about a third of you that are reading right now are saying, "No one is interested in what I made for dinner." Actually, take a picture of it, and they may well be. This is typically when I get, "That's crazy." No, it isn't. I love to cook, and my wife (although she may be biased) thinks and tells me that my food is generally excellent. She even tells others. I can't tell you how many face-to-face conversations I have about recipes and cooking with other people. So, I post some pictures on Facebook of my culinary creations, and—what do you know?—the responses and interaction sound eerily similar to the same conversations I have face-to-face. Now, it is true that not everyone is interested in what I cooked for dinner, but it is one thing I do that I enjoy and I share it. It is a very authentic part of who I am, and many people seem to respond to my enthusiasm. My point is for you to be the authentic person that you are. If you take a trip, share some photos of your adventure. Did you see a sign that made you chuckle? Share it.

I am spending a great deal of time talking about photos, so this is probably a good place to explain why photo sharing is so important on Facebook. Dan Zarrella, a leading researcher in social media, has discovered some interesting data with regard to posting: Photos on Facebook receive far more likes and shares than either text-only posts or videos.[9] Why? Because humans are visual creatures. We make judgments based on what we see because it is a simple format that requires little interpretation of emotion; our eyes tell us what we need to know.

Now, for another interesting finding: What gains the most comments, according to Zarrella's research, is text-only posts. There is a caveat to all of this: It is better if your text is either very short (less than 100 characters) or long (over 350 characters).[10] What is the takeaway from all of this? Post a status update! Although there is some scientific evidence for the power of photos, text, and video, the overwhelming point is to post something that you find interesting and personal so you can become present to others on Facebook and show them the real, likable you.

What Time Is Best to Post on Facebook?

As you are posting all this great content, consider what time of day works best for your audience. According to Dan Zarrella's research, it appears that the best time of day to post is generally after 5 p.m. and on weekends.[11] Why? Perhaps it is because many businesses do not allow their employees to use Facebook, even blocking Facebook use in some workplaces. Many users catch up with their news feeds on their phones immediately after work, or perhaps they catch up when they get home by reading their news feed on their tablet or desktop. Many people also have access to their Facebook news feed on the weekend because they tend to be away from the office and have some free time on their hands; it follows that they may be the most active then. Although this finding is interesting and you may read differing opinions on the days and times when you should post, also consider that your audience may be unique. If your target market tends to be stay-at-home moms or retired seniors, you may find that it's most effective to post at other times of day on weekdays. Be willing to experiment and pay attention to the results.

Share the Facebook Love: Commenting and Liking

Consider, for a moment, the possibility that you cannot think of something to post on Facebook. Perhaps you have experienced one of the sins of memory called *blocking,* where you just cannot think of anything. No problem: Comment and like other peoples' posts. Why is that so important? Recall our earlier discussion of reciprocity? It is powerful. If you spend a great deal of your time simply commenting and liking others' posts, when you do post something, you will find that people respond pretty quickly. It is an amazing phenomenon, as if people are just waiting for the opportunity to return your encouragement. It is also a compliment to others when you comment or like their posts because it is social validation that they have posted something that has value.

Did you see the psychology here? These three principles of psychology are all working in conjunction with each other simply through your commenting and liking, and let's not forget the power of sharing. When you share someone's post, this is similar to telling someone, "Not only do I like this, I like it so much I have to let my friends see it." Now the real power of Facebook can take over, and it cost you nothing. This doesn't mean that you should comment, like, or share every post on your news feed; it means to genuinely and honestly comment, like, and share those posts with your Facebook friends that you believe have value for that particular group of people.

Facebook does try to help you when it comes to figuring out what to post. For example, Facebook will remind you about your friends' birthdays, engagements, marriages, and other important events. Keep in mind that for some of these, you do have to adjust your settings to make sure you see them. I want to see these kinds of announcements because I know that these are significant events for my friends. In most cases, my friends live out of town and I cannot make their wedding or birthday party, but I still want to make sure that I recognize these milestones. One of the first things I do in the morning is to check these life events. In this way, I am assured that I have stayed in touch with the right folks at the right time, even if it is on only this simple level.

Keeping in Touch and Following up: The Power of Lists

One of the most important features of Facebook for you as a businessperson is the one that allows you to categorize your friends in different lists so you can post for one group but not another. Why would you want to categorize people into lists? Well, first of all, having a list allows you the option of posting a particular update to a particular group of people. For example, I have a list I've named Clients. This is a list of people I either currently consult or have consulted with previously. Many times, I will run across a link or piece of information that I believe is beneficial for people on this particular list but maybe not for other people who follow me. Facebook allows me to customize who I want to post to, so I may choose this list because I believe the information is especially important to them. It also allows me to continue posting more personal information for close friends and family that I don't necessarily want to post for clients.

Also, I realize that my best source of future business is my current and past clients. I can pull up my Clients list and I will see only those posts by my clients without seeing all of my friends' posts. Because I want to focus on the clients, I can now quickly scroll through their posts and comment on, like, and share those posts in particular. Facebook, in this sense, is follow-up made easy.

I find that one of our greatest weaknesses in business is follow-up. Follow-up is difficult because it takes time. If you have a fairly large number of clients, trying to make a phone call or hand write a note to every client you want to keep in touch with can be time consuming. It is so much faster and easier on Facebook to have a list and run through what is going on in the lives of these very important people. I can look at nearly 25 posts in a matter of minutes and stay connected with these clients in a personal way that I just do not have the time to in real life. Having the Clients list allows me to follow up and stay in contact with those people who, first of all, have supported me with their hard-earned dollars and, at the same time, keep me at the forefront of their thoughts as a result of our regular exposure on Facebook. Of course, Facebook is not the only follow-up you should do, but it is certainly an easy way to stay connected and maintain relationships. There is still nothing like a casual lunch, quick phone call, or personal note to demonstrate another person's value. I am merely suggesting that Facebook can help to fill in the gap when you simply couldn't otherwise stay in touch with people on such a frequent basis.

Try This!

It's time to start using Facebook for your business. Make a list of the clients you have a good relationship with and send them an invitation to become Facebook friends if you aren't already connected. Are there any individuals that you are hoping to do business with in the future that you feel would be okay with adding as Facebook friends? Invite these folks, too. Over the coming week, chances are that some of these individuals will accept.

Now put a note on your calendar to check back in a week to create a list of Facebook contacts called Clients. Be sure to add all of those Facebook friends you are already doing business with or hope to do business with. Next, add a quarterly reminder to your calendar to invite new clients to friend you on Facebook.

Going forward, make a habit of clicking on this Clients list when you visit Facebook so that you can view your Clients news feed. Like, share, and comment on your clients' and potential clients' posts in an authentic way and enjoy the opportunity to interact with them on a regular basis, helping to keep you top of mind and increasing the chances that they will think of you when they or their friends are ready to do business.

The Dreaded Facebook Business Page

Now that we've reviewed the ins and outs of your personal Facebook page, it's time to look at that pesky Facebook business page. The best way to define the business page is to think of it as a free fan page for your business that has the look and appearance of a personal page but has limited interactive capabilities as compared with your actual personal page.

If you are a small business, the business page is probably one of the most difficult things to work with on Facebook. I say that because there are a ton of people sharing a ton of ideas on how best to use the page, and, quite frankly, some of it is good, but most of it is not so good. I know one thing for sure: Facebook has not made the business page easy if you are on a limited budget. The page may be free, but it is difficult to get it seen. This is because Facebook does not allow everyone who "likes" your page to see it, and, what is more, the business page does not fit neatly into Facebook culture, because people are more skeptical of the motivations of those who have set up the business pages.

When it comes to Facebook, do not forget why people are using it: to connect with other people. If they are interested in connecting with a business, they want to interact with the business on their time and their schedule; they do not want the business to force itself on them by popping up on their news feed with a promotional type of post or by hanging around as a sidebar ad.

I recently conducted a small, impromptu survey to get a feel for what people think about advertising and sponsored posts on Facebook. I asked people to indicate on a Likert-type rating scale, where 1 = *I like it,* 5 = *I do not care,* and 10 = *I hate it,* how they felt about ads on Facebook. The average rating from more than 30 respondents was 7.2, a pretty strong indicator that people do not like business-sponsored advertising on Facebook. To most folks, business-sponsored ads on Facebook simply create noise and clutter their news feed.

Lab42 conducted a study of social media and brands.[12] One of the questions they were attempting to answer is why people turn away from brands on social media. According to their study, 73% of people have "unliked" brands on Facebook. The number one reason was that the brand posts too frequently. Nearly half of those surveyed reported they did not like brands on Facebook because they "clutter my newsfeed." It is pretty good evidence that Facebook, for businesses, is a one-way street and that business pages are often like outlaws in a friendly land.

I am well aware that you will run across many social media marketers who will say that paid advertising is advantageous and inexpensive for a business. Unfortunately, these individuals are not calculating the true cost that this kind of advertising can have for the business. When businesses add advertising noise to a place where people go to create, maintain, and enhance relationships, it begins to invade the freedom the user desires to have in regard to these personal conversations. When the user feels that his or her freedom is being threatened, it creates something called *psychological reactance,* which often reveals itself in the behavior of the user to regain freedom.[13, 14]

In the realm of social media, psychological reactance might involve unliking your business page, unfriending you personally, or hiding your personal posts. I say this after interviewing hundreds of Facebook users, both online and face-to-face, who have told me how they will do anything they can to avoid seeing ads or they will simply try to ignore them. It is easy for the user to do. You are merely one click away from your business being gone forever, simply because of the perception that you have taken away one's freedom to use the platform as they wish through your advertisement.

What's more, there is a growing trend of users who are seeking out and using ad blockers to customize their Facebook news feeds so they no longer can see or have to deal with the noise associated with sponsored business-page advertising. Many have also said that they use mobile versions of Facebook to avoid having to deal with the advertising visible in the news feed when viewed on their computers (although advertisements are coming soon to our mobile devices as well). It is true that some small businesses have reported doing well with paid-ad social media; however, if you are in a service industry, it can be extremely expensive. When I have asked how these companies are measuring success, rarely have I found that they can put a dollar value on how their paid-for Facebook advertising has increased their bottom line. The fact is that the value of Facebook advertising for the small business is tremendously difficult to measure in actual dollars. (We talk more about this in Ch. 8.)

So what do these mixed results mean for you? Simply this: You don't have to spend any money advertising on Facebook to be successful using it. I have experimented with both paid-for advertising and business-page paid-for postpromotion. What I have discovered is that the non-paid work will be more effective, not annoy your friends, and allow you to avoid adding to your marketing budget. That being said, it will cost you some time in developing your strategy; however, for the small business, especially the microbusiness owner, the benefits of using your business page in the right way for free will be of far greater benefit to you and your business than spending marketing dollars on paid ads that can get expensive.

A Better Way to Do Business on Facebook

There is a better way to use your Facebook page that will not cause as much angst and negativity as paid advertising and that will likely get you better results without costing money. Here are a few fundamentals critical to your success.

Choosing a name for your business page. First, the name of your business page is important. Facebook only allows you to change your name one time, unless you have over two hundred likes on your page, at which point, you can no longer change the name of your page. This is important, as companies are gobbling up names. Even if you do not have a page active right now but plan to in the future, I would strongly suggest that you claim your business page name now. If your business page name is taken, and it may be, try to find a way to still use your business name by adding a word like *The* in front of your business name, or perhaps add a descriptor of your business to the end of your business name. For example, if your business name is A Touch of Class and you sell clothing, you could add the word *Clothing* to the end of your name. Another strategy is to create a name that is a descriptor of what you do. So, let us say that you're in the consulting business, your name is already taken, and adding the word *Consulting* to the end of your name has also already been done. If you consult with small businesses, you can possibly add *Small Business Consulting* or *Consultant to Small Business* to your business name. Certainly, your business name is the best route to go if it is available, and I highly recommend you find a way to incorporate it into your business page name.

Completing your business profile. It is also important that you fill out all of the fields in the profile of your business page. That is, as you are creating your business page profile, make sure that you have filled out all of the information possible, such as your business address, website URL, and hours of operation. Do not frustrate the potential customers you have enticed to a business page by not having a way of contacting you or not providing a description of the business. This also means that you want to control your privacy settings to allow as many people as possible to be able to see your business, for example, selecting "Public" for "Who Can See My Stuff?" (explore your Privacy Settings to see this and related options).

Selecting your photo. Next, make sure you have a high-quality cover photo (the large photo that starts off your business page) that meets with the guidelines of Facebook. These guidelines are not difficult to follow, and recently Facebook simplified them. They read as follows:

> All covers are public. This means that anyone who visits your Page will be able to see your cover. Covers can't be deceptive, misleading, or infringe on anyone else's copyright. You may not encourage people to upload your cover to their personal timelines.[15]

This is very different from what was previously true about Facebook photos for business pages. This now means that we can include our web address, physical address, phone number, and even a call to action within the cover photo. Previously, this was not allowable. For some reason, Facebook did not announce this change publicly. The rules may change again, but until they do, you should certainly take advantage of the new guidelines, especially as a small business owner. When it comes to your cover photo, make sure it looks crisp, clean, and clear and is easy to read. Do not force your user to struggle to read or see something. It also can create a bad first impression of your business if your cover photo looks blurry, pixelated, or low quality. You get one chance to make a first impression, so make it count. Include your logo somewhere on the photo as well. Remember, we want the mere exposure effect to start working with your brand, because the more your Facebook audience sees your brand, the more they will be attracted to it.

The next photo to upload is your thumbnail photo, which is located on the lower left corner of your cover photo. There are a couple of options here. You can use your logo, which I think is the best option for most small businesses. However, if you, like me, are your own brand—that is, the entrepreneur who offers a service and the person who will be in contact with your potential client—then it is perfectly acceptable to use a photo of yourself. Keep in mind that Facebook is a person-to-person, relationship-first platform. Any chance that I have to give people the face of a real person that they can emotionally connect to, I am going to default that way.

That being said, although as a small business you should maintain some sort of personal connection, it does not mean that a logo for your thumbnail photo is inappropriate. Perhaps you include people in the cover photo to ensure that personal touch, whether it contains a group of your smiling employees or some of your satisfied clients with your product. Keep in mind that people are influenced when they see similar others modeling behavior. If you have a picture of your clients on your business page news feed, it will go a long way to bridging that emotional gap of how Facebook users initially feel about business to help them have a more personal relationship with your own business.

Populate Your Business Page with Content

Now that your profile and cover photo are set up, it's time to start posting good content on your page. The goal is to post information that your target audience might find interesting or care about. This is critical even before I mention that you can invite people to your page. If you do not have good, useful, or even fun content on your page, then why would people visit? The answer: They would have no reason. You need to make sure that you have good content.

What does good content look like? It can be a variety of things. Here are some of the possibilities:

- Share client success stories.
- Offer discounts and promotions.
- Show photos of clients with your products or different people who work in your store or business.
- Provide videos of client testimonials, or perhaps take short video of some things that people may be interested in around your place of business, creating a virtual tour of your products or information that may engage prospective clients.
- Hold a contest such as funniest holiday picture, in which people can win a gift certificate to a nice restaurant.
- Give away sports or entertainment tickets so people have to come to your office to pick them up and meet you and your employees.

As you post on your Facebook business page, try to be fun and interesting. Also, not everything has to be about your business, and it is okay to share things that may be relevant to your business but are not business-y. For example, post things that are happening in your area, or perhaps a funny cartoon. Last, test, test, test: Pay attention to what you post and what is getting the most responses, whether in the form of likes, comments, or shares, and use that to inform what and how you post in the future.

Photos. Whether it be photos you find on the web, pictures you take, or others' photos or pictograms that you choose to share, pictures are a great way to engage your followers on the business page (see Dan Zarrella's research findings earlier in the chapter). Again, psychologically, humans like pictures. We are visual by nature. It only follows, then, that pictures will help your business page. Facebook does do something very cool when it comes to links and photos. If you find a link to some content that you believe would be of interest to your Facebook page fans, put the link in the status box, and Facebook will generate a post with a picture. Here is the cool part: Many of these links have multiple pictures, so you can click through the arrows on the photo that is being shown and select which picture that you want to be associated with your link.

Donna and Jen Hankin are a mother–daughter team and, along with the rest of their family, own two small businesses: Venture Joint Jewelry and Peachy Keen, which is a retail women's fashion and accessory store (http://www.facebook.com/thepeachykeen). Jen plays an active role in all aspects of the store, but one of her favorite roles is serving as the communication and social media manager for both businesses. When it comes to demonstrating a great combination of pictures and consistency, Jen does an amazing job. She posts pictures of new fashions, discounts, and specials on the Peachy Keen business page. Jen takes a fabulous approach to showing off her fashion and accessories: Many times, she uses her current clients as her models!

The psychology behind this is genius. As Jen has discovered, most people, when asked to be a model for clothing, very rarely, if ever, say "no." What is more, when people are put in a position where they are going to be able to be publicly acknowledged as the model, they are given a sense of fame. It is a tremendous compliment. It boosts self-esteem and confidence and serves as a public compliment that creates a powerful role of influence with our friends. What a great way it is to get a page likes is when one of our friends can say, "I modeled some clothes for Company X. They are going to post the pictures on Facebook; go over to their page and check them out."

With her Facebook approach, not only has Jen created a raving fan that is a client, but now that client is influencing her friends to like the page. Further, now those friends have a desire to become clients because they may also get an opportunity to be a model in the future. With over 1,500 page likes as a small business, Peachy Keen is using its Facebook fan page as a client maintenance tool as well as a future client generator.

How can you use Facebook photos to your advantage? What creative ways can you find to post visual items for your audience? Maybe you share travel photos from a recent conference, post pictures of new products, or have a contest in which your Facebook friends submit photos—whether relevant to your product, service, or industry or even to celebrate the season. A dose of creativity is useful here, so take some time to generate ideas and bring in others to help you brainstorm when needed.

Video. After photos, videos are becoming major elements on Facebook business pages. Video is popular on Facebook simply because it is visual. The user can be passive: He or she does not have to read; the user only has to watch and listen. I fully understand that video is another layer of technology; however, many of today's smartphones come with high-definition video recorders on them, so making and posting a video is much easier than it has ever been. I strongly suggest experimenting with it. I encourage you to record videos of clients in the store or office, or have them submit one of their own in which they talk about their experience with your business.

I have found that the better the quality of the video, the better the response, especially when it comes to the audio portion of the video. This is probably true because speakers on the mobile devices on which your video may be seen are small; therefore, clear audio enhances the viewing. All this being said, I would also note that a professionally done video is completely acceptable, but not necessary. You may be amazed by the results of video and how giving other people the spotlight on your business can, in turn, give them the authority to influence others to visit your page and your business.

Contests, promotions, discounts, and giveaways. Another way to use your Facebook business page is to push people to your website to capitalize on an offer or a discount. Perhaps you are able to make an offer or highlight a discount that is directly related to your business, but if that is not an option for your particular type of product or service, I have found that businesses will offer, say, tickets to a movie, special event, or sporting event instead. Facebook now allows you to do contests from your business page, such that you can have a promotion or contest contingent on likes, comments, or shares. However, you can also drive traffic to your website from the business page with a post such as, "Go to our website to register for a chance at two tickets for [the ballet, opera, baseball game, etc.]." Either way, people like getting things for free. This may cost you a little money for the tickets or giveaway prize, but it is far less expensive than regular, paid Facebook ads and far more acceptable to users if they have an opportunity to get something for free. Even better, it generates a great amount of goodwill. Many times, you can get gift certificates, tickets, or other discounts contributed from other businesses if you give the business a shout out from your business page. Or you can get creative and think about what best to give away from your own company to generate more business. For example, if you are an interior decorator, you could create a contest in which you ask people to post a picture of the ugliest room in their house, ask people to vote for the worst-looking room, and then give free design advice to the winner for that room. Afterward, you can post the winning picture, showing off your design expertise to the group.

You do two things with a promotion like this. First, you create buzz, as people will tell their friends about the contest and ask them to click on the pictures they posted to your site, generating traffic for your page. I hope your business website is full of good and useful content, because then you have an opportunity for those people to see more about your company and to understand what you do and what you have to offer. This is also a great way to increase your search engine optimization (SEO), because part of SEO is the popularity of your website. Therefore, by getting more people to come to your great, content-filled website, you positively affect your search engine ranking.

Whenever you can positively affect the SEO of your website, you help build more branding and awareness for your business. For example, research conducted by the KRDS marketing agency demonstrated that Facebook folks interact (e.g., like, comment, or share) six to seven times more with a post when it involves a contest versus a noncontest status update.[16] This approach may not be right for all businesses, but it's worth considering as you design your plan for getting the most out of Facebook.

Try This!

It's time to start posting content on your business page. For those who are planners by nature, make a list of the kinds of things you'd like to try posting (client success stories, web links, product photos, video clips), compile this content in your files, and then commit to posting one of these things daily around the same time each day so you start to build a habit, whether it be during your morning coffee, over your lunch break, or before you sign off at the end of the day. Also, be prepared to post real-time links and news as timely information comes across your desk.

For those of you who prefer a more spontaneous approach, commit to paying particular attention to happenings during the day to come up with fresh, authentic, and relevant things to post on the basis of what you are reading, doing, and receiving. As you come across a news article that seems relevant to your crowd, post the link on Facebook. If you attend an industry event, take a photo of a famous speaker, you and your colleagues, or an interesting display at an exhibitor's booth. Or just share a thoughtful comment or piece of expertise with your clients the next time it pops into your head.

Regardless of your approach—planned or more spontaneous—aim for posting daily and see what kind of interaction you can generate. Experiment with times of day and content to see what gets the most likes, shares, and comments for your business.

A Question of Likes

After you've built your business page, it's time to get people to "like" it. Liking your page is, of course, important because the more people that like your page, the more people who will have the opportunity to interact with you by either liking, commenting on, or sharing a post. Getting likes is not often an easy thing to do, which is why I suggest that your current marketing efforts include a call to action for people to like your page with your page address. I find that a small sign in your place of business that simply says "Like Us on Facebook" is actually quite effective. This invitation should also be on your business cards and any other marketing that you do.

Another way to generate page likes is to directly ask people to like your page. A strong word of caution here, though: Do not ask everyone you cross paths with to like your page! This is like spamming for business. Instead, be selective. You should only ask certain people, such as those whom you think might have an interest in your business on the basis of common interests or those in geographic proximity if you are a regional company. Only ask a few at time and not every day.

It is perfectly acceptable to ask current clients to like your page if they have not already. After all, they are clients; you clearly have a personal relationship with them; they are doing business with you; and if they like you as a person, they typically are more than happy to like your page. The biggest mistake that people make is just going down the list of suggestions that Facebook offers and asking people to like their page without regard to the relationship they already have (or do not have) with them. I can say from experience that it is quite irritating to have some random business that you don't know and barely heard of asking you to like their page.

Also of relevance here is that the more people who like a page, the more people who will come to like the page in the future. It is a form of social proof and applies not only to getting people to like your page but also to getting people to like, comment on, or share your posts. This appears to be part of Facebook's strategy for *top stories*; that is, the stories that have the most interaction float to the top of people's news feeds. It only follows that as people see and read the top stories that they, too, want to be part of the commentary. This is especially true if they see their friends making comments. A peek into psychology will help us understand why.

In the 1950s, psychologists discovered through experiments by Solomon Asch[17] that people would answer a question wrong (regarding which line was the longest) to conform to the answers given by others. A significant percent of individuals would conform to the group consensus even though they thought the group's answer was wrong. What was the point of the experiment? That, as humans, we do conform to the opinions of others. Why? It is a form of social validation when we are in situations where a task may be ambiguous or difficult or we simply do not have much knowledge: If our friends like, believe, or think something, we have a very high likelihood of liking, believing, or thinking the same thing, many times even if we do not agree deep down. Social proof is that powerful.

This is where Facebook is especially powerful. More and more individuals are using their Facebook personal pages as a form of Internet search, getting answers to questions, looking for specific businesses and services, and so on. When our friends publicly and consistently say on Facebook that this is a great place to shop, eat, or receive a service, we are extremely likely to do as they say, because we know if those friends like it, we may too.

In the 1989 baseball movie *Field of Dreams,* Kevin Costner's character heard a voice whispering in his head, "If you build it, they will come." When it comes to building your business page on Facebook and getting the most out of it, this statement is only partially true. You can't just build it; you have to build it right. This means focusing on posting useful, interesting, and entertaining content for your audience. It also means being willing to personalize your business page, whether through your status updates; your own photos or videos with people; and/or fun promotions, discounts, and events.

Be careful about asking for "likes" and "shares." Occasionally encouraging people to like, comment, and share is okay. However, in Facebook's most recent algorithm, this practice has been referred to as "like-baiting."

While it may in fact increase the numbers of "likes" or "shares" you receive, Facebook considers it SPAM, and overuse of these types of phrases can have your page on warning. Use it judicially, meaning I do not recommend it on every post....

Also, do not be afraid to occasionally share your own Facebook business page's status updates on your own timeline. You can do this from your business page—simply scroll down to the post of interest, click on the *Share* button, and indicate that you'd like to put the post on the timeline of your personal page. I like to do this with my business page posts that involve information regarding other people or entities, such as a link to a great blog or news article. In this way, my business site gets a quiet shout out without my being overly promotional.

In Sum: If You Build It Right, They Will Come

When it comes to success on Facebook, patience, commitment, and consistency are key, whether for the personal or the business page. If these three characteristics do not resonate with you, I suggest that you forget doing Facebook and jump to the Twitter chapter—or simply stick with LinkedIn. For those of you who are interested in giving Facebook a try, patience, commitment, and consistency can be very useful.

Patience is key, because you are going to build your likes and comments organically, not by paying for them or exchanging likes with other businesses. You are going to build good content on your business page and that takes time. Even when you do have things for people to read, you are not going to get a huge influx of people chomping at the bit to get on your Facebook page. You must be patient; they will come, but it is going to take time.

This leads to *consistency*—posting regularly. You cannot expect people to come to your business page if you lack consistency. If you only give followers something once a month, they will see no value in making time to visit your page. True, earlier in the chapter I noted that people unfriend some businesses because they overpost; however, this is, in large part, due to major companies that are spending money to promote posts. I do not advise doing that. Therefore, unless you are posting ten times per day, chances are you are not overposting.

Dan Zarrella, whom we met earlier in the chapter, shared research that suggests that Facebook business pages with new posts approximately every other day receive the most page likes.[16] This, again, requires consistency. However, it is also going to require some other thought strategy as to what to post. As mentioned earlier in the chapter, you have quite a few options at your disposal, whether to announce giveaways that drive traffic to your website or post photos of your clients or merchandise. Again, consistency is critical here. It is important that I note, however, that you do need to try different things. There is not a "one-size-fits-all" way of doing things on Facebook: Every target market is unique. For you as a small business, do not be afraid to experiment, but, more important, plan to stay consistent.

The last word I am going to talk about in regard to success on Facebook is *commitment*—the ability to use Facebook over the long term. What I mean by commitment is that even if you do not see Facebook working immediately, you will stick with what you are doing. You will work with the platform over the long term so that there is enough time for you to really show your personality to friends, build relationships, meet new people, and reap benefits in the form of referrals and new business.

I believe the biggest challenge for most small businesses is that ability to stay committed. Yes, patience and consistency are important, but without commitment, these characteristics have little to no value when it comes to Facebook for business. There will be many days and sometimes weeks where it appears that nothing is happening with your Facebook business page. You are being consistent; however, there are few, if any, new likes and/or few, if any, comments or shares. For the personal page, you will be busy staying in touch with potential and current clients without your efforts seeming to yield new business. The temptation will be to give up on it. If you'd like to see whether Facebook is of value to you or to your business, stay the course and don't give up. It is normal that some days on social media are better than others and that it takes time for your efforts to pay dividends. Using social media in the way I have suggested is like any other sweat marketing. Some days are going to generate better results than others, but the sum total results will be worth your ongoing efforts.

If you have ever been to networking events, you know this to be true. Sometimes you can go to a networking event and not seem to make any great contacts. Yet, unbeknownst to you, you actually made an impact and hear back from someone months later. By the same token, you may have been at a networking event where you really felt you nailed it. You were sure you were going to get business from it, yet ultimately nothing happened. The one thing I am sure of, though, is that like those networking events that you go to more regularly, which, in turn, yield more results than those you don't attend, the more regularly you post on Facebook and interact, the more positively you will affect the income of your business. It does work and it can be effective, but you have to stay committed to the process.

If this chapter (also see Ch. 8) has convinced you that Facebook may be of value to your business, follow the suggestions that I have given here and use them as a foundation to create some of your own ideas. If not, feel free to focus on one or more of the other great social media options out there.

Above everything else that you do with your pages, personal or business, be human. Yes, even on your Facebook business page, recent research has demonstrated that a human picture and human voice have a greater effect on page and post interaction versus acting simply as the business.[19] If you look human and sound human, whether on your personal page or your business page, you will increase your interaction. The research also suggests that this human voice of communication from your business page gives the user more of a feeling of transparency and increases word-of-mouth marketing. As we know, word of mouth is how people, places, and things go viral, and that happens for free.

Build your relationships personally and let them translate professionally. Nurture your friends as friends and, over time, they will become your biggest fans: When you do the right things in the right way on Facebook, some friends will become clients and others will become your biggest referral source for your business. In the end, when it comes to Facebook and small business, do what we do as real friends on the platform: Be human, be genuine, be patient, be consistent, and stay committed. Who could ask for a better friend or business than that?

The Lowdown

- Businesses, especially those that do paid promotional-style posts and paid advertising, are often seen by Facebook users as outlaws in a friendly land. Why? Facebook is a place of friendship, conversation, connection, and self-expression, not business promotion.
- If you're going to be successful on Facebook, show up as your real self and be human. Sure, have a simple business page presence, but focus mostly on using your personal page to share a sense of who you are and to make personal connections that can lead to business and referrals over time.
- Facebook is follow-up! Create a list of clients and potential clients, and Facebook will let you see their latest posts at a glance. Staying in touch is as simple as making a cheery comment, adding a quick post on someone's wall, or clicking the *Like* button.
- What do you post on Facebook? The same things you'd talk to a friend about: recent movies, what you cooked for dinner, how your favorite hobby is going, what made you

sad yesterday, or what inspired you today. Don't think of it as mundane, think of it as personal—a chance for potential clients to get to know, like, and trust the authentic you.

- When in doubt, remember the principle of reciprocity: Give and receive. "Like" others' photos; comment on their posts; and wish people a happy birthday, congratulations, or a happy anniversary. One of the easiest ways to garner Facebook love is to comment on and like others' posts.
- When it comes to your business page, make sure you have a complete profile and then plan to periodically post content, such as once every couple of days. Experiment with different approaches—giveaways and discounts, client success stories, or an interesting photo or video clip. See what your community responds to and build from there.

Twitter: To Tweet or Not to Tweet, That Is the Question

> I thought if I had a Twitter feed and say I had a following of a 100,000, that means 100,000 of them would be interested in my book. It was logical, but it didn't turn out to be true. It turned out if I had a Twitter feed of a 100,000, four of them were interested in my book.
>
> —Steve Martin

For most small business owners, questions abound about whether Twitter is or should be a significant part of their social media strategy. It is a great question, which should lead you to equally probing questions, such as, "Does my target market use Twitter?" "When do they use it?" "How often do they use it?" and "How does Twitter convert followers to clients?" There may even be a more general question:

"How in the world do you use Twitter for business?" I must confess that I debated whether I should title this chapter "Twitter: Why Bother?"

I understand the questions surrounding Twitter's usefulness. In fact, as much as I love Twitter, I will admit that for the entrepreneur and small business owner, Twitter probably generates more questions than answers. I mean, what can you possibly say in 140 characters—not words—on a regular basis that will translate into some sort of business? It is a great question.

In spite of the uncertainty and confusion that often surrounds Twitter, it can potentially have some value for business. As I discuss in this chapter, some benefits are

- Twitter's search feature, which allows you to locate those tweeting in search of services like yours
- the massive amount of timely information available on Twitter, which you can use to stay on the cutting edge of information in your industry, field, or specialty
- the opportunity to position yourself as a credible source in your industry, field, or specialty via the kinds of information that you tweet and retweet

Twitter is by no means the perfect social media platform for most business owners, and keep in mind that Twitter is not as big as claimed in terms of number of users (as I have noted in the past on my blog.[1] Recently, with Twitter's IPO filing, these exact questions are now arising. Even advertisers are questioning if there really is enough of a marketing opportunity on Twitter.[2] For the small business on Twitter, it's a question of finding and keeping the right followers that are in your target market.

Leveraging Twitter is not easy for many reasons, and this difficulty starts when one begins to understand its culture. As a result, I do not evangelize about Twitter, and yet I feel it is important to share with you what I have studied and observed about it so that those who are interested in becoming active can gain insight into where best to direct their Twitter zeal and those who are curious can simply learn more.

Understanding How Twitter Really Works

Twitter is a conundrum. It is not easy to define nor is it easy to explain. As a result, it is the most misunderstood of all of the social media platforms. Typically, you will hear people describe something like, "Twitter is nothing more than people talking about where they eat and when they poop." In some respects, this claim is false, and in other respects it is true. It is true in that Twitter is filled with *tweets* (the name given to updates that people post) on the most mundane matters; however, it is not true, because if you are following specific people for specific reasons, you are less likely to see such minutia.

Traditionally, Twitter has been referred to as a *microblogging* platform because it is 140 characters of everything a blog can be. It can be personal, impersonal, informational, nonsensical, professional, academic, and more. Here is a list of sample tweets you might find on your feed, posted by different users, on a given day.

Personal: "I went to the store today and ran over a shopping cart."

Random: "I really need a sandwich and a beer."

Informational: "Great article for starting a small business" (followed by a link to the article).

Professional: "The least expensive way to improve your business is to improve your customer service."

Academic: "Neurology research finds dopamine release with social media use" (followed by a link to the article).

Quotes: "'The real problem is not whether machines think but whether men do.' ~B. F. Skinner"

Twitter is probably the most frenetic of all the platforms, as it is estimated that there are more than 400 million tweets per day.[3] How many folks are out there tweeting? According to a Pew Internet Study, 16% of all Internet users interviewed had a Twitter account. This means that about one out of every six or so people on the Internet are possibly using it—not nearly the staggering numbers of Facebook, and bear in mind that some people have more than one Twitter account, which may dilute this number even more.[4]

Twitter has evolved over time. When Twitter first started, it was a private network that was for sharing personal information via an intranet. According to Shel Israel (whose Twitter name is @ShelIsrael) in his book *Twitterville*, Twitter's real public moment started at the South by Southwest music, film, and technology conference in Austin in 2007.[5] It was there, according to the author, that Twitter allowed anyone in attendance to sign up and use Twitter to communicate about anything and everything, from where the best band was playing, to where people were drinking and eating, to the subject matter of different conference speakers, to what new technology was being discussed at the event.

The point of Twitter was, and still is to an extent, about updating your status. It was personal, it was informational, and it was communication. However, since Twitter has allowed the general public to join the platform, the culture has certainly changed. It was once mostly made up of technology gurus, search-engine marketers, a few celebrities, and some regular folks. In the beginning, there was far more interaction and conversation. Today, it is much different: There are fewer conversations; it is far more informational; and, clearly, although all those folks I mentioned are still using it, it is far more dominated by celebrities and news media folks. I recall that when I first used Twitter (back when there were fewer people using it), the platform was about having a conversation about things that were important or interacting with people regarding a blog or article that someone had written. Today, so many tweets are scheduled in advance and automated that attempting to have a meaningful conversation (in which a person actually responds) is far more difficult.

The Culture of Twitter

What is Twitter culture, then? It is not easy to pin down, but let's look at the name used to refer to Twitter users to get some insight. Whereas LinkedIn users are called *connections* (given the professional culture) and Facebook users are called *friends* (given the personal, friendship culture), Twitter users are called *followers*. Why? Because when you are on Twitter, you are said to *follow* what other people are saying and doing on Twitter. Twitter is also about who is *following* you. In some cases, it may be more important to know how many people are following you than which people you are following. It should stand to reason, then, that the key to success on Twitter would be to be a leader. However, as much as I would like to say that this is true, Twitter has evolved into and is more dominated by a culture of fame and popularity than leadership. This is why Twitter is not only difficult for small businesses to leverage but also difficult for the average person to wrap his or her mind around.

Fame. Leadership, especially thought leadership, is still important when it comes to Twitter; however, the real dominant forces on Twitter are those who have fame. Recently, I decided to analyze the top one thousand accounts that are followed on Twitter. What did I find? More than 97% of these accounts were national or international celebrities from movies, sports, music, politics, and the like, or media outlets such as CNN and YouTube. The number one followed account at the time of this writing, with more than 39 million followers, was pop musician Justin Bieber. What is more astounding is that Justin Bieber, Lady Gaga, and Katy Perry together have more than 100 million followers!

The remaining less than 3% were businesses such as Starbucks (@StarBucks), Whole Foods (@WholeFoods), and Samsung Mobile (@Samsungmobile).[6] In nearly every case, those businesses were retailers or otherwise had some product to sell. They were also major brands with large marketing budgets. I did not find a service industry business in the top one thousand. It makes you wonder, what chance do you have as a small business to wrestle your way to prominence on Twitter?

Before I tackle that question, we can't just leave fame and celebrities alone. After all, they are the ones who truly dominate the culture. As a matter of fact, celebrities and famous individuals are now being paid by companies to tweet! Athletes, movie stars, media personalities: Some of the tweets you will see from these folks are paid for so that the company's product will be mentioned. I don't know how much money celebrities get for this service, but it must be enough to make it worth their while.

What can the celebrities who are doing so well on Twitter possibly say that is of such great importance? I think that is up for tremendous debate. Seriously, I have yet to read anything from these folks that will fundamentally change a follower's life or business. So why so many followers? Answer: fame and popularity. As humans, we are fascinated with fame and celebrity status, which is why people follow celebrities on Twitter. Psychologists call it *parasocial contact*.[7] Parasocial contact is typically a one-way relationship with someone, usually a celebrity, who does not know the person, yet the person doing the following through some sort of affiliation (in this case, Twitter) feels connected to the celebrity. I have been told by several people, "Well, that sounds like stalking." Maybe it is, but, in this case, it is acceptable. Just look at the hundreds of millions of people on Twitter following people with some sort of fame!

What is also telling is that a significant portion of this massive group of the one thousand most followed Twitter accounts follow very few people, even no people, in return. In many cases, some of these famous people have millions of followers and tweet very little. A great example of this is Beyoncé Knowles (@Beyonce), the famous singer and actress. She has nearly eight million followers, but she only follows eight people; she has been on Twitter for more than six years and she has a grand total of four tweets at the time of this writing.[8]

If you are a small business owner, don't look to Beyoncé for tips on how to tweet your way to eight million users. Clearly, fame is at work here, and most small businesses do not have the good fortune to have that working for them. What positive insights can we take from this example? When it comes to Twitter, the more fame you have, even on a local level, the greater the advantage you have over someone who does not. If you are someone who is the face of your brand or someone who is recognized wherever you go in your local area by a significant percentage of people, you will have a tremendous advantage on Twitter.

Not so social after all. Another important characteristic of Twitter is that it really is not all that social, which is a bit funny given that it's considered to be part of social media. For starters, not many conversations happen on Twitter. For example, if you follow a celebrity, media outlet, or major business and you happen to tweet them a reply or you post something on their Twitter feed, you probably will not get a response from them. In my experiments of following certain people, I have found, in general, the celebrity, including the local community celebrity, will not respond to your tweet. This has proved to be true even if when I was responding to something he or she said that appeared to be a tweet that was looking for a response. However, I have found that if it is another celebrity who makes the comment on another celebrity's feed, they typically will interact in the conversation. It is, after all, the privilege of fame. They do not have to respond to you and, quite frankly, they probably shouldn't, as they do not know most of the people that tweet to them or at them.

I am also reluctant to call Twitter true social media because one of the cofounders of Twitter, Jack Dorsey, doesn't even consider it social. Speaking at the Digital-Life-Design conference in Munich, Germany, Dorsey responded when asked, "Is Twitter social?" in this way:

> "Not so much," Dorsey said. "Twitter is a way to learn about what your friends are doing, but more than that it's a way to learn about what other people who are relevant to you, from all over the world, are doing. We definitely see social as just one part of what people do on Twitter. We think of it as an information utility and a communications network."[9]

Well, there we have it. Jack Dorsey thinks of Twitter as an "information utility" and a "communications network." This is where we need to probe a little deeper when it comes to using Twitter. We need to consider what our potential followers will value so that we can use the platform to gather and communicate specific information of relevance to them. Of course, with limited interaction, it is difficult to gauge whether your followers are finding what you say is valuable. Perhaps a very gross measure of value is if you do not lose followers, your followers favorite one of your tweets, and/or they retweet a tweet (i.e., share what you've tweeted with their followers). The fact is that you may not know for sure. Folks may be reading your tweets, but unless they favorite or retweet them, you'll never know. That's one of the difficulties of Twitter and social media in general.

A younger demographic. So we know that Twitter is a culture of fame and information; it may be helpful to look at what types of individuals are playing there so you can see if they match your particular target market. What is known about Twitter users? It appears that 62% of Twitter users are women versus 38% men, while it is estimated that 58% of Twitter users have an annual income of $100,000 or more,[10] and 51% have a college or graduate school education.[11,12] This makes sense because many actors, athletes, and other celebrities may not have a college education and yet have very high incomes.

We still need to exercise caution interpreting these statistics in terms of what they really mean regarding who is on Twitter. Sometimes statistics can be misleading. If we were to eliminate the celebrities on Twitter from the demographic information, it may be interesting to see how the income levels would change. I am not exactly sure what the revised numbers would look like, but given that so many athletes and celebrities have high incomes, my guess is that we would find that if we eliminated these groups of people, Twitter users may not be as affluent as the statistics indicate.

It is also worth noting that an estimated 27% of all Internet users between the ages of 18 and 29 years are Twitter users, and, as age increases, the percentage of users significantly decreases.[13] What is more, Twitter's users appear to be getting younger. In a recent survey, 24% of teenagers who are online are now on Twitter, up 8% since 2011.[14] So if your target market is young people—say, you are selling skateboards, young adult fiction, or new teen fashion—Twitter may be a good spot for you.

What does this all mean when it comes to Twitter culture? Younger folks like teens may be migrating to Twitter, and yet there are still plenty of others on Twitter as well, with more than half being college graduates making $100,000 or more a year. Almost one third of all Internet users are on Twitter, so it is possible that your target market is there, even if it's not yet clear how best to engage them.

In addition, Twitter is a "pop and information" culture. It is, in fact, a combination of celebrity status and valuable information. For you as a small business, this means that if you have any sort of celebrity status, even on the local level, you will have a significant advantage on Twitter. However, even if you do not have fame, you can still create an advantage for yourself by providing useful and valuable information to those who do follow you. And as I presently show, you can also use Twitter to identify individuals who may be looking for your services.

What's the Point: Why Should You Use Twitter?

Although Twitter's value is not as clear for the business owner as is the value of some of the other social media platforms, let me just say that, personally, I use Twitter and I like it. A tweet can be no longer than 140 characters, which is a short sentence at best. Thus, it is a great way for me to post information quickly. I post things that I have read that will give people further insights into their business, social media, and the psychology of their consumer. I am always trying to find ways that I can save businesses money, help them attract more consumers, improve sales, and be more effective at using these social media platforms, and Twitter is a quick and easy way for me to share some of those ideas. Let's look at each of the possible business benefits of Twitter more in depth.

Staying Informed

In thinking about the value of Twitter, I would have to say that the most useful feature is that it is searchable, meaning that you can do a search for specific information, people, or subject matter there. The search function is beneficial in identifying individuals you would like to follow who provide information that you are interested in. The people and entities I follow are those who are consistent thought leaders (e.g., Seth

Godin [@SethGodin]), industry groups (e.g., Society for Consumer Psychology [@myscp] and Journal of Cyberpsyschology, Behavior, and Social Media [@cyberpscyh_jn]), the media (e.g., *Wall Street Journal* Small Business [@WSJsmallbiz]), and research/academic services (e.g., @PsychCentral). This is helpful to me as a business owner because I can stay on top of what is happening in my field in a very quick way. This makes me better at my consulting work and allows me to be more credible, knowledgeable, and readily able to speak about my industry to my potential and current clients.

Regardless of your field or specialty, there are people on Twitter who are talking about how to make your industry better. You would know much better than I would who those people or entities are that would benefit you most. Think about some of the leaders in your industry or those whose books you've been reading and look them up on Twitter. If they are there, follow them. If not, this is a good opportunity to use your Twitter search skills. Enter some terms that relate to your field and see what comes up. Take a chance and follow several individuals; once you see who you like over time, you can continue following the individuals you appreciate while unfollowing the rest.

So much information is being posted on Twitter that I believe it is the best way to get the most up-to-date information available on any given topic. Instead of sorting through millions of tweets, you can simply type in the search field what it is you are looking for. For example, if you want to find out about the stock market, you have several ways to search: You could enter the word *stocks* or *stock market* or *Dow Jones* and pull up information about what is happening on the stock market. However, if there is a news or top trend that several sources or people are commenting on, then you can search via a hashtag, which is the # sign. You will see what is trending when you go to the home page of your profile on Twitter. Just type #andthewordorphrase (with no spaces), and anyone that has used that hashtag in their tweet will show up in the search results. This can certainly be useful if you are trying to organize or follow a particular subject. For instance, if you search for #socialmediology, you will see all of my tweets related to social mediology.

Think about some key terms related to your business, region, or industry; you can then try each of these out with the hashtag to find out what people are tweeting about right now on that topic. There will be some junk in there, but you may also find some interesting information.

Finding Prospects

Twitter search is also helpful in identifying people who are looking for your services. Here's where things really start to get interesting for you as a business owner. So, if you are in the real estate industry, try searching for "looking for home in ______" or "need realtor in ______." When you do so, Twitter will yield all of the tweets in chronological order from the most recent to the oldest of anyone who used those words or phrases in their tweets. There is generally someone out there that you may be able to connect with that you can help. The same is true of the retail industry. Say you sell a particular brand of clothing or shoes. Simply search on Twitter for "want to buy ______" or "where can I buy ______," and, again, up will pop all of the tweets with those words and phrases with your specific criteria. You can see how there could be a benefit from this way in which Twitter allows you and your business to identify potential customers, whom you can then transform into clients.

Just as a test, I decided to do a Twitter search of the phrase "looking for book editor." How interesting it would be for a business that specialized in book editing to try this search and see if they could find anyone who was looking for an editor. Perhaps the search term seems a bit obscure or like wishful thinking, but guess what? The very first tweet that came up was the following:

> @AdebukolaOAA I'm desperately looking for a GREAT book editor. Any recommendations please?[15]

At the time I did the inquiry, the post had been up for forty-seven minutes. If an editor had been a bit more savvy and created a running search on a Twitter management platform, he or she could have been notified immediately of the person and what the person was searching for. Now this was not the only person looking for a book editor, and many book editors also had tweets broadcasting their services. However, within the first twenty-five tweets I read, there were four people looking for an editor to help them. That is pretty powerful.

I know the next question is, What about the quality of the inquiry? That is, of course, up for debate. What I can say is that I have not found any empirical piece of research that demonstrates that the prospects generated on Twitter are any better or worse than those found via any other source. I can promise you that you will have to sort through the results and you should review profiles, because, quite frankly, some people are phishing for people to sell to and this type of tweet could be bait. However, it's hard not to consider the search element of Twitter and the way it may be able to help your particular business.

I encourage you to be creative and get into the psychology and behavior of your potential clients who may be on Twitter. Think about how they would write what they are searching for if they wanted something from your industry. Try saying it different ways. Experiment—you will find that searching with the right words will lead to better and more qualified responses. The reason why people are putting these requests out there on Twitter is because Twitter, compared with the other social media platforms, has been associated with fast responses. Even if you are unsure about Twitter from a business standpoint, consider leveraging at least the search feature of Twitter, which seems to provide some value.

Try This!

Take five minutes to brainstorm a list of possible search terms to identify other Twitter users who might be interested in your business (e.g., "looking for interior designer," "seeking good accountant," "in search of vintage bridal gowns," "need affordable car detailing"). Consider what types of words your potential client would use to search for the products or services you sell. If you do not know or simply are not certain, then start asking your current client database.

Once you've generated some ideas for keywords, enter each of them into a Twitter search and see who and what come up. There will likely be some unrelated or unhelpful tweets. However, did you find any interesting potential leads that you want to follow on Twitter so you can get connected? If not, brainstorm three more search terms and see what happens. This can be an effective, real-time way of finding Twitter users who are potentially interested in your business.

You will read a great many things from the social media experts on the value of Twitter and how easy it is to use. I want to be clear: If you do not have fame, Twitter is not easy. It is difficult to gain and maintain the right followers, provide the right content, and manage it correctly, and all of this takes time. What's more, not all businesses are created equal, nor are all industries equal. Some small businesses will be far more successful than others simply because of the product or service that they have to offer. You will find some success stories; however, when you analyze them closely, it will be very difficult to trace a cause-and-effect relationship between profits and Twitter usage. Yet, every single industry is represented on Twitter and some are using it in unique ways that help their business—maybe not from a traditional return-on-investment standpoint but from a branding and awareness standpoint, all at zero marketing cost. Is Twitter a must for your business? In many cases, the answer is probably "no." Yet Twitter is a free tool in the world of social media that is at your disposal. If you are intrigued, interested, or ready to learn more about how to leverage Twitter for your business, read on.

Your Business Rx: Getting the Most out of Twitter

If you are new to Twitter, take one look at the list of tweets on your feed and you may quickly start scratching your head. Your eyes may glaze over and your brain may go into overload as you try to make sense of the symbols; the abbreviations; the strange web links with things like "bit.ly" in them; and short, seemingly undecipherable phrases. Perhaps more than any other social media platform, Twitter may be the most foreign and confusing; it is truly another language and another world.

As with all social media, however, if you take things one step at a time on Twitter, breaking the procedures down into small chunks, you can get comfortable using the platform over time. In fact, as you read the following pages on how to use Twitter for your business, you will likely begin to see some similarities with the other social media platforms, which might put you at ease. You will be building a profile to give yourself a presence, you will be creating your own personalized community of users, and you will be posting and reading information. Sound familiar? We could just as easily be speaking about LinkedIn or Facebook with those terms. Of course, Twitter is still its own unique animal, so take a deep breath and get ready. It's time to learn more.

The Necessities

On Twitter, as with Facebook and LinkedIn, you will have an opportunity to post a picture and complete a profile. Whereas with LinkedIn we needed to look more professional and on Facebook more friendly, Twitter appears to have fewer rules. Having a picture is important, but you have some flexibility in the picture you use. If you are a small business, my advice would be for you to use your logo. Or, if you are your own business, your face is great, too. Remember, though, that the Twitter icon is small, so make sure that if you are using your face in your icon, followers can see you.

Next, please make sure you have your full profile filled out. Recent research suggests that people who have a full profile have more followers on Twitter than do those who do not.[16] In your profile, tell what you do, who you are, and what makes you special. This is the one place where you should not be afraid to call yourself an expert, and let followers know what it is you can do for your current and future clients. Also, feel free to be creative and allow some personality to come through. I think @ JohnnyCupcakes really captures the idea in its headline:

> @JohnnyCupcakes: My favorite thing to do in the world is to bring out the kid in everyone. Not in the sense of getting loads of people pregnant—but I enjoy making others happy.

@JohnnyCupcakes has more than 78,000 followers. You do not have to use this same approach, but I want to make the point that creativity is perfectly acceptable on Twitter. It does make you stand out. Creativity in a profile creates curiosity. It also creates a personality for the business. If you have never been to a Johnny Cupcakes, the heading alone may inspire you to go. We find here another example of classical conditioning, where a place of business is associated with both fun and tasty cupcakes. And who doesn't like a good cupcake? It appears, at least on a cursory view, that creative profiles have higher follower counts. Certainly, they attract additional marketing, as many bloggers have commented on the creativity of the @ JohnnyCupcakes profile.

One last thing about your Twitter profile headlines: Please list your website in there. I am amazed at the number of business profiles I see where the company's web address is nowhere in sight. Give yourself every opportunity to gain clients by including your web address!

Following Is Easy, Getting Followers Is Not

That was the easy part. The next part—getting followers—is not so easy, and, quite frankly, it is time consuming. But your Twitter account is meaningless if you don't have followers, so we must spend some time looking at how to get them.

Finding followers. As mentioned earlier, followers flow like wine for the famous. What is more, these individuals don't even have to interact in a conversation. However, for the average person, the entrepreneur, or the small business, it is likely that you do not have that kind of fame or status, so we'll have to turn to something else. Over the years, I have asked social media marketers, gurus, and strategists, "What is the best and fastest way to build your Twitter account?" I had an answer, but I wanted to see if there was something that perhaps I missed. Nope. Every person gave me the same answer: If you start following a number of people, you can expect to get followed back by a percentage of them. Again, enter the psychological principle of reciprocity that has been mentioned throughout the book; give and receive.

There is no way to know the exact percentage of followers you will gain by following others, but I have seen estimates from 20% to 50%. That being said, you must be careful about who you choose to follow: Do not just randomly start following people. Instead, have a strategy, and I suggest a three-pronged approach. First, follow people that are in your industry, doing what you do and using Twitter extremely well. That is, they have far more followers (more than one thousand) than how many they follow, and they are active. This can help you see what works well on Twitter.

Second, follow thought and information leaders that you are interested in. I find that a few people who share common interests also tend to follow each other. It is a double benefit: Not only do you get useful information, but you also can be connected to like minds that may want to follow you as well, because of the common interest.

Finally and the most important prong, you should follow people that would be considered part of your target market. Fortunately, Twitter makes this fairly easy to do, but adding them is time consuming. You can simply go to any profile where your target market is likely to exist, click on their followers, and—lo and behold!—a list pops up of all of their followers with their profile headlines and you can start clicking *follow*. That sounds easy, except you need to carefully read the profiles of the people you are about to follow, because not everyone is a perfect match. Also, look at a person's activity level before choosing to follow him or her. If someone has only tweeted five times, chances are that person is not really using Twitter—the account may be abandoned and of no use to you in building a true followership.

I wanted to get a better handle on the ease or difficulty of adding followers, so I decided that I would go to the Fox Small Business Twitter Account (@fbssmallbiz), which has more than 22,000 followers. I felt this would be the best account to start with because chances were that the type of businesses I work with would be there. What happened? Well, some small businesses were there, but approximately 50% of the Twitter profiles I reviewed were people in my industry! Certainly, those are not the people I am looking for. Then I found that several profiles were not relevant to my target market at all. I also avoided any profiles that did not have a picture or a description because I felt they were either not serious about their Twitter use or not serious about their business. I finally selected sixty profiles that I felt I could follow that were legitimately in my target market. All of this sorting, reading, and checking took me approximately forty-five minutes. I am not sure how many hundreds of profiles I reviewed, but, after a while, I felt my eyes roll toward the back of my head from sheer boredom, and my eyes blurred. I cannot imagine how a small business owner who doesn't do this for a living would feel. This is my profession and it was tedious.

Upon following these 60 profiles, I simply waited. Yep, waited. I can't force people to follow me, so there was nothing left to do but follow and hope. I went off to do other things. One was writing this chapter. Many social media strategists suggest that you should see a response in an hour, and, in fact, I did: I lost two followers. Well, that was not exactly the outcome I was looking for. I laughed, thinking to myself, I can only imagine a small business owner going through all this effort and checking his Twitter account later only to find that he lost two followers. If I were him, I probably would close my Twitter account and possibly throw my laptop or phone out the window while driving down the interstate.

However, here is the good news: After nearly two and a half hours, I had gained eight followers. After seventy-two hours, I had gained a total of thirteen followers. So the return rate for my effort was approximately 22%. Was it worth my time? I don't know. Will I get a client? I don't know. The fact is a follower is a follower, not necessarily a prospect, even though, deep down, I believe most small businesses see their followers as prospects. I would not necessarily make that assumption. I have to keep in mind that, psychologically, they may have followed me simply because I followed them first, not because they actually are interested in anything I have to say or offer them. All of this being said, I need to be cautious here, because this was a one-time trial. Perhaps if I did this again, I would get different results, although I am pretty convinced that 20%–30% is probably a pretty good estimate of an expected return. If you are on Twitter, try it and see how you compare.

Try This!

Now it's your turn. Jump on Twitter and start searching for people to potentially follow. You may want to do as I did and check out Fox Small Business if that's relevant to your target market, or you may want to look elsewhere. For example, if you are a book editor, look at the Independent Book Publishers of America (@IBPA) account and start following some of the people that follow IBPA. Clearly, you need to personalize the search to your type of business, industry, space, and so on, so think about things like what type of media your target market might like to read or watch (Aerospace Times Magazine? Travel Club Television?), what groups they might be associated with (International Widgets Association? Dollhouse Furniture Makers of America?), and what thought leaders they may be listening to (Yoga Guru Jane? Blacksmithing Expert Joe?).

Once you are on the Twitter profile of these folks, you can click to see who is following them. Scroll through and select at least 15 good prospects to follow on Twitter. Click follow for each of them and check your number of followers in a few days. If you have gained three to five new followers, try this exercise once a week for the next month and watch your followership grow. Over time, perhaps you will not only gain more followers but also occasional clients.

Keeping followers. When you set up your account, it is a great idea for you to start tweeting, even if you do not yet have any followers. There are two reasons for this. First, if people are doing a search for information on specific keywords, perhaps you have written something they are searching for. However, and more important, when people do start looking at your profile and are deciding whether to follow you, they can see what you talk about and what your expertise is. It's hard for someone to feel motivated to follow you if they can't assess the kind of material you like to share via Twitter, so begin to build a base of tweets.

Of course, once you have followers, it is important that you continue tweeting to keep these followers as best as you can. I say, "as best as you can," because you will never know why someone unfollowed you. It may be because you said something they didn't care for, it may be because you didn't say something, or it may be that the person checked their Twitter feed and you tweeted at the wrong time of day so they never saw you and they felt you were inactive. Perhaps they were paring down their list and you simply didn't make the cut; maybe you tweeted too much, or maybe they shut down their Twitter account. The fact of the matter is that we rarely know why a person unfollows another; it just happens. So what's a person to do?

Some Twitter experts say that to continue to grow your list, you must provide your followers something of value in your tweets. Well, that isn't too terribly helpful. What is value? Value is in the perception of the reader, and it's hard to know how that varies for each person. Let's say you have five hundred followers. I can promise you that whatever you tweet will have value to some and no value to others. This then encourages you to tweet numerous things so that maybe something will be valuable to someone. Of course, then you may be told that you tweeted too much and that will cost you followers, which can make the Twitterverse look like it has a dissociative identity disorder.

My point is that it is a bit of a guessing game when it comes to knowing what to tweet that is of value. But if you've decided to engage on Twitter, keep in mind that not everything you tweet needs to be original: You can also share tweets that have something your followers will appreciate or like. Makes sense, right? It might be links to interesting articles, updates on newly released books in your industry, or thought-provoking statements that get people in your field or target audience to reflect. Will your followers find these tweets to be of value? If they retweet what you've posted, that's a good sign. If not, don't despair. They may simply have missed your tweet or read it and then moved on. All you can do is experiment with posting different items you believe to be of value to your followers and target market and see what kind of return you get.

The next piece of advice I have read and heard to help you keep followers and even gain them is to be "part of the conversation." If you are a newbie on Twitter, you may be asking, "Which conversations? How often? When?" Or you may simply look at your feed, full of tweets and retweets, and panic, thinking, "How do I jump into *these* conversations?"

It is true that, occasionally, conversations will come up. If your account is more personal, then you can expect normal, personal conversations that are filled with mirth and fun. However, if you are having conversations about professional things, it is likely that those conversations will be staid in nature. Keep in mind, too, that Twitter users are limited to only 140 characters, so the conversations are not going to be all that long or as in depth as a normal conversation or even what you would see on Facebook. Many times, you will find that the conversations are limited to a few words or phrases and that you and/or the other people will simply be making a point. When it comes to these more professional conversations, I have generally found that they do not last all that long; they often allow someone to clarify or exemplify something and that is all. If you choose to participate in a conversation, it can be useful simply because you are taking the time to respond, which shows you are active and engaged. Conversations on Twitter can also lead to an additional conversation somewhere else, such as on another social media platform or via e-mail if the conversation moves in that direction.

That being said, you must always remind yourself that many of the tweets that you read have been previously scheduled, so chances are that the real person may not even be paying attention; he or she is simply putting out content. Dan Zarrella stated the following from his research: "Highly followed accounts tend to spend a lower percentage of their tweets replying to other accounts—they are less conversational—than less followed accounts."[17] Zarrella's research is consistent with what I have said about Twitter to this point: It is just not that social. What is more, if you have an account that has more than a thousand followers, you are more than likely less social. What does this mean for those with fewer than a thousand followers and for the small business?

To gain followers, you are going to have to experiment with finding the right content. I cannot tell you what to specifically tweet because every business has a following of different types of people, and no two businesses are the same. In other words, it is not possible to wear a one-size-fits-all Twitter shoe. However, I do know a few things that can help you.

- Tweets between 100 and 115 characters appear to get retweeted more often than longer tweets do.[18]
- Links placed toward the beginning of a tweet get clicked on more frequently than those placed toward the back.[19]
- Sunday afternoons and evenings, as people get ready to go back to work, appear to be great times to tweet. Experiment and see what times of day seem to work best for you and your followers.

Twitter is a social, informational medium. Although it is not as social as other platforms, Twitter still has a social component in the sense that people are reading what you tweet—not all of your followers, all of the time, but certainly some of your followers, some of the time.

The biggest complaint I receive from Twitter users pertains to one particular group of businesspeople that I work with on a regular basis: the real estate industry. Dear real estate agents: Stop putting the houses you have for sale on Twitter! It is killing your present and future following. Most people are not paying attention, and you will find it more difficult to gain the right followers. Perhaps your fellow real estate agents will follow you out of courtesy, but the person that you want to follow you is not other real estate agents: It is the people that may want to buy or sell a property. I use this example because it is such a clear case of self-promotion on Twitter, and I hope it makes anyone in a line of business where it is easy to directly sell oneself pause and reconsider such an approach. Remember, Twitter is still a two-way medium. When you simply promote your business, you are no longer acting in a bidirectional way; you're acting in a unidirectional way that does not open the door to even the most remote possibility for communication.

Retweeting people is also extremely important. Retweeting, also known as *RTing,* is simply sharing someone's tweet with your group of followers. You do not want to retweet everyone or everything; instead, make sure it is something that you believe a significant percentage of your followers would be interested in. Perhaps someone posted an article about a new app that one can get for a smartphone that will make one's life easier as it relates to business, or maybe there is a link to an article about a new and groundbreaking study on your industry. If you think your followers might appreciate these articles, then go ahead and retweet them.

The psychology behind the retweet is particularly interesting. When we retweet another persons' tweet, we elevate the original tweeter's status. We have said, in a public way, that this person has something of value. If you retweet the tweet of someone you are following that is not necessarily following you, you often will receive a new follower afterward.

Now let's put the shoe on the other foot: When your tweet gets retweeted, this helps you greatly. We know that more than likely, no two people have the same group of followers. Hence, when someone retweets your tweet, your thoughts get pushed to their list of people and the chances of your gaining followers have dramatically increased. This is the power of authority at work. If someone on Twitter is seen as an authority by the majority of his or her followers, when that person retweets our post, that authority has just endorsed you among their own following. Because we know that power of authority has tremendous influence on how people act and behave, in this instance, it can be a powerful source of followers and help in developing your own credibility and authority.

I already know the next question: How do I get retweeted? The best way to get retweeted is simply to ask. In marketing terms, it is a call to action. At the end of your tweet, make sure you save enough room so you can simply include the words, "Please retweet." That's it. Again, Dan Zarrella, in his most recent research, demonstrated that using the words "Please retweet" increases your likelihood of getting retweeted, versus using "Please RT" or saying nothing at all and hoping you will get retweeted.[20]

Invite, experiment, explore. If you want to have the best followers who will give you the best experience on Twitter, I encourage you to personally ask your current clients to follow you on Twitter. Then I would ask them what type of content would be most valuable to them. Once you know what they want, give it to them!

Next, you will find that the number of followers you gain on Twitter will depend on your business. For example, it may depend on the age of your target market. If your clients are older, you may find you have very few, if any, that use Twitter at all; if your clients are younger, you may have a ripe audience waiting for you on Twitter. Either way, ask for followers. In addition, if you are going to use Twitter, make sure all of your marketing has your Twitter handle. This includes your website, blog, and print advertising. This strategy is grassroots and not very technologically advanced, but the fact of the matter is that like any other platform, Twitter works best when you combine it with other forms of marketing. In the end, Twitter may be right for you or you simply may enjoy using it. If either of these scenarios is true for you, do it, but, more important, do it right.

In Sum: Twitter—If You Build It, They May (or May Not) Come

Twitter can be both difficult and time consuming. If you are not a celebrity or not nationally or internationally known, Twitter is going to be challenging. You are not going to be able to simply build a profile and expect people to follow you. You will have to do some work, which will take time. You will also have to engage in regular upkeep. Honestly, Twitter can be a black hole that consumes your time with no immediate or obvious payoff, or what I like to call a *time hole*. My one-week experiment of trying to gain followers in the ways I have mentioned and attempting to keep them by tweeting took more than five hours. For a single week, that may not seem like an overabundance of time, but this kind of activity should be kept up every week to be really successful on Twitter. Keeping your activity level up is an important part of Twitter because, on the basis of my experience and that of other noncelebrities, when you are not tweeting, you quickly disappear from the Twittersphere.

So what is the bottom line when it comes to Twitter for business? Before I answer that question, I want to be very clear. I like Twitter. I enjoy doing it. Then again, I have a pretty good following of people. We don't talk much, but I knew we wouldn't going in. I say all of that before I note that, of all of the platforms (depending on your business), I am not convinced this platform is a must. As a matter of fact, if you do not use it, I am not sure it would hurt your business, especially when there are more interactive social media platforms out there. I say this because statistically and timewise, Twitter does not make as much sense as, say, LinkedIn or Facebook.

First, I have already told you that 16% of Internet users are estimated to be on Twitter, which means only one person out of six is using it. Second, we really do not know how many individual people are using Twitter because of all of the fake accounts, inactive accounts, and people with multiple accounts. I personally have two, but I have colleagues with as many as nine Twitter accounts. It is interesting that the person with nine accounts told me that he has pretty much abandoned Twitter for Google+ because everything was so automated on Twitter and there were far fewer conversations. Third, Twitter's demographic is getting younger, so if your target audience is older, Twitter may not be the best place to spend your time and effort (again, depending on your business).

I know that what I am saying here is flying in the face of the advice of nearly every social media marketing guru or expert. However, Twitter is just not statistically or demographically as good as we are led to believe. In addition, for a small business to gain followers, keep them, and find interesting information to post is extremely time consuming. (Beware: I don't suggest simply repurposing your Facebook posts for publication on Twitter, so you will have to find new, Twitter-specific content.)

I know that you, as a small business owner, do not have enough hours in the day to follow a bunch of people, tweet, try to add followers, and keep some margin for a personal life. Also, for many people, Twitter becomes emotionally exhausting as they watch their follower count change or their tweets attract no responses. This is where Twitter can become psychologically punishing. You can tweet a great number of times and have good information, and yet you may never get retweeted or favorited. Part of this is because with so many tweets being posted, your great information may never be seen. Very few people dig through their Twitter feed—maybe they go back one page, but, ultimately, if you do not say the right thing at the right time, when the viewer is on and looking for the right thing, you simply posted into the Twittersphere, where it is flying around doing who knows what. When this happens over time, you may no longer have a desire to tweet, because there is no reinforcement for your efforts. In fact, you may even feel like you are in time out.

I am aware that many articles by social media people insist that Twitter is an absolute necessity. In contrast, I am telling you it is not. As a matter of fact, if you do not use it, your business will do just fine.

That being said, you may nonetheless encounter a business owner or two who think that Twitter is the greatest thing since sliced bread. Good for them. They have their demographic, it fits for them, and it is working. If you have found a sweet spot on Twitter for your business, enjoy it, too. And if you'd like to give it a go, please experiment and see where it takes you.

However, far more businesses are demonstrating success without Twitter than are successfully leveraging it. I know that a certain segment of social media marketers will say that those who tried it and failed were just using it wrong, but the statistics on fake and inactive users, the percentage of people who use it, and the time required to gain and maintain followers that I have shown you speak for themselves. As much as I like Twitter and enjoy using it, I would probably say to the vast majority of all of the small business owners that I work with, "You don't have to use Twitter, and you will find better platforms that will generate more business faster and with less effort." In other words, I give you permission, business owner, leader, or social media manager: It's okay to not tweet!

The Lowdown

- Twitter is a microblogging platform where people publicly post tweets (text) of 140 or fewer characters that can be personal or impersonal, informational or nonsensical, professional or academic, and more.
- Although Twitter was once the haven of techies, thought leaders, and cultural gurus, it is now largely dominated by the famous and those in the media. This can make it hard for the small or local business to break in and create a following; if you have fame—even on a local or regional level—this may make Twitter more suitable for your business than if you do not.
- I don't see Twitter as an essential marketing element for most businesses. If you do choose to use it, think of its benefits as helping you to stay informed on business-related topics, establishing your credibility as a business and/or persona, and finding potential clients by using the Twitter search feature.
- One of the simplest ways to grow your following on Twitter is to follow others, as a certain percentage will almost surely follow you back.
- To maintain and grow your followership, aim to tweet regularly on topics you feel are of interest, relevance, and/or value to your target market; periodically retweet the tweets of others; and avoid directly promoting yourself via your tweets. Twitter is not your personal billboard, and you are sure to lose followers if you start plastering ads and marketing announcements everywhere.

- Should you use Twitter? It's frenetic, it involves a unique language, and famous people have a real advantage over the regular guy. Yet some folks really like Twitter. If you're feeling adventurous, give Twitter a try to see how, when, and why it might work for you. If not, move on to one of the other promising social media platforms.

Exploring Other Frontiers: Google+, Pinterest, and YouTube

I had a teacher, he was 86 years old and his name was Luigi in New York City, and he said, "Never stop moving. You get to reinvent yourself." So you have to find ways to reinvent... yourself. Especially today, because it's a whole different market—social media is so important.

—Ben Vereen

I have spent a great deal of time covering the "big three" social media platforms—LinkedIn, Facebook, and Twitter—and with good reason. They are the most widely discussed in the media and by the public at large, they are the most established as platforms, and they have (for the most part) the majority of users. As convenient as it might be to stop there, there's always something new on the horizon, and business owners simply can't afford to bury their heads when it comes to staying tapped into what's next, including in social media.

As of the writing of this book, what's next is Google+, Pinterest, and YouTube, which, in reality, are probably the biggest players in social media, with the biggest upside for businesses. What? Yes, you read me right. The next big three could be even better for your business than the first three. It would be a mistake to ignore these platforms, as they are likely going to continue to grow in popularity, and they offer some of the best ways available to reach customers. I'm not saying that you have to immediately jump onto any of these bandwagons (although I'm sure that many readers have watched their share of YouTube videos), but I do want you to take enough time to learn more about each of these so you understand them and are well positioned to take advantage if and when the time is right for you.

Google+: Growing, Maturing, and Still Changing

If I were to describe Google+ from the user perspective, I would say that it has taken the best elements of LinkedIn, Facebook, Twitter, and blogging and combined them into a single platform *without all of the advertising*. Intrigued? You should be. Google+ has some distinct advantages over other social media platforms and certainly some useful tools that you, as a business, can take advantage of.

I am just going to come right out and tell you that I like Google+ a great deal. It is becoming possibly my favorite of all of the social media platforms. I have been using it since the beta release, and the more I use it, the more I like it. The biggest advantage that Google+ has over every platform is that it is owned by Google. As we are well aware, Google is the number one search engine in the world, and Google search is still the number one way for businesses to be found online. So, rather than displaying advertising on their social media platform, Google displays their search function at the very top of the Google+ platform. This has two distinct benefits. First, if you need to find information as a result of something you have read or seen while on Google+, you simply type it in the search field. Second, you don't have to deal with the annoyance of advertisements intruding on your social media time while on Google+.

In addition, I recently discovered a bonus benefit of Google+, in that it appears that you can make your Google+ posts easily findable on the web by others interested in your topic when you use a hashtag (# followed by a key search term with no spaces) in your post. In my own experiments, I have discovered that by adding a hashtag with certain keywords somewhere in my Google+ post, I can later Google that hashtag and find that my Google+ post shows up relatively high in the search results. (I should mention that it did not show up internationally, but it did in the United States.) So if I create a Google+ post with a link to my latest blog article on social mediology and include a hashtag of #socialmediology, other Google+ users who search for information using #socialmediology will likely see a list of results that include my Google+ post. None of us should be shocked if it were true that Google+ posts may have some added value in terms of search engine optimization. If this is, in fact, true, then Google+ has a huge benefit over every other social media platform. The hashtag is a great way for a business to not only build some search engine optimization but simplify the process of telling people how to find the content that it posts.

Google+ also allows URL shorteners such as bit.ly and goo.gl so that you can post abbreviated web links of interest to your readers that don't take up much room and thereby keep your posts simple and easy to read. At the same time, Google+ allows you to post as long (or as short) of a post as you would like (cf. Twitter, which is limited to 140 or fewer characters).

As of the first quarter of 2013, it has been reported that Google+ is the second largest social networking platform behind Facebook.[1] Although we cannot be sure of the exact numbers because Google+ does not release their numbers (as is the case with many of these platforms), according to *Business Insider,* Google+ has 359 million users.[2]

The breakdown of Google+ users is rather interesting. Statistically, it has been male dominated, as approximately 70% of users are male.[3] This skew toward men may be a result of the reality that Google+'s first user base was predominantly IT Engineers, an industry typically dominated by men. That being said, the number of women using Google+ is growing. Additionally, the Google+ age demographic is split at the age of 24 years, with approximately 50% of the users below the age of 24 years and 50% above the age of 24 years. In other words, young and older people alike are currently using Google+. From an occupational standpoint, college students and people in technology-related occupations lead when it comes to the users of Google+.

Why are folks using Google+? According to Google Plus Demographics, the majority of users (41.99%) are motivated to be on Google+ to make friends, whereas almost one out of three (32.21%) are motivated to use Google+ for networking. Although the culture of Google+ is still developing, this gives us a glimpse into the current atmosphere. It is educated and technological, with business and friendships sprinkled in. This does not mean that all that is talked about on Google+ is academics and technology. On the contrary, there are interesting side stories, humor, and current events as well. Your experience on Google+ will be dictated by who is in your *circles,* as Google+ refers to an individual's networks.

When Google+ first started, it was quite dominated by what I would call the "Google elite" and the "social media famous." However, as it has evolved and is still evolving, people from all walks of life and industries are joining. As on Twitter, social media celebrities on Google+ are typically not all that interactive. They tend to post information, and dozens or sometimes hundreds of people make comments without the celebrity responding. However, for the not so famous, interaction is happening. In fact, Google+ can be an ideal environment for the frustrated Twitter user, in that it is both socially and professionally reinforcing.

For example, whereas Twitter is not as conversational and has fewer opportunities for interaction, Google+ allows you to freely comment, +1 (which is akin to a Facebook like), share, and more. Professionally, Google+ has advantages because you can easily set up a business profile that allows you to directly interact with real people and other businesses. Whereas Facebook business pages do not allow you to freely connect with others, you can easily include people from your Google+ circles in your business posts to generate interaction. This Google+ advantage can also be seen when the platform is compared with LinkedIn, where you cannot call people out in a group, only from your individual status update. In other words, whereas Facebook and LinkedIn have boundaries around when, where, and with whom you can interact (i.e., call out and notify by name), Google+ allows you to do so from anywhere—from your personal status update, in hangouts, from your business page—and with people that aren't even in your circles.

While trying to define Google+ culture, I happened to have a conversation via Google+ that further enlightened me on the topic with a colleague, Mike Allton (+mikeallton), who is a social media and Internet marketing consultant for small- to medium-sized businesses and an editor at The Social Media Hat (http://www.TheSocialMediaHat.com). As we were discussing the evolution of Google+ culture, Mike said, "If we think about Facebook as being a place where people 'reconnect' with friends and family, Google+ is a place where we create new relationships both personally and professionally." Perfect. I 100% agree with his conclusions. My relationship with Mike was, in fact, created through Google+, and I certainly have other relationships that resulted from my experience and interaction on the platform as well. Very cool! Now, how does that apply to you as a business owner? On Google+, you can get connected to potential clients and, just as important, to people who have the power and influence to be brand ambassadors for you and/or your business, singing your praises, increasing your credibility, and spreading the good word about you and your business.

Google+ is not nearly as friendly as Facebook, but it is far more friendly and interactive than Twitter. Certainly, there are numerous ways to interact with a post that very much resemble your options on Facebook. For instance, as I've mentioned, you can +1 someone's post, which is similar to Facebook's like. You can comment on a post, and you can tag someone in that comment by simply adding a + or @ in front of that person's name, so he or she will be notified of your mention. You can also share someone's post, just like you can in Facebook. And, just as you can create lists of people in Facebook with whom you communicate (close friends, clients, knitting group, softball team, etc.), Google+ allows you to add people to "circles." For the avid Facebook user, it is actually quite an easy transition to Google+.

More recently, Google+ has allowed the creation of business pages, similar to Facebook. However, unlike Facebook, where you cannot directly interact with a person from your Facebook business page, from a Google+ business page, you can put a + or @ sign in front of a person's name to notify them directly of a communication. Wow! A major obstacle experienced by businesses on Facebook business fan pages has been removed!

I know that the potential for spamming people is there with this type of thing; however, you can stop it by simply muting the post or removing the person or company from your circle. The advantage here is that if you already have a clientele that is using Google+ and you have posted something that you know is of particular value or importance to one of your clients, it is a nice feature to use occasionally (do not overdo it!) to bring them in and have them interact with you on your post.

Another area in which I think Google+ is absolutely succeeding is in bringing communities of like-minded people together. In LinkedIn, you are able to create or be part of groups that facilitate specific discussions about issues and industries. Google+ does the same thing, but on this platform, they are called *communities*. They work in a way similar to LinkedIn groups. For example, you set up a group; manage the members; start discussions; join in discussions; add photos, links, and video; and create interest around a specific topic.

Mike Lovas, the founder of the Psychological Marketing Network on LinkedIn, and I recently created the Psychological Marketing Network on Google+.[4] Mike and I believe that Google+ is more interactive than LinkedIn and that there is a large enough academic and marketing demographic that will have an interest in psychological marketing to make this community worthwhile. Although the LinkedIn group is currently our primary focus, we also do not want to be naïve to the fact that Google+ is growing and may be an ideal place for us to grow the network of individuals interested in this topic. The Psychological Marketing Network is in its fledgling stage, but we both believe that Google+ is the right target market to enhance our discussions of psychology and marketing. Google+ is also great for bloggers. For example, you may find that you are having difficulty setting up a blog. Not to worry. You can do your blogging right from your Google+ personal profile or business page. Technically speaking, the blogging setup on Google+ can eliminate any worries you might have about setting up a blog, adding plug-ins, and addressing other minutiae and still get you really good search engine optimization in Google search.

Google+ even has some amazing features that no other platform currently has. For example, when you type a post or status update into Google+, you can bold, italicize, and strike through words and phrases. What is more, whether you write an update or comment on someone's post, you always have the option, no matter when, to edit or update your post. It is a very cool feature (which Facebook has now caught on to and added as well). No longer do you have to delete and start over; simply hover, hit *edit*, and make your corrections. For people like me, who hurry while typing and sometimes make mistakes, it's an invaluable feature.

If you were to ask me about the best way to start on Google+, I would suggest that you create a profile. As always, make sure it is complete. Next, use a real photograph of you. Again, people are connecting with people, not your dog, cat, antelope, children, or some avatar. Your picture can be casual or professional, but make sure it is you. If there is one commonality I have found among the biggest users on Google+ when it comes to a photo, they all have some easy-to-see picture of their face. This makes sense because if Google+ culture is about creating new relationships, then we need to offer up someone, not something, to have a relationship with.

In case you were wondering about fake profiles, when it comes to social media platforms, Google+ probably has the best verification process of them all. It is very difficult to have a fake profile and be successful on Google+. It does not mean that fake profiles do not happen; it only means that Google uses quite a few safeguards to limit the number of fake profiles. One such way they are able to verify Google+ profiles is through what Google calls *Google Authorship*. It is a way to connect your already existing blog and anything you say to your Google+ profile. This is a creative way of claiming your blog content and your Google+ profile content. It is actually pretty cool, because once you verify your Google Authorship, typically when you post something online, if you search for it, your picture will appear next to whatever you posted (unless the user has chosen to block that setting).

After you have created your profile, Google+ will make suggestions of people that you know. Like on Twitter, the power of reciprocation takes over. You start adding people to your circles and people will add you back to their circles. There is a major difference from Twitter, however, when it comes to Google+: Even if no one is following you, posting still has major value for you and your business. This is because your posts from Google+ are typically indexed on Google search, especially if you use hashtags. This provides you with some extra organic search engine optimization that you might not otherwise have. So whereas with Twitter, you may feel the frustration of not having as many followers as Justin Bieber or Beyoncé, with Google+, you can know that every time you post, regardless of your number of Google+ followers, your post has meaning and potential impact. Essentially, if a tree falls in the forest, Google+ will try to make it as easy as possible for those interested to hear it.

This is not to say that followers via Google+ aren't desirable. When you start adding people to your circles, they will see what you post and you will see what they post, creating opportunities for valuable communication and interaction. If they have not blocked commenting, you will have the opportunity to +1 an update, comment, or share. You can create conversation by simply being interactive. Like Facebook, if you are willing to do some initiating of conversation, you will quickly be interacting. Do not forget to use the + or @ sign before a person's name, because when you type it out, their name will be highlighted and they will be notified that their name has been mentioned. For example, if I want to get feedback on something I have written and if I have some specific people in mind that I want to be notified, I simply put a + before their names (as long as they are in my circles) and ask them to comment.

You can see the advantages of doing this. First, you have the capability on Google+ to directly ask one or more people to interact with you. Second, when those people start interacting, the idea of social proof kicks in, and now others are more likely to also interact. One thing is for sure: If you give people credit for what they write and you engage them, you will create an influential reciprocal relationship that can begin to take shape and be cultivated by you.

What's the Point: Why Should You Use Google+?

I have heard the following question quite frequently: "Why should I use Google+?" Well, I hope that after having read the number of useful features available on Google+, you are starting to see how it can be of value. As a recap, here are three benefits that you can gain from Google+, which I present with the note that in my own business, I reaped these benefits immediately and could not have gotten them from any other social platform. First, Google+ enhances search engine optimization faster and better than any other social media platform. Your posts from Google+ are put up on Google's search platform about as fast as you hit the *Submit* button. Okay, maybe not quite that quickly, but it is really fast. Remember, Google owns Google+, so they own how and who will be seen; it doesn't take a brain surgeon or even a consumer analyst to know that Google's own social media platform is going to get priority.

Second, because Google+ is what I would consider a pretty educated platform in terms of user demographics, you can develop a sense of credibility by interacting there that rivals that gained from participation in LinkedIn groups. In fact, I have found that the relationships I have developed on Google+ with people in my field have led to tremendous opportunities that I would not have gotten from any other platform or that would have been difficult for me to otherwise develop.

Third, there is no advertising noise and thus no distractions on Google+. This is one of the greatest benefits of all. On Google+, there are no sponsored posts, advertising on the side, and so on. It is all about the people, their posts, and the interaction generating conversations and relationships.

Finally, there are some smaller yet significant benefits unique to this platform to take advantage of. You are allowed to interact with people from your business page, not just be another "liked" business, as on Facebook. In addition, there is no limit on how many people can see a post from your business profile, whereas Facebook does not allow something you post on your business page to show up on all of the news feeds of people who have liked your page. This is so they can sell more advertising. In Google+, everyone who has included your business as part of his or her circles will see something when you post it. What is more, your business posts will be indexed by Google search: That is not going to happen on any other platform.

As you can see, I really like Google+. It is my favorite of all the platforms: no advertising and so much business benefit. As a result, I would rather see you use Google+ than Twitter, perhaps even more than Facebook, depending on your target market. However, there is a downside to Google+. As big as it is, there probably are not as many active users on it as Google claims. A significant number of people use it and that number is more than likely larger than the number of people on Twitter and growing, but maybe not as many users are on Google+ as has been stated, whether that be due to individuals having multiple accounts or having an account but never actually using it.[5] Also, Google+ is currently pretty much male dominated; I have noticed that, typically, there are not as many women using Google+ as men. I believe there are many reasons for this. First and foremost, it is not as casual or relational as some of the other platforms. This is by no means an indictment or a chauvinistic viewpoint. Statistically, women tend to be on the platforms where there are more sharing and relational interactive aspects to the platform, such as Pinterest and Facebook. I do think this is subtly changing, however, as more professional women are using Google+ and reaping the benefits for their business and business endeavors.

Before I close on Google+, I truly encourage you to build a profile for yourself personally and for your business—if for no other reason than because it will be indexed on Google's search platform. Within these profiles, you can link to your website and other social media profiles. There is a huge advantage to creating your Internet social media footprint so that you and your business can be found, and, with the power of Google behind you, you and your business will be even more accessible. Like all of the social media platforms, none of which are perfect, Google+ may not be the best platform for your target market (only time will tell), but create yourself a profile there because this is a social media platform with true fringe benefits.

Try This!

Go ahead and set up your Google+ account if you haven't already, and be sure to also set up Google Authorship (https://plus.google.com/authorship) in the process, which will entail uploading your photo. Then, write a post on Google+, including keywords or phrases as well as a hashtag of the words or phrases in the post, for example, #socialmediology, #marketingtips, or #organicskincare, depending on your industry, line of business, and what you think would help people find your post on a search. Then, do a Google search in the next twenty-four hours and see where your post winds up. Don't be surprised if it initially winds up on the first page for that search word or phrase!

Women Are from Pinterest

Pinterest, a photo-sharing social media platform, has been around for a very short period of time, but it has grown quickly and gained a lot of popularity with certain parts of the population. Here's how Pinterest works: People post photos (called *pins*) of different things (e.g., vacation destinations, clothes, furniture, antique cars, recipes, room-decorating ideas), put them into categories, and then share them with others. The greatest interaction for people using Pinterest is that they can "repin" others' Pinterest photos, meaning add them to their own Pinterest boards. Although people can certainly upload their own original photos to pin on their boards (e.g., family snapshots, garden photos, family dinners), they can just as easily pin photos and websites that they find online, for example, coupons to local stores, home improvement ideas, sales flyers, and literally anything that you can imagine in pictures.

Recently, Pinterest even created a way to pin your blog post. It will be interesting to watch and observe whether this significantly affects how people use Pinterest. I say this because Pinterest has traditionally been a picture board of sorts (which is what makes it so unique), whereas blog posts require reading. I would guess that this addition will have some effect on how people view and use Pinterest, but we will just have to wait over the next year to see how users react to this new feature.

The sum total of all this pinning and repinning is a dashboard of different virtual bulletin boards that the Pinterest user can access at any time, whether to see a favorite holiday cookie recipes or to consider different paint colors for the master bedroom. So, if you run a baking company, local paint store, jewelry shop, or any small business that lends itself to showcasing your product or service in pictures, Pinterest may be a natural platform for you to develop a presence on.

You may wonder why people bother pinning material from the web when they can simply bookmark websites of interest. It's a matter of utility and visual appeal. Whereas a bookmark is simply the static name of a website on a drop-down menu that a person can click to be taken back to that website, pinning allows people to store photo representations of all of their favorite materials from the web in one place (by category) that can be browsed and enjoyed at a glance—pictures of different Italian meals they hope to make, front-porch decorating ideas, or potential birthday gifts for a loved one. Looking at Pinterest boards is a bit like window shopping.

Where does the allure of Pinterest come from? Photos and pictures influence people. Although we may remember an event, a two-dimensional picture enables us to relive it. In his online book *Photographic Psychology: Image and Psyche*, John Suler's research suggests that one reason why people recall specific pictures from a long series of pictures is to create a sense of tranquility or happiness.[6] There is no doubt that pictures are powerful: They elicit an emotional connection in people. As a testament to the power of visual imagery, there is an entire sub-branch of psychology called *photo psychology*.[7] It is an interesting field that covers the entire gamut of why people look at photos to what are some of the psychological meanings of what the photo has captured. I have already discussed how powerful pictures are when it comes to Facebook and other social media. If there is a social media spot that exploits the psychology of pictures more than any other, it is Pinterest.

I joined Pinterest when it first started, and I found it interesting. However, as Pinterest quickly evolved, I found myself struggling to stay in tune with it. I like to pin infographics on psychology, the Internet, social media, and business that I think may be helpful to others, but I am not one who typically peruses other people's pins. I have many friends who love Pinterest and can spend hours looking through pictures. This is probably in part because Pinterest is a great place to find categories of things you are looking for. Trying to decide what kind of fence to put up? Search *fences* on Pinterest. Want ideas for your upcoming party? Search "Mardi Gras decorations" or "Dora birthday cakes." A list of relevant pins will pop up for your viewing pleasure. I also have friends who post pictures of recipes that they share with each other, coupons to local stores for discount shopping, and do-it-yourself home improvement ideas.

Demographically, the Pinterest culture has distinguished itself among the social media platforms for its dominantly female usership, as I recently highlighted in a blog post titled "Men are from LinkedIn, Women are from Pinterest."[8] I have read several studies on the Pinterest demographics, including one that indicates that a full four out of five Pinterest users are female.[9] According to Nielson it appears that 84% of Pinterest users are female, making it the most skewed demographically of all the social media platforms.[10] Also of note, Pinterest is not demonstrating any significant growth in active male users. What else can be said about Pinterest's demographics? Eighty-one percent of Pinterest users are between the ages of 25 and 54 years, 25% have a bachelor's degree or higher, and 65% have an income between $25,000 and $75,000 per year.[11] This puts Pinterest in a unique category when it comes to culture and business: Of all the social media platforms, Pinterest is clearly skewed demographically to women, meaning that if you have a business that is more female-centric, this may be a great place for you to focus your time and energy. That being said, as with all of the social media platforms, it will take some time and experimentation to assess whether Pinterest is right for your particular business.

What makes Pinterest social is that people can share their pins with others as well as allow others who are searching Pinterest or Google to peek at their pins or to follow their pins regularly. (People can also choose to keep their pins private.) Although you can like and comment on other people's pins, in reality, when compared with other social media platforms, there is very little conversation on Pinterest. As with Twitter, Pinterest is not the most social of the social media cultures. According to RePinly (now known as Postris), a statistical component of Pinterest, the behavior of a Pinterest user is unique when compared with the behavior on other social media platforms. Pinterest users spend 83.4% of their time pinning, 16% of their time liking other pins, and a whopping 0.06% of their time commenting on pins.[12] This indicates to me that psychologically, people are spending a huge amount of time putting up their content or the content they find rather than interacting with each other. Perhaps, then, it is the photos and pictures that are creating the emotional connection (as John Suler argued) rather than any sort of relationship development with other people.

In an attempt to get a better understanding of the Pinterest culture, I used RePinly to assess what types of information get pinned and who is most followed on Pinterest. First, looking at the top one hundred accounts with the most followers, I found that Pinterest was overwhelmingly dominated by female pinners, none of whom I recognized (unlike Twitter's top folks). Only a few male pinners made the top one hundred, as did a few brands. Then, I looked at the top categories that made up at least 50% of pins and discovered that they were (in order) as follows:

- Food & Drink
- DIY (Do It Yourself) & Crafts
- Other (a catch-all and not a very helpful category)
- Home Décor
- Hair & Beauty
- Women's Fashion
- Weddings[13]

Given that these categories are areas that typically would generate a much higher percentage of female interest than male, the theory of the female-centric nature of Pinterest is further reinforced.

What's the Point: Why Should You Use Pinterest?

Pinterest clearly has a place for certain businesses. When you look at the top-followed pinners on Pinterest, you will find that the majority of them are in design, fashion, food, arts, crafts, architecture, and the like. These types of industries can take advantage of this platform because their output is visual in nature and can be captured in photographs. It really comes down to understanding who your future client is. If you are selling mutual funds, Pinterest would probably not be the best platform for you. However, if, for example, you have a women's clothing store, then it may be time to start snapping photos of some of your new fashions to pin on Pinterest. This is why it is critically important to know who your client is demographically as well as who the users are of each platform to help make sure it is a good fit for your product or service.

Although Pinterest originated as a noncommercial site, it has recently created a business platform. You can either convert your personal profile into a business profile or create a separate business profile. The reviews on the efficacy of a business profile are still mixed. However, whether you like the business profile will largely depend on what your business offers in terms of products or services and how that fits in with the Pinterest culture. It may also change as the Pinterest business profile evolves over time.

I also believe that success on Pinterest has less to do with *who* pins and more to do with *what* is being pinned. In other words, you don't need to be famous to get repinned, but you do have to provide something that is visually appealing and relevant to people's lives. Although it's true that beauty and value are the perception of the user, some photos simply look more professional and enticing than others. It will be important, should you choose to use this platform, that you consistently check how many repins and likes you get on the pictures you post to find out what is and is not working.

Like Twitter, Pinterest's value to your business will be about *followers*: that is, those people who choose to follow what you post. Much as I would like to, I cannot provide you with some shortcut to getting followers. The key is having the right pictures, in the right categories, that people are interested in. The top-followed accounts as of the writing of this book are related to the design industry (as touched on earlier) and do not follow many people. I believe this is because these pinners have, for lack of a better term, an eye for what is appealing. Unlike Twitter, where celebrity status will land you more followers, on Pinterest, what you do, not who you are, gets you noticed and followed.

So what psychological principles should you keep in mind when you are posting on Pinterest? First, do your very best to post images that elicit positive emotions. Does this picture make you smile? Might it make others smile? Does it make you laugh? Feel peaceful? Feel hopeful? All of those positive emotional states are signs that you might be posting something that will also appeal to others.

Second, pin DIY projects. Can you show a picture of something that a do-it-yourselfer would want to try? If so, post it.

Third, pin vision and inspiration. Give people pictures of things that most only dream about. A word that came out of my research on Pinterest is *fitsperation,* sometimes called *fitspo,* which refers to pictures of fit people doing fitness activities that inspire you to do the same. Give your viewers something they can shoot for in their future, something they can imagine creating or attaining someday. Perhaps it is a beautiful home, luxurious bedding, hand-crafted furniture, or an exotic beach getaway. We may never truly know what makes people pin specific pictures, but I am convinced that if you pin content from these three areas, you will be followed and repinned.

How does any of this translate into business? There are several ways. First, your Pinterest account can be indexed by Google: Go to your privacy settings and click "No" in the area that says, "Keep search engines (ex: Google) from showing your Pinterest profile in search results." This is important because you and your business can get some search engine optimization if you let search engines in.

Second, Pinterest allows you to verify your website. This is important because this verification process separates the real users from the pretenders. When you verify your website, you are also attaching a sense of trust to your profile. Third, you can add links to your website from your pins. This is terribly important in driving people who are interested in your pins to also perhaps be interested in your business.

If you are selling a product that fits within the Pinterest demographic, you certainly have a tremendous advantage. If you are in the service industry as a designer, interior decorator, or even a real estate professional (posting unique and interesting ideas you see in homes), I believe you can also do quite well on Pinterest. Certainly, I am not saying that Pinterest's scope is limited to these industries, but some industries are a more natural fit for Pinterest than others.

The other side of this, however, may be that you just like how Pinterest works. Even if your business or industry is not an obvious fit for Pinterest but you enjoy it, then use it and be creative; perhaps your passion can translate into trust that can translate to your business. You will only know if you try. The bottom line of Pinterest is this: Know your target market and know the Pinterest demographics. If they match up, Pinterest may be a good option for your business.

Try This!

After you create your Pinterest account, start following a few boards that you find interesting. Repin some pictures and organize your boards, and then start pinning some pictures related to your product or service. Make sure the pictures are of good quality, and then write a description of your pictures using keywords. See how long it takes for people to start repinning, liking, and even posting comments. If you see things happen in twenty-four hours or less, you are in the sweet spot. If nothing happens in seventy-two hours, change your pictures and descriptions to see if this generates more interest.

YouTube: The New TV

Many people love watching TV, for many reasons. For some, it is an escape; for others, it's about entertainment or to learn something new. The fact is, we like having the ability to disconnect from our preoccupations while connecting with television programming, whether it's in the form of a crime drama, tragic love story, news exposé, or comedy sketch. Television certainly has provided all of these and more, even if they are occasionally interrupted by advertisements.

What if there was a place where you could pick and choose what you wanted to watch and when you wanted to watch it, with limited or no commercial interruption? That is YouTube. (Of course, it's also on-demand TV, but we won't be discussing that here since it's unrelated to our topic of social media.)

YouTube is a giant, with more than 170 million people in the United States visiting YouTube per month, according to Quantcast.[14] One billion people come to the site every month from all over the world, according to YouTube. What may be even more impressive is that one hundred hours of video are uploaded to YouTube every minute.[15] And, of course, YouTube videos aren't just being uploaded and/or watched: They are being shared as well. That's what makes it social. People love sharing videos to which they have an emotional connection. If you look at Facebook, Google+, blogs, Twitter, and other platforms, you find that people share video. Video creates conversation. Video creates interaction. YouTube has given people an easy way to share videos we like and enjoy with others, whether through Facebook, Twitter, or personal websites.

As for who is using YouTube, the demographics are pretty evenly distributed across age groups, income levels, genders, education, and so on. In fact, among all of the social platforms, YouTube easily represents our world better than the others. Why? It is probably because most people like to watch moving pictures—once on film reels, now available in digital—and that moving pictures have been around for more than a century, making them mainstream and familiar.

What is our fascination with watching videos? There may be no single psychological answer to the question. That being said, there still appears to be a common denominator: The biggest reason we like what we like is because we are making some emotional connection with whatever we are watching. It may be subtle, offering us a pleasant escape from everyday life. It may be more overt, like when a movie causes us to experience a sense of emotional intensity. Is there anything that feels better than a huge belly laugh? And even a good cry from a sad movie can be cathartic. If one were to pinpoint a single reason for people's watching behavior, it is to stimulate emotion in some fashion or another.

YouTube does that better than any other social media platform. And YouTube is better than TV for many simply because we can search for exactly what we prefer to watch while, at the same time, getting the pleasure of stumbling across something that often stimulates us emotionally in a surprising way. Today, YouTube allows lengthy videos and movies; however, the YouTube videos with the most views are only a few minutes long.

This may provide some insight into YouTube viewing culture—perhaps we enjoy it so much because we can quickly view several different videos in a relatively short period of time that stimulate our emotions again and again. (Clearly, this topic needs more study, and if you are a psychology doctoral candidate, here's your dissertation, perhaps? Ha!) The fact remains that billions of videos are being watched for a variety of reasons, and the popularity of this type of visual media is growing. Simply because of the sheer number of people watching videos, there is a place for YouTube in any business.

How can you maximize your effectiveness on YouTube? There are a number of ways.

Go for High-Quality Video and Audio

First, make sure your video and audio are of the highest quality. Creating a YouTube video today is easier than it ever has been. You can buy very good high-definition (HD) video camcorders for less than $300. Even many smartphones now capture video in HD quality. Your biggest challenge will be getting good to great sound quality. Do not underestimate sound quality, because we "see" with our ears quite often. What do I mean by that? Merely that when we are at home watching a TV show, movie, sporting event, or other video, many times we look away or perhaps move to another part of the room so that our eyes are no longer directly focused on the screen, yet we can hear whatever it is we are watching and feel as if we have not missed anything simply because the audio quality is so good.

A friend of mine who was a professional videographer said to me in a conversation about video, "We have all these high-quality, low-cost HD videos, and more often than not we have low-quality audio. The two do not match up and the video will never be as effective as when both are at the highest quality." After watching probably thousands of YouTube videos, I must agree: It is frustrating when the video looks good but the sound quality is poor. This can lead people to quickly move on to something else.

Give Us Something Good to Watch

Second, when putting together video for YouTube, give people something to see, not just hear. Many times, businesses will produce great videos with good information, but they are so long and so lacking in visual interest that you probably should have made it a podcast. I think the businesses that have a tremendous advantage on YouTube are those that can actually demonstrate how to do something. Give viewers something to observe that they can do. I saw a video that I thought demonstrated this nicely: An owner from a small clothing store for women demonstrated how to tie a scarf in different ways to dress up a look. Not only was this an excellent demonstration, but it also gave her great credibility. She was showing viewers her knowledge of not just clothes but how to creatively wear them. What can you visually demonstrate or teach on YouTube to your clients and potential clients? Use video when you actually have something for people to see. Remember, people are perusing YouTube to be stimulated visually, not to simply listen to you.

Show Us What You Got

Third, don't sell viewers a product or service; sell viewers on your knowledge, skills, and abilities. We are strongly influenced by people of great knowledge, especially if they know something we do not know. This does not always translate well to video, but perhaps you can apply your knowledge in a creative way that would make someone want to watch the video. This is where adding some nice production value, such as movement, cutting away to an example, or clever titling can be beneficial. If you have specialized skills and abilities, those are even easier to demonstrate and will give you quite an advantage. For example, if you sell high-end, handmade light fixtures, record your team blowing the glass and forging the iron. If you are a marketing agency, create a video presentation that gives tips on how to put together an effective brochure, or record your creative team as they brainstorm new company names with a willing client to educate potential clients on the process. Always keep in mind when you are creating your video that an audience will be watching, and ask yourself, "Did I give my audience something worth looking at?" If your answer is no, ask your clients what questions they would like to have answered by you, the expert, and build from there.

Make Us Laugh

Fourth, using humor in video is a great way to encourage shares and views. When you look at videos outside of music that have high numbers of views, humorous videos seem to rise to the top. I find it interesting that corporations are more willing to be humorous with their videos than smaller businesses are. It has taken me a long time to figure out why, but I believe I stumbled on the answer. Many times, owners of small businesses and entrepreneurs believe that to be competitive, they have to maintain a professional image in everything they do. Therefore, they are reluctant to put on displays of public humor, because they fear that their businesses will not be taken seriously. However, if you watch TV at all or see commercials on YouTube, even the most professional companies are using humor to attract new clients. Why humor? Because it is memorable. The more humorous something is, the more people remember it.

Now, let's go back to Pavlov's classical conditioning model that I have talked about in other situations. If a company can pair its brand with a smiling or laughing reaction enough times, what happens when you hear the company name? Of course, you smile or laugh. Even better (from the company's point of view), you also immediately recall the commercial.

Consider how successful GEICO has been with "I just saved hundreds of dollars on car insurance" with the cavemen, now the gecko? Who took Progressive Insurance seriously until they gave us the flighty Flo? The fact is, humor works. That being said, it is also important to note that humor is in the eye of the viewer. It is not always easy to know what will be considered funny. However, that doesn't mean you shouldn't try it; it only means that before you post a humorous video, you should have a few folks preview it. If you see smiles or chuckles in reaction, put it up. I don't believe you always have to be humorous, but I do believe that humor has an important place in video. If you are able to get past your fear and condition people to associate your business with a smile, you will reap the benefits. At the very least, experiment with it.

Be Real, Be Natural

Fifth, be organic. One of the other characteristics I have noticed in my research of highly viewed videos is that they have an organic element to them, meaning that they are not necessarily overly produced. Now, this may be intentional or unintentional for these videos, but regardless, these particular popular videos make viewers believe that they just naturally occurred as part of a day. These videos draw people in because it is easy to believe something like this could happen, or maybe it has happened to us or to someone we know, but now there is actually a video of it. In essence, it is like a slice of reality TV, which has been increasing in popularity since 2000 and remains incredibly popular.[16]

Find a Need and Fill It

Sixth, when thinking about what content to put into your video, consider how you can offer people information that is not already available. Here's my own example of doing just that, even though I fell into it a bit haphazardly. A few years ago, I had to get a knee replacement. I watched as many videos as I could about how the surgery was going to be done. Some of these videos showed me the full graphic nature of the surgery. At the time, though, very few videos depicted the recovery after knee surgery, especially in terms of the physical therapy. I decided I would film from my perspective the first couple of days of my physical therapy, complete with the view of my gross-looking, freshly scarred knee.

To date, I have more than 68,000 views on the Day 1 video and more than 45,000 for Day 2. What is more, I have had hospitals and therapists request permission to use the videos. (I agreed.) Now, there is nothing particularly great in regard to my production of these videos, but they are real, and my anguish is equally real. If I learned anything from this experience, it taught me that there is something powerful about realism. I know most businesses will not have a video quite as graphic as mine, but you should absolutely know there is something very attractive to the viewer when videos have an authentic and organic feel to them, as I just discussed. This video was also likely a success because it provided information that was not already out there. If you, as a business, can fill a gap in the knowledge with your video, you may find yourself getting many views and shares.

Keep It Short and Pithy

Finally, shorter is typically better. This is not just because shorter video fits the original culture of YouTube, where longer videos were once not allowed (to keep download times fast), but because it fits the attention span of most viewers today. For example, the average viewer is more willing to view a one-minute or two-minute video than a five-minute video, particularly one that is not professionally produced.

The psychology here is simple: On a shorter video, even if the video is bad, a viewer will not lose much of our time, whereas a five-minute video that is bad can feel to the viewer like an eternity. So viewers may be predisposed not to click on longer videos or, when attention spans are short, to simply navigate away from a video soon after hitting the *Play* button.

All of that being said, lately, I have observed more and more videos that are longer than three minutes are garnering millions of views. This is because the videos in question contain some sort of drama or suspense that keeps the viewer engaged. As more and more TV programs are being posted in ten- or fifteen-minute segments on YouTube and receiving a decent number of views, I am discovering that length, although important, may be becoming less important, especially if a video is interesting.

As you are experimenting with making videos, get your social media network to comment honestly on their views of what you post; ask them how to improve your videos and what would make them better. Their feedback can be extremely beneficial in helping you to produce better videos that have a greater impact for your business in the future.

A Few Tips on Professional Video Production

So far, I have said very little about professional production. This is because for small businesses, professional video production is expensive. Fortunately, your videos can be surprisingly well produced in house—and I do believe you should do them well. As mentioned earlier, this starts with an HD digital video recorder and attention to good sound quality. One way to really improve the quality is to make sure you have a high-quality microphone that allows you to be clearly heard while reducing the ambient noise. Personally, I use a lavalier microphone that can be attached to what I am wearing and that can be fairly easily concealed while still giving clear sound.

Once you've got the audiovisual equipment, put some time into organizing your video's content. Even in so-called reality TV, some planning must happen. In sum, you should have a plan; your video should look good and sound good; and, clearly, there must be something of value on display for your current or future client.

What's the Point: Why Should You Use YouTube?

Through videos, you, as a business, have ways of giving people a sense of what you and your business are about. No other medium can bring you and your employees to life better than video footage of you speaking, smiling, teaching, and showing. Whereas web text is flat and two-dimensional and written posts and comments on social media are just words, video is movement, three dimensions, personality, and spice.

Rather than trying to simply write a clever advertisement, you are giving the viewer a more realistic preview of you, your business, your knowledge, and your creativity.

In addition, most people watch video and like video; as a result, video can be a nice addition to your business's marketing output. It's one more potential point of contact with your client who learns best by seeing and observing or who is simply attracted to clicking the *Play* button when faced with video content.

As touched on earlier, video can be done, and done well, for relatively little money and with no extra marketing cost. Keep in mind, too, that YouTube videos are indexed by Google (after all, Google owns YouTube), so if you put keywords and phrases in your video's description, they will be indexed in Google search. Video is also valuable because if you are clever and creative enough, you give people something that is easily shared via all the social media platforms, plus e-mail. As more people click on your video, it can help strengthen your brand and give people another reason and way to spread the news about your business.

Next, YouTube can have benefit for your business because it helps people, especially the younger generation, see that you have some Internet savvy. Internet prowess is especially important to under-35 digital natives who more readily connect with those who are digital. Even though you may be a "digital immigrant," the fact that you are at least making an attempt to enter the digital natives' world and speak their language demonstrates that you are willing and able to interact with them on their natural turf. If you are not using video, I highly recommend you experiment with it. You may find that video gives you a competitive edge, and you certainly can give your business a great boost by being creative.

So, yes, there is a place for video in your business. However, you must be realistic about what you expect to accomplish with it. For the typical business, it will not be realistic to think you will get several hundred million views. This is because it is difficult to make that kind of emotional connection with viewers. That is saved for the likes of music videos, reality–videoed incidents (e.g. extreme athleticism, live tragedy), and humorous home movies that happen to go viral. You are more than likely not going to be doing a video on kittens playing the piano (although, if you can somehow fit it in, it may not be a bad idea), dogs saying "I love you," or a three-year-old getting bitten by his one-year-old little brother.

If you are going to use YouTube for your business and make a real impact, then you will have to understand that you are creating videos for a smaller group of people, namely, your current and future clients. This is where I believe most business owners, when using YouTube, make a big mistake and end up frustrated. They see videos with millions of views, so when they make a video and it may get a few hundred or maybe even a few thousand views, they feel disappointed.

Don't despair! If the video is being seen by the right people, its impact can have tremendous influence. It only takes one video seen by one right person who shares it with their circle of friends to create some buzz and, with luck, will cause it to be shared again by others. What is more, this video can give you credibility because rather than just reading about your credibility, people actually can see and listen to you demonstrating your expertise. As I have mentioned before, high credibility contributes to one's ability to influence—a powerful capacity for the businessperson.

Admittedly, determining success on YouTube is subjective, at best. Certainly, the number of views is a good determinant—a sign that you have piqued the interest of folks enough to click on the video, maybe even enough to play it multiple times and/or share it with others. The comments are a sign of success as well.

If a video does not seem to be getting much play, you may want to share your video by shortening the URL with goo.gl or bit.ly, posting it on your other social media business platforms, and seeing how often it is clicked on. In any case, do not dump a video simply because it is not being clicked. Do what you can to get the word out via the other social media channels or specific interest forums and message boards. If that still doesn't attract many clicks, it may then be that you have not created the right video; from there, you can try something new.

Of all the social media platforms, YouTube is probably the most time consuming. Yet, this is also why YouTube can be such a benefit. That is, because it is so time consuming, chances are your competition is not doing it! Video can make you stand out, so don't be afraid of it—try it! Make a sample video and send it out to your friends and clients. Ask for feedback. Improve it. Ask for more feedback, and try improving it again, until you are satisfied with the results.

YouTube can greatly benefit your business, but like any particular social media platform, you will never realize the benefit if you don't use it. I really hope you will take the time to give it a try. In doing so, you will be able to observe how video allows you to offer your potential clients a new touch point for getting to know you and your business, whether that be hearing from those who have trusted your organization in the past or seeing you and/or your professional team come to life on-screen. In the process, you can create a nice collection of video testimonials from your clients so others can hear just how skilled and knowledgeable you and your team are, thus creating powerful social proof.

Try This!

It's time to create a business video on YouTube. Even if you do not have an HD camera and special software, try creating a short video using your computer or phone. Most computers today have a built-in video camera and some sort of easy editing software included.

Start by brainstorming on what you are going to do in your video. One idea is to do a referral video, by talking about why one should refer you and your business. Another idea is to create a demonstration video where you teach your viewer something or an unboxing video, where you open a sealed box and describe what is found inside. In addition, consider creating a testimonial video, where one of your current clients explains what they love about you and your business. Remember, social proof of someone endorsing you on video can be a powerful tool of influence to get people to talk and inquire about your product or service. Whatever idea you ultimately choose, give yourself permission to keep it simple and focus on creating no more than one minute of video.

After you have rehearsed and captured the video to your satisfaction, upload it to YouTube, creating your own YouTube channel. Next, copy the link generated, shorten the link using either goo.gl or bit.ly, and then send a copy of the video to a few people in your referral network. Get some feedback and, over the course of the next few days, also check Google search to see where your video is being indexed. Let me know what you posted (send the link to jay@socialmediology.com), and let's see how you did.

In Sum: Pick and Choose, but Choose Wisely

Although we may have once thought of social media as a yes–no proposition—either we were on it or we weren't—as the number of platforms out there multiplies, we are left instead to decide which ones to use to draw the most clients to our businesses. We can pick and choose which platforms we use and then put them together in a way that lets us present our businesses as well-rounded entities.

Some of the more recent newcomers on the scene are Google+ and Pinterest. Then there is YouTube: Many of us are more familiar with this one, but that may be more from a perspective of watching video than creating it, so there's still room for many of us to grow here. If you have not had a chance yet to consider these three social media platforms, now may be the time to learn more about them and to test them out.

When should you use which platform? On Google+, you can interact with others from your status posts, your business page, and your hangouts, and there are no ads, unlike on Facebook and LinkedIn, where there are limitations on who you can call out to interact with. You will also get big search engine optimization benefits by using Google+, in part because Google search gives Google+ posts a lot of credibility (no surprise there) and in part because fewer businesses are on Google+, so you have less competition. As for Google+, there are so many promising features here, I have to suggest that every business owner take some time to get to know it, whether now or in the near future.

Pinterest is a good option for those with something visual to show, such as clothing, cuisine, travel destinations, book covers, antique cars, DIY projects, arts and crafts, merchandise, or home interiors. If your demographic is women, get creative and figure out how to show your stuff on Pinterest, as many women are spending time there.

As for YouTube, it's a fabulous way to bring you, your employees, and your company to life with video testimonials, personal interviews, product demos, service overviews, and more. Short, upbeat, funny, clear, and educational all work on YouTube, where people are happy to look at a quick video that is relevant to their lives and then share it with others when it makes an impact.

Spend some time reviewing which demographics play on each of these social media platforms and considering what the benefits of each are so you can match up your business needs with the right new platform or platforms. With the interesting features of each—Google+, Pinterest, and YouTube— it's all within your reach: stamping all of your writing with Google Authorship, producing a catchy series of videos, and putting together stunning displays that give your followers a visual sample of you and your business.

The Lowdown

- Like technology, social media will continue to evolve and change over time. Google+, Pinterest, and YouTube are up-and-comers, each with their own unique value for the business owner.
- Google+ is a tribute to the best of social media: You can use it to post comments, +1 others' posts that you like, share information, talk from your business profile to everyone in your circles (not just a select few as on Facebook) or to any other Google+ user (even if they aren't in your circles), and even blog—all without any advertising. It also provides search engine optimization benefits and lets you take ownership of all your writing with Google Authorship.
- Pinterest is a photo-sharing social media platform, currently dominated by women, that allows users to pin different photos from the web, creating a dashboard of virtual bulletin boards on topics such as cooking, home improvement, dining out, and traveling. If your demographic is women or you have a product or service that displays well visually, Pinterest is a good social media platform to consider.
- YouTube gives you an easy way to post and share videos to give your client a taste of the real, live you and the human side of your business, whether through product demonstrations, client testimonials, employee interviews, or another sort of presentation.

Social Media: ROI or ROLie?

When I hear people debate the ROI of social media? It makes me remember why so many businesses fail. Most businesses are not playing the marathon. They're playing the sprint. They're not worried about lifetime value and retention. They're worried about short-term goals.

—Gary Vaynerchuk

When it comes to social media and business, the question of investment dollars is a fundamental and serious one. If you invest your money in social media marketing, will you have enough of a return on investment (ROI) to spur you to continue investing, or is the promise of a return on your investment simply not true (ROLie)? If you spend a certain amount of time engaging on social media during the workday, will the benefits outweigh the opportunity costs, or do the efforts outweigh the benefits? These questions must be explored from not only a financial point of view but also a psychological view. That is because so much of the benefit of social media comes from the intangible social capital, relationship building, and influence that you can generate when social media is used effectively, in many of the ways already suggested in this book. On the flip side, the drawbacks relate to the dangers of pushing potential clients away when you use social media improperly, say, as a personal billboard or as business advertising space.

There are many issues to consider when making a choice to invest in social media, whether through paid-for initiatives or via those suggested in this book that involve more time than money. In addition, each platform is culturally different, so we can't expect to find one simple answer to this question of ROI. Instead of asking whether social media is worth it, I hope by the end of this chapter you will start to ask yourself instead, Which forms of social media are best for my business? In the pages that follow, I give you my best advice on the unique benefits of each social media platform, so you can ultimately decide for yourself where you want to invest time and money. Notice that I said *benefits* there, not *ROI*, because it is much easier to see what benefits can come out of social media for a business than it is to track a direct dollar amount that results from each action performed on social media.

That being said, remember that it has always been hard to assess which marketing efforts generate the most ROI and to determine which are truly the best for your business. Just think of traditional advertising and marketing methods, such as the roadside billboard, the television or radio ad, or consumer giveaways like pens and tote bags marked with a company's insignia. When a company engages in one or more of these traditional marketing methods, they often have no idea how much revenue is generated in return, except for those rare cases when a coupon code or call to action is involved or when a consumer is able to specify what moved him or her to contact the organization. Does this lack of direct trackback mean that the ad or giveaway wasn't effective? Hardly. Instead, it points to the fact that we can't always quantify exact ROI, that we may not be able to match a specific marketing activity up with new business generated, and that it is often the cumulative effect of all the marketing that we do that pushes a potential customer our way. It is the same with social media.

Put quite simply, ROI refers to the amount of money you get back from marketing dollars spent. So if you spend $500 to advertise your company in the newspaper and you win $1,000 worth of business from that ad, then your ROI is $500, or 100%. The bottom line is that it cost you $500 to make $1,000. Now consider social media and ROI. There are all sorts of problems in trying to calculate it, simply because it is nearly impossible to measure any sort of cause and effect. Note that I said *nearly impossible,* because if you are selling a product through a link on a social media platform, then you can track that person all the way through the transaction, making it entirely possible to detect cause and effect in that particular case. However, this process becomes far more difficult to track and trace if you are in a service industry. You can and should certainly ask how your clients found out about you and why they chose to do business with you, and perhaps that will give you some idea of how much social media has influenced your sales, but as Phil Graves points out in his book *Consumer.ology*, consumers rarely know why they do what they do.[1]

Herein lies much of the problem with trying to calculate a real ROI from social media: We can never be truly sure why a person has done what they do. Did someone do business with you because of what you posted on Facebook? Was a referral made because of the way you handled yourself on a particular LinkedIn group discussion? Did a new client pick up the phone to call you because of the blog entry you just posted on Google+? Was it some combination of these activities or something else entirely? Although we can calculate so much of what we do in business, to accurately measure business ROI in the realm of social media is nearly an impossible task because it may be a cumulative effect rather than a one-off incident, or a social media post may be the icing on the cake that helps push a new client to reach out to you.

The honest truth about ROI is this: No one, and I include myself in this group, can demonstrate exactly what it is that you specifically do on social media that will produce a single dollar for your business. In a statistical sense, it cannot be said, "If you do X, you will get Y." This is because no one is exactly sure what behaviors you must perform to produce a single client, buyer, or sale. That does not mean that there is no ROI; it simply means that it is harder to track.

So instead of making vague or specific claims on the ROI of social media for your business, I will simply discuss the benefits of using social media and let you assess its value for yourself.

ROI: Now You See It, Now You Don't

Although it's not always clear what the ROI on certain marketing activities is, this does not necessarily mean that those activities are not worth your time. I'm reminded of the value of reviews on Yelp, where some businesses are spending time to actively solicit positive reviews and to address any negative reviews that happen to show up. If I were to ask you, Mr. or Ms. Business Owner, "How much is a positive review worth in dollars on Yelp?" could you tell me exactly how much ROI you will receive from one positive review? Probably not; it's hard to detect. But wouldn't you say that a positive review on Yelp for your business has some value that translates into revenue? I am sure the answer would be "yes."

Now let's look at it the other way. Would you say a negative review concerning your business hurts your revenue? Sure you would. How many dollars did that negative review cost you? It's not possible to actually know, is it? So, if you don't know what the ROI of a positive or negative review is, then does that mean these reviews have no value to the bottom line of your business? I think we can all agree that a positive review is good for business, whereas a negative one is not.

The same questions may arise with ROI on social media. There is value to positive interactions, and the more you use social media properly, the more you may start to see and feel the benefits; in contrast, a poorly executed social media campaign can certainly push potential clients away. In sum, you may never know the exact financial return (or loss) on your time invested in social media, yet, if done effectively, you are likely to see a growing base of followers over time who will want to work with you and who will send referrals your way. Will this business success be wholly traceable to social media? Of course not. It will be based on your whole marketing outreach effort, of which social media is one effective part.

LinkedIn

In reviewing social media's benefits, let's start with LinkedIn. Every business owner needs to develop credibility and a sense of authority. When it comes to the social media platforms and what they can offer you, Mr. or Ms. Business Owner, that's where LinkedIn comes in. If there is one major benefit to LinkedIn, it is that it can give you credibility. Even for the person who is just starting out, LinkedIn is a resource that allows a person to be known for what he or she does and how well he or she does it. For example, you can demonstrate expertise on LinkedIn by

- showcasing your professional experiences in a well-written and complete profile, which can include descriptions of successful projects you've worked on
- exhibiting recommendations from others that demonstrate your knowledge
- having a high number of endorsements that specify the different types of knowledge that you have

- knowledgeably answering questions that get posted on your LinkedIn groups and sharing links to useful articles of potential interest to those in your LinkedIn groups

Some people have the advantage of demonstrating credibility simply because their profiles are filled with amazing professional experiences and expertise. However, even if you do not have a long and storied history of experience, you can be involved with different LinkedIn groups in which you can demonstrate your knowledge, giving you credibility in your business. Being a regular contributor of useful information to these groups can naturally help you demonstrate expert status.

There is no doubt that a person with authority has a greater ability to influence others than someone without such credentials does. In fact, recent neuroscience research has demonstrated that when someone encounters a product or service that is associated with an individual seen as having expert status, parts of the brain that are associated with memory and positive feelings become activated.[2] I found it interesting that this same study gave an example of how celebrity chef Jamie Oliver, when associated with a particular cookware company, was estimated to have added approximately $400 million dollars to the company's profits over a five-year period. I am not suggesting that you can expect this type of result, but what I can say is that the more you develop your expert status, the greater the opportunities you will have.

The biggest benefit of LinkedIn is the way that it can give you credibility as you develop yourself as an expert authority via weekly posts, contributions to group discussions, a compelling profile, and a portfolio of positive recommendations and work samples. To try to build a business without credibility is a long and arduous task. LinkedIn creates opportunities that you would never otherwise have—whether that be a chance to connect to people in positions of power that are otherwise unreachable or an easy way to showcase your work and recommendations. Then it's up to you to convert those opportunities into business.

Consider Using LinkedIn If...

- you are interested in a social media platform that delivers professional networking benefits without taking up a great amount of your time
- you are little known as an expert in your business and would like a free and easy means to develop your credibility and reputation
- you want to develop relationships with people whom you are very unlikely to connect to in your face-to-face life and whom can help you further your business and credibility

Facebook

Ah, the dilemma of Facebook. It is a true conundrum for many business owners: whether to spend time on a platform that seems faddish, super casual, and not particularly appropriate for the business realm. Vacation photos, posts about what you ate for breakfast, and rants about your latest pet peeve—do these really have a place in the realm of gaining new clients? It's an understandable question given the history of traditional marketing and business development. The lines between business and personal have often been clear and formal; Facebook entices us to consider blurring those lines quite a bit. Is this a problem? Not at all. If you are trying to determine whether to spend your time and resources on Facebook, consider its most important benefit: *the power to build and maintain personal relationships that can lead to business over time.* A secondary benefit of Facebook, although not as unique, is that you can also build and grow your business's brand via your Facebook business page. Let's focus first on the personal page, because that is where Facebook offers unique value.

In my interviews with dozens of small business owners, one thing that has become apparent has been how much more business originated from their Facebook personal page versus their Facebook business page. In nearly every interview, people reported that as a result of their interest in others and posts about what was happening in their personal lives, some person walked into their shop, called them on the phone, or wrote them to do business with them.

So a major benefit of Facebook is the way it allows you to make personal connections with people who may eventually turn into clients. You may be thinking, "Well, I only have a finite number of friends—then what?" Know that although it is true that we start making Facebook friends with people we already know, for most users, the list grows to include people we either did not know well or did not know at all that have become our friends through Facebook.

As we continue to use the platform, it is amazing how quickly our list of friends can grow. You meet someone at a dinner or party and decide you want to become Facebook friends. You are having a conversation with someone on Facebook and one of their friends who is not a friend of yours also comments; as a result of the conversation, you become Facebook friends. Let me say that this is extremely common and that I personally have made some amazing contacts as a result of what seemed to be ordinary, innocent conversations. Next thing you know, your Facebook friend list is growing and you have the potential for more of these folks to come to you for business in the future.

This list of Facebook friends represents people who you influence and who influence you. Why is this personal influence so important? Consider this: Nielson conducted a study of more than 28,000 Internet users from more than fifty-six countries. In this study, 92% of those people said that they trust recommendations from their friends and family.[3] The collective of friends and family was by far the number one trusted source of information, as compared with about one third for social-media-sponsored advertising. This is critical to understanding the power and benefits of your personal Facebook page. It is the power of friends—even your social friends—and word of mouth that will help to promote your business.

We are all aware of the power of word of mouth; it is just that we have a tendency to ignore it. Perhaps this is because it is a time-consuming process or because we have the illusion that we don't have a lot of control over it. (The fact is, we have plenty of control over it because as we communicate with and serve people in the right or the wrong way, we will positively or negatively affect how word of mouth will be generated.)

No matter the reason, we must not ignore it, as evidenced by researchers like Trusov and his colleagues, who demonstrated in an elegant social media study that when it comes to new customer acquisition, word of mouth in social media lasts twenty times longer than traditional marketing methods in terms of referrals.[4] They further suggested that for the small business, it could be even higher. This is because small businesses do not have big marketing budgets and so they do more grassroots campaigns such as social media to enhance their business. This is very important, Ms. and Mr. Business Owner: Your personal network of friends is your best source of making your business grow and of having financial success, and Facebook is a great place to grow that network.

This leads me to the second benefit of Facebook. In addition to helping you build personal relationships with individuals, Facebook also helps you maintain them. You may not see this as a benefit; however, in my experience, one of the most neglected and weakest areas of most small businesses is personal follow-up. Facebook is quite good at helping you to follow up on a personal level with your customers and clients.

For example, Facebook allows you to create friend lists in which you can put different people into different categories (Potential Clients, Existing Clients, Industry X, Industry Y, etc.) so that you can organize people into groups through which you can see what they are doing and remain in more constant contact with those friends that have special influence. At the start of every day, you can quickly review the feed of just those on a given friend list and briefly reply to comments where it seems appropriate—congratulating someone who has just bought a new home, sending well wishes to someone who has shared that a family member is sick, or simply letting someone know that their post was funny or interesting. It is here that we can keep up with our clients and friends, letting them know we are thinking of them and staying at the top of their minds should they need our services or encounter someone that could be referred to us.

Last, as mentioned earlier, Facebook can also be valuable in that it gives you a place to expand your brand through a business page. Just as you should hang up a shingle on the web (in the form of your website) to establish your presence, show that you are a professional entity, and become searchable, you can also hang up a shingle on Facebook. Facebook business pages are searchable within the search engines as well as within the Facebook search feature itself, which means that if someone hears of your business and decides to try to locate it, they can do so from Google or the Facebook search bar. As a result, creating a Facebook business page is another way for your business to be found online.

In addition, if you have the right product or service for which you can offer discounts or coupons, these can be an effective way to get people to come to your Facebook business page as a threshold to your business. I say *the right product or service* because for many industries, it is not possible to offer discounts or coupons for a variety of reasons. Yet, just having a business page presence can help for branding purposes alone. Also, the business page gives you another link to your website, which has benefits from a user standpoint and some positive search engine optimization.

In sum, an interpersonal aspect to business that many of us do not consider very frequently is social interaction, which is extremely important to our marketing and professional business.[5] These personal social relationships open communication and build trust. Facebook's greatest benefit is the opportunity to develop these relationships, socially opening up lines of communication. When used correctly and within the unwritten rules and expectations of the culture, Facebook has, potentially, the greatest benefits to date of all of the social media platforms. If you are not using it, you may be missing some great opportunities. If you have stopped using it, start again but use it differently and begin to work your way toward the referral business. If you are using it only from a business page standpoint, consider changing your strategy to include the personal page and open yourself to the possibility of referrals.

Consider Using Facebook If...

- you value the power of personal relationships and word-of-mouth referrals to generate business
- you'd like to have an easy tool to follow up with potential clients and to stay in touch with existing and former clients
- you'd like to have an additional means of disseminating your brand beyond your web page and you'd like to increase your ability to be found online

Twitter

As with Facebook, many businesspeople are asking the question of whether Twitter is worth the time and effort. Can you really grow your business one tweet at a time, in 140 or fewer characters? I was pretty hard on Twitter earlier in the book, with good justification. However, as I stated before and I will state again, I like it. At the same time, I do not believe it is right for every business simply because of the time and effort required to establish yourself and keep yourself going, unless you already have notoriety, celebrity status, or fame. That said, if you are interested in being on Twitter, there are some benefits to using it.

Like all of the social media platforms, Twitter gives you another avenue by which to brand your business. If no one or very few people are following you, it may be less of a benefit, but, as with all the platforms, your profile is indexed by the search engines so, at the very least, you have created another place where people can get to your website.

Twitter also has the benefit of being easily searchable. You can search for people who may be looking for a product or service that you offer, immediately get back in touch with them, and create a dialogue. This, I think, is one of the most valuable benefits of Twitter, because people are constantly looking for recommendations of businesses and people to help them solve their problem or lead them in the right direction. You can be their superhero, no cape required.

Tweets are also indexed by the search engines. This means that when you put out information on Twitter, the things you say find their way to the search engines. This means that you do want to be intentional about what you say and how often you say it. There is no doubt that with Twitter, when people search and see a consistent message that comes from you, it does add to your credibility.

Speaking of credibility, the information that you tweet also adds to your credibility. If you are putting out good and useful information on Twitter, people will respond to it. Perhaps it will be retweeted by someone (i.e., shared with others) or made a favorite—either way, these two ways of interacting are beneficial for you because others can and generally do see how others are responding to what you are saying, and that may add to your social influence. Certainly it can be said and it has been demonstrated that Twitter can help develop your credibility and position you (and/or your company) as a thought leader.

Again, I do believe that Twitter can have some benefits for the right type of business. However, unlike LinkedIn or Facebook, this platform is much more difficult to leverage for a small business, and the returns for some industries will not be robust.

Consider Using Twitter If...

- you are looking for an additional means of building your brand and generating clients for your business
- you want to be able to identify people looking for your product or services right now (through Twitter search)
- you want to further establish your credibility by demonstrating your knowledge through the sharing of interesting information

Pinterest

What about this newer platform called Pinterest that has a predominantly female usership? If you have something business related to visually show and it fits within the current Pinterest demographic of women, this particular platform can have positive benefits. First, it has the potential to be the most direct way of showing your wares by giving you an opportunity to share a visual portfolio or collection of photos of what you have to offer. Those in the retail, fashion, food, and do-it-yourself industries will have a distinct advantage here over other kinds of companies. When you have something to show that the demographic is likely to tune into, Pinterest can enable branding and awareness in a way unlike any of the other social media platforms.

That being said, if you are from other industries and you are a bit creative, you can also use Pinterest to bring some eyes to your business and brand. For example, I have seen some success in this regard in the real estate industry, where real estate professionals are taking pictures of unique and interesting interiors, decorating ideas, patios, pools, and so on that give people ideas of what they may like to do in their own homes or perhaps to put on their board for future reference. How is this a benefit? Because rather than just selling a house, the real-estate business owner is giving her knowledge and expertise in a fun and interesting way that creates a positive association with her name and brand.

Finally, like the other social media platforms that have been mentioned to this point, there is also some search engine value for your website when you are present on Pinterest. You lose nothing by just having your name, your business, and a link to your website out there on Pinterest so that people have another way of finding your website and contacting you.

Consider Using Pinterest If...

- you have a product or service that lends itself to a presentation that can easily be shared through pictures
- you have a significant number of women in your target market, a demographic that currently dominates Pinterest
- you specialize in products or you conduct business in the do-it-yourself or fashion industry

YouTube

YouTube is the most unique of the social media platforms. It is not traditional in the sense that it lacks the element of social interaction found on the other platforms, yet it is important given that video is one of the most shared entities on the web today. In fact, it is the sharing that makes YouTube social.

As for its value, video offers tremendous benefit in getting your message out in a visual way. It provides people with an opportunity to get a "live" look into your business—your company's attitude, values, sophistication, or sense of humor. If you are creative, you may even be fortunate enough to have your video go viral so that thousands or millions of people will click to watch it. I am not even sure how to estimate the value of a viral video, but certainly it has taken people and companies from obscurity to fame. One company in particular that stands out is called Dollar Shave Club (http://www.dollarshaveclub.com). Their hilarious video of supplying razors for one dollar helped launch the company, and over ten million views later, they are now a serious player in the razor blade industry.

In addition to giving you a way to showcase your business in three dimensions, YouTube can also be a gateway to your web presence in that it allows you to put links to your website in the description of the video as well as to add clickable links on the video itself. As a result, during the video or after, a person can click on the link and be directed to a place on your website or perhaps a social media page.

Another large benefit from YouTube, perhaps the greatest benefit, is how YouTube ranks on the search engines. Recently, *Forbes* magazine synthesized a report from Forrester Research that indicated that a YouTube video has fifty times the chance of written content of landing on the front page of Google search results.[6] We all know the value of the first page of Google! If you are not using video, perhaps these statistics will motivate you to start.

Consider Using YouTube If...

- you do not like to write blog posts but you are comfortable with talking
- you want to get noticed more on search engines
- you would like to build trust by allowing others to see your verbal and nonverbal behavior as it relates to you and your business

Google+

Although this is the newest platform on the block, Google+ may actually be the most powerful platform out there when it comes to search engine optimization for your business. We all know that Google is the most powerful search engine in the world, and it probably also goes without saying that Google's search is still the number one way for businesses to be found. Now, when you post on Google+, your posts will also be available on Google search results, and that is a tremendous benefit. I have tested this over and over again: If you are a Google+ user and you have your search opened up (which it appears is typical of most users), it is often the case that your posts show up on the first page of Google's search for specific keywords and hashtags within your post. It is plainly evident that Google gives priority to its social media platform, treating those that post there as having authority. It should not be ignored.

Another benefit of being on Google+ is that it allows you to claim authorship of anything that you write online. If you have a blog or you write something else online, you can set Google Authorship for yourself and your business. As a result, your picture or the picture of your company will then show up right next to anything that you have claimed authorship for (assuming a user's settings don't block this option). This is powerful, as now Google+ members have a distinct marketing advantage within Google's search platform: Google Authorship essentially helps these members brand themselves and build credibility at the same time.

Google+ also allows you to create special interest or professional groups, called *communities*. Like LinkedIn groups, these communities allow you to demonstrate your knowledge and expertise by interacting with others in that community. It is a great way to develop additional credibility, and some businesses may even find Google+ communities to be better than LinkedIn groups because Google+ allows more flexible options in terms of posting, such as video and photos. Also, the Google+ mobile application allows quicker and easier access to group discussions.

David Williams, a professional photographer and cinematographer (https://plus.google.com/+Dwppc) in Wake Forest, North Carolina, started to experiment in 2013 with how much interaction his photos would receive on the different platforms. Following a photo shoot, David would post what he thought was the best photo to his Facebook personal account, business account, and Google+ Photography community. Over the course of approximately six months, his Google+ community had more interactions, at a rate of fifteen to one, than any of his Facebook profiles. Depending on the photo, the rate would sometimes be thirty to one more interactions.

Although Facebook was limiting the number of folks who could see David's Facebook business posts of these photos, Google+ was allowing his circles free access. Certainly, the advantage of the additional interactions is clear. As people interact with his photography, this generates conversations that lead to referrals from others, but this also generates public questions to him from other professional photographers about what equipment he used and how he created the shot, putting him in a very high position of expertise among peers and readers.

Google+ offers the option of a business page. Although it has a feel similar to that of the Facebook business page, it has a distinct advantage over Facebook business pages. Google+ allows you to intentionally interact with individuals from your business page by including them in a post, by putting either the + or the @ symbol in front of the person's name, which will notify the person of their mention in the post. Facebook does not allow this same type of interaction. That is, even though your business page may be liked by an individual, Facebook does not allow you to call out that individual from your business page; you can only call out another business page from your business page.

On Google+, you can do either or both. Why is this such an advantage? One of the keys to success on any social platform is interaction. It is especially important if that interaction is commentary, as this creates discussion that leads to knowing, which leads to liking, which ultimately leads to trust, which translates into a greater probability of direct business and referrals. As an up-and-comer on the social media stage, Google+

should get your attention, whether because of its ease of generating interaction, ability to name-stamp your text, or generate the much sought after search engine optimization benefits.

Consider Using Google+ If...

- you are looking for a platform that is more interactive than LinkedIn and yet less personally interactive than Facebook
- you want the ability to initiate conversations and create discussions, either from your personal page or business page, with individual people
- you seek the additional web exposure you will get when Google displays your timeline posts in the search results, for both your personal page and your business page

A Well-Rounded Approach

When trying to assess which social media platforms are right for you and your business, it may help to think of each platform as representing a different part of you, the whole business owner. As people, we are multidimensional. Each platform allows us to express a certain part of us that people can come to know, like, and trust. This is why each platform has its own unique value to business.

- *LinkedIn* represents our professional side. It allows people to see what it is we do, how knowledgeable we are, and how our history of professional work has brought us to a place where we are able to demonstrate in a professional manner why we are experts in our field.
- *Facebook* represents our personal side. It allows us to talk about what we are feeling, thinking, or paying attention to in our per-

sonal lives on moment-by-moment and day-to-day bases and, in the process, make emotional connections with those who friend us.

- *Twitter* is about the information we believe is important. We share things that we believe will interest others to promote goodwill, build credibility, and show expertise. Although it is not as interactive as Facebook or LinkedIn, Twitter certainly demonstrates to others what interests us and what we believe interests the Twitter searcher.
- *Pinterest* allows us to share our passions, hobbies, and things we like in pictures. It creates a pictorial painting, if you will, and a showcase for all things visually related to our business.
- *YouTube* is a view into what we enjoy watching. It allows others to see what we find entertaining and perhaps even absorbing. YouTube can also provide you with a unique opportunity to introduce others to you and your business on a visual level and to provide them with information that does not have to be read.
- Last, *Google+* gives us a searchable identity. It incorporates the facets of Google search and Google Authorship, from both a personal and a professional side. Because it is powered by the most powerful search engine in the world, it allows people to discover what we are truly known for—our expertise.

Some of these social media platforms overlap to a degree. Some allow for a more professional flavor, whereas others allow for a more personal touch. In my view, it takes all of these social media platforms to reveal the multidimensional nature of you, the business owner. This is the beauty of social media. As we follow, friend, and connect with others on these platforms, we offer glimpses into not just the person behind what we do but who we really are as people. It is that authenticity, that piece of vulnerability, and that genuine part of ourselves that others will want to connect with, friend, and follow. It can create a sense of trust that helps others not only to develop a relationship with us personally but also to support us in business and make referrals.

The Invisible Impact of Social Media

Throughout this book, I argue for the value of generating interaction and conversations on social media (e.g., comments and replies to your posts). And although this is certainly a useful way to measure the impact we are having via social media, it must be said too that there is an invisible impact of social media that we may not often hear about. Here's a personal example.

I was working out at the fitness club when one of my friends who has been a friend on and off of Facebook came up to me and said, "I just want to let you know, I love your Izsoisms. I read them all the time, and they really make me think and they get me motivated." (*Izsoisms* are statements and questions—sometimes funny and sometimes serious—that I think of and share that are philosophical or psychological in nature.) I replied, "Well, thank you for saying that. It really means a great deal to me to know that I am making a positive impact." She said, "Oh, you do! I love reading them. I have even saved them, but I do not reply to them." I stopped, my mouth fell open, I looked at her wide-eyed, and I asked, "Whoa, why do you not reply"?

"Because I do not necessarily like to reply. I like staying in touch, and I like reading, but I really do not feel like getting involved with conversations," she replied. "Wow!" I exclaimed, "That is huge. It never dawned on me that if I were to say something that had an impact that someone would not respond." She continued, "Oh, they do, I love what you have to say and post. I look forward to it." I said, "thank you" and she went to yoga and I went on to lifting.

During the remainder of my time in the gym, I found myself pondering this conversation. The more I thought about it, the more I realized that the impact with our words within these social media places goes far beyond what we can measure. The fact is that even measures of influence such as Klout and Kred (social media influence measurement tools) cannot possibly measure your true impact on others. We are only able to measure a very small percentage of people who actually do respond; what about those you are reaching who don't respond? In reality, you are being read on social media and are influencing more people than you know.

Bear in mind that there is a large segment of social media users that I call *social media introverts,* those who are present on social media but who do not interact. Some marketers and other social media people refer to these people as *lurkers.* However, like introverts in the general population, there are people who want to keep up with their friends or colleagues but who do not want to say anything. They feel they are a part of the conversation just by reading and watching it. They do not have nefarious intent, nor are they creepy. They just do not want to participate.

Does this mean that they are not engaged by social media or not impacted by it? Not at all. But they don't interact on social media, so you may not hear about them. The one thing that is evident from my conversations with social media introverts is that we are developing and impacting relationships and creating a referral network often unbeknownst to us, which can ultimately benefit us both personally and professionally.

In Sum: The Choice Is up to You

It is easy for me, as a frequent user and lover of social media, to talk about the benefits of social media. I find the cumulative effect generated by the emotional, psychological, credibility, influence, and branding benefits of social media to be sufficient to justify its use and so am less hung up on attributing specific revenue output to my exact actions and behaviors on social media. At minimum, I know I can always count on the search engine optimization and branding benefits of being on these platforms.

Of course, you have to be the one to ultimately judge which benefits are right for your business. In my view, it is not important that you be on every platform, but it is important that you are going to be on the platforms that make the most sense for your business and, more important, that you will be committed enough to consistently use them. There is no benefit to any of the platforms if you are not going to use them. The truth is, no one, not even I, can motivate you to use these platforms. It should be motivation enough to get on social media because you can brand yourself there without having to spend a dollar. However, this benefit may not be sufficient for some.

Some of you will say that you do not have time for social media; I would argue that you just refuse to take the time because you do not want to do it. I have always found it interesting that certain top-producing individuals who work on and grow their business will come back from a conference and add something that they learned to their new way of doing things and will not think twice about implementing it into their day. However, when it comes to social media, some of these individuals simply do not have time for it.

If you are convinced you do not have time, that is your choice. I can only tell you that if you consider social media to be important, you will find a way to put it into your day. Remember, you do not need to be on all of the platforms. I would rather see you be on one or two of these platforms, be committed to them, use them regularly, and get proficient with them than struggle to be on all of the platforms just so you can check off all of the social media boxes. Even if you ignore the rest, regularly using one of the platforms can help to increase your connections, multiply your interactions with them, and provide the different benefits of that particular platform.

Admittedly, some people do not use social media simply because they are not sure of where to start and it seems too overwhelming to them. I completely understand those feelings. Even though I live, study, and research these unique cultures, I too get overwhelmed at times when trying to stay on top of them. Honestly, I do not use all of them equally. I have had to make decisions about where to put my time and energy, and you need to do the same. Select a couple, and then, over time, add another if you can. If you do not like how things are working out, perhaps stop one and move to another.

My hope for you and your business is that you do not allow your emotions to keep you from reaping the tremendous benefits of a social media program customized for you. Think LinkedIn for building and maintaining credibility, Facebook for follow-up, Google+ for search engine optimization, YouTube for offering a live sample of you and your business, and so on. Each social media platform has its own gift to give.

The Lowdown

- It's next to impossible to show a direct ROI from social media in which a specific social media task converts a specific new client (but, then again, the same is true for most billboard and television ads). Instead, focus on which social media platforms offer the right benefits for your business and think of social media in terms of its cumulative effects to generate business over time.

- LinkedIn gives you a free and easy way to develop a sense of authority and to demonstrate your expertise online.
- Facebook can help you build and maintain personal relationships that can lead to business over time. It makes follow-up with existing and potential clients easy—with birthday reminders, specialized lists of clients, and opportunities to like and share with the click of a button.
- Twitter can be a time sink, but think of it as an option if you'd like an additional way to demonstrate your thought leadership, brand your company, and find new clients.
- Pinterest gives you a great way to connect with female buyers as well as to feature your business in a visual way. It works particularly well for those who offer products or who have services related to home improvement, fashion, cooking, or travel.
- YouTube offers an easy way to post and share videos for your potential clientele, providing a more human view of your business before people buy.
- Google+ gives you the chance to initiate conversations with potential clients directly from your business page (unlike Facebook), to blog with ease, and to get your name and photo associated with everything you write on the web.

Managing Social Media: From Chaos to Control

Lack of direction, not lack of time, is the problem. We all have twenty-four hour days.

– Zig Ziglar

Perhaps at this point, you are saying, "Okay, I see the benefits, and I even acknowledge that social media has value in terms of sending more traffic to my website, but, quite honestly, I do not have the time to use it." Others may be adding, "Even if I had the time, I wouldn't know where to begin. There are so many platforms to manage, each with its own set of tools and options." Whether you're hesitant to jump into social media because you find it a little bit overwhelming or you just feel short on time, I am going to give you some clear guidance in this chapter to bring social media within your reach.

Social media is not and should not be a time sink. But it will take some time—time that is worth the effort. Think of it as part of your marketing and follow-up strategy. I ask you this: Is there any value in having a human conversation with people in a face-to-face situation? Is there any value in getting your brand seen by thousands or perhaps millions of people? Is there any value in being able to personally follow up with your past, current, or potential clients? No one in their right business mind would deny the power and value of these behaviors. Social media provides you with an opportunity to do all of these things in an efficient, virtual setting...for free!

It's not a matter of whether you want to use social media, or even if you enjoy using it; the fact is that your business can and will benefit from your using it. It does not matter if you think social media is stupid, insane, ridiculous, childish, or nonsense or if it gives you an emotional rash; there are things in business we do not like to do yet need to be done, and social media has the potential of huge payoffs for your business. Turning away from free marketing, networking, and word of mouth is certainly not logical. If your business is going to succeed, doesn't it make sense to take advantage of as much free or low-cost marketing as possible?

The good news is that most of you can monitor and update your social media in under an hour per day. The allotted time doesn't even have to be in an unbroken chunk; it only needs to be a handful of minutes here and there, and much of it can be done while you are doing something else. At the end of this chapter, I provide a checklist for keeping your social media efforts to forty-five minutes a day (or as little as fifteen minutes if you would like to start by dipping your toe in the water). Before we review that handy checklist, however, let's start with an overall prescription for taking control of your social media efforts—something that I call SPICEY—so you can get the most out of social media for your business without being overwhelmed in the process.

Make Your Social Media SPICEY!

Can you imagine food without the right spices? I don't know about you, but as a foodie, I am definitely of the belief that cuisine is much better if it is seasoned correctly with the right herbs and spices. Just as putting the right spices together can bring out the best flavor in your food, so can adding the right ingredients to your social media mix make your efforts work better for you and your business. I like to call it SPICEY:

- **S**trategize
- **P**lan
- **I**nteract
- **C**ommit
- **E**xperiment
- Be **Y**OU

If you focus on being SPICEY instead of being bland, your social media will be tremendously effective. Like really tasty, exciting food that requires the right combination of spices and flavors, so too must you have the right combination of ingredients to give your social media the flavor that not only will people want to sample but will entice them to come back for more!

Strategize

The first step of managing your social media efforts should be to *strategize*. This is where you must clearly decide which social media platforms are right for you and your business. LinkedIn, Facebook, and Pinterest? LinkedIn and Google+? Twitter and YouTube? To strategize, mentally go through the different platforms, check the demographics (see the earlier chapters), and compare them with your target market. Determine up front which social media platforms have the most potential benefit given your goals for your organization. This doesn't mean that you might not add others later, after you have a greater comfort level, but I would like for you to begin by picking two that you feel are the best fit, bearing in mind that I strongly recommend that LinkedIn be one of them.

A huge consideration when developing your social media strategy is how much you would like to grow your business. Are you content with your current customer base or are you looking to expand? How you answer that question will change the way you use social media, leading to a more aggressive versus passive approach.

Strategies to grow your business. If you are trying to grow your business by bringing in new clients, then your strategy will likely take on a twofold approach. First, and perhaps easiest, is using social media to stay in contact with your current and past clients so that they are subtly reminded to refer their friends to you for business. Second, start adding new contacts to your social media following. For those of you who have been using social media for a longer period of time, you are more than likely already receiving several connection requests each week, so take a look at these closely. If you do not know the individuals, check out their profiles and determine whether they would be a good fit for your social media community. If so, make that connection.

If you are relatively new to social media (or even if you are not), go out and look for people that you may already know who can be added to your social media community. When you go to casual parties, especially around the holidays, you know a card or two gets passed on; keep them, and if you can envision any of these individuals as a potential client for your business, request to connect with them on LinkedIn and friend them on Facebook if they have an account. Many times I have done this right from my phone during the party, and the people were so impressed with how quickly, efficiently, and proactively I added them that I wound up with a consultation later.

My point here is that as much as you may say, "I have enough friends," when it comes to growing your business, you want more clients, which ultimately means more relationships. Whether you are just starting your business and care about getting people to come through your doors for the first time or you have a more mature business and are interested in growing your existing clientele, the previous techniques will help you grow your business via social media.

Just as important as making connections is determining which social media platforms are right for your business. You can make this assessment by reviewing the demographic profiles and benefits of each and matching these up with your target market and business goals. For example, you may find that engaging friends on Facebook who already support you and talk about you and your business may be a great way for you to get more referrals. Or you may be an aspiring author or speaker who needs to develop additional credibility, such that LinkedIn would be a great place for you to start interacting within group settings. You might also consider using Google+ and Twitter to establish yourself as a thought leader and to generate further credibility by showing people what you know and how your knowledge can help them. Each social media platform has its own set of unique benefits; take some time to get familiar with these (see Ch. 8), and you will begin to see which platforms are right for you.

Strategies to maintain your business. Although many of us are trying to grow our businesses, the truth is that some of us are actually quite happy with our current level of incoming business. If you are in this group, you feel that you have the right amount of clients and you are not really interested in further growth. Ring true? If so, you may not choose to get involved with many of the social media platforms to any depth or degree.

Remember that LinkedIn is still important, however, because it gives you a social media presence that you can easily ramp up when and if you become ready to be more active. It also, at the very least, has some search engine optimization value that keeps your name out there as a player in your specific industry. As a result, you should plan to periodically update your LinkedIn profile to reflect your current work experience, get connected with new individuals on occasion, and possibly even contribute to some group discussions. Try not to let the sound of these activities overwhelm you, as you can probably do all of this in about half hour to an hour a week.

If you are not trying to grow your business, you are likely to spend less time on the other social media platforms (as mentioned), but I do, however, encourage you to at least know how these platforms work in terms of posting and interacting, even if it is on an extremely casual basis, and possibly even set up your profiles. I suggest that you watch how others are using them, go to an introductory class (many free ones are available), experiment on your own, get a basic social media book, and incorporate the suggestions from my book. Find people that you know are using the different platforms successfully and do not be afraid to ask questions. You would be surprised how people like to be an authority on a subject (plus, giving people a position of authority means that you have increased the likelihood they will positively reciprocate for you in the future).

In this way, if you should decide that you want to grow your business in the future, you have the necessary foundation for getting your social media off to a good start. In addition, you will know what is happening in the world around you. At the very least, you should see what your competition is doing and start to develop a plan of what you might use in the future. My point here is, regardless of what position you are in, at least start organizing which platforms you would consider using. Make sure your platforms are ready for use, so if you should choose to grow your business in the future, you can jump right into creating your daily plan.

Try This!

Complete the following questions to help you strategize about what kind of social media marketing approach will work best for you and your business. (For a review of the demographics of a given platform, see that particular social media chapter.)

	Strongly disagree	Somewhat disagree	Neither agree nor disagree	Somewhat agree	Strongly agree
1. I am motivated to use social media.	1	2	3	4	5
2. I am motivated to use Face-book.	1	2	3	4	5

	Strongly disagree	Somewhat disagree	Neither agree nor disagree	Somewhat agree	Strongly agree
3. I am motivated to use Google+.	1	2	3	4	5
4. I am motivated to use LinkedIn.	1	2	3	4	5
5. I am motivated to use Pinterest.	1	2	3	4	5
6. I am motivated to use Twitter.	1	2	3	4	5
7. I am motivated to use YouTube.	1	2	3	4	5
8. My target market aligns with Facebook.	1	2	3	4	5
9. My target market aligns with Google+.	1	2	3	4	5
10. My target market aligns with LinkedIn.	1	2	3	4	5
11. My target market aligns with Pinterest.	1	2	3	4	5
12. My target market aligns with Twitter.	1	2	3	4	5
13. My target market aligns with YouTube.	1	2	3	4	5

After answering these questions, compare and contrast your motivations to use specific platforms (Questions 1–7) with where members of your target market tend to spend their time (Questions 8–13). The platforms to which you have given the highest numeric ratings indicate where you should spend your time on social media. Start with the platform that you've given the highest rating and expand from there.

Plan

After you have strategized about which social media platform or platforms are right for your business, it's time to formulate a *plan* for how you are going to use these platforms. Because LinkedIn is your anchor, I will use that as an example for how you might plan your time on social media. I highly suggest that you spend thirty days (after you have created and completed your profile and joined your groups) using LinkedIn as part of your plan. In those thirty days, I want you to spend a total of fourteen minutes a day working with LinkedIn: seven minutes in the morning and seven minutes in the evening.

The plan is to have your morning cup of coffee, tea, or other beverage and simply check to see if you have any notifications and any interesting discussions in your groups. Comment if you find it necessary, endorse someone, and/or make a connection with someone. However, stop when your seven minutes are up. That is about the time it takes to drink your beverage. If you find it helpful in staying on task (or at least on time), you can set a timer that goes off after seven minutes. Initially, even if you are tempted to spend more time, do not do it. Stay in control of your social media so that your social media does not take up all of your time and get out of control.

As you get more and more comfortable with LinkedIn (or any other social media platform), you will find that you know exactly where to look to discover the information you are looking for. By Day 30, you will more than likely be able to use that platform in less than seven minutes, because you will come to understand that you only need to do specific things. You do not need to see or use everything, only those things that are necessary. I find that when people work a social media platform on a daily basis, it no longer overwhelms them. However, they do have to spend a little time each day to get used to the platform.

When you start adding other social media platforms to your outreach efforts, you need, as with LinkedIn, to have a plan. Designate a specific amount of time you will be on the platform, with goals for what you will accomplish in that time, for example, stay on top of notifications, accept connections with others, share a bit of something interesting with your followers, and comment on other people's posts.

As part of your plan, you should also consider what your approach will be to measuring how effective you are within each platform. That is, are you going to measure likes, comments, shares, all of them, or just some of them? Are you going to give them equal weight, or are you going to consider a like, for instance, worth less than a comment or equal to it? The point is that you should have a plan of measurement to see how effective your efforts are on each platform.

If you control your social media with a daily plan, you will find that you will be able to stay in touch with more people in social media in less time than you can with either phone calls or e-mails, and you will have a greater sense of accomplishment because of it.

How Often Should I Be Using Social Media?

As you lay out your social media plan, ask yourself whether you are comfortable with using social media a few minutes at a time multiple times throughout the day, or would you prefer a little longer period of time twice a day? I know some of you are hoping for a once-a-day plan. However, visiting only once a day is going to have limited effectiveness. This is because if you only post once a day, the chances of your post being seen are going to be slim.

First, people in your social media community may not check their social media accounts until later in the day, at which point your post will have moved so far down on their feed that they may never even see it (kind of like showing up on the third page of Google search results). Second, even if the people in your community happen to be on the given platform around the time that you post, if they have a large base of friends, followers, or connections, your post may get lost among all of the other posts being made at that time. Third, Facebook now gives preference to those individuals who post and interact more often, putting their posts higher on people's feeds. Bottom line: The more often you post, the greater the chances that at least one of your posts will get seen that day.

There is another reason that it is important to be on social media more than one time a day: Social media is not only about posting, it is about interaction. If you just post and walk away for the day, you will not be able to respond to any comments, likes, or shares that you get in a timely manner, and you will be missing the whole point of social media. These are bidirectional platforms that require interaction for effectiveness.

If all you are attempting to do is post and run, you are trying to leverage this medium in a one-way direction and it simply will not work. It is just as important to respond to comments and replies that people make to your social media postings as it is to post your own. In this way, you can validate others for what they say and further build the connection and trust between you, which may lead to business over time.

The reality is this: Once-a-day posting is not a reliable or complete plan for effective social media; if you want to be successful there, you need to be present on it a minimum of twice a day. Yes, a once-a-day intentional contact with clients through commenting on their posts will certainly have a positive effect, but it is not a complete approach to using social media and it won't be able to give you its fullest effect.

However, don't let the need to be on social media two to

three times a day overwhelm you. By organizing yourself a bit better within the platforms to make sure that people are in the appropriate lists, you can easily and quickly scan where and to whom you want to post. And don't forget, the more comfortable you get with social media, the faster you will be able to use it and move on to other tasks.

Interact

Now that you've got a strategy and a plan, it's time to *interact,* Step 3 of getting SPICEY.

As a quick review, interactions come in three forms:

- interacting with the things others write, post, or tweet
- others interacting with the things you have written, posted, or tweeted
- you and others actively interacting at the same time in the form of social conversation within the platform

To be successful on social media, you absolutely need to interact—to be active in a way that connects you with other people. I am talking about dialogue, real communication between you and others.

The first important piece of interaction is the *what* part of the equation and has to do with the content of the things that are posted, whether they be links to interesting articles, questions (or answers) to stir thinking, or tidbits of industry-related advice. Posts can also involve wishing people a happy birthday, sharing someone else's tweet with one's followers, or +1ing a Google+ post. Yes, I do think likes, favorites, and +1s have value; however, remember that for people to truly learn about you, what you are about, and who you are, you need to go beyond these, because dialogue is what creates the relationship. In the case of a like, favorite, or +1, there is no dialogue and there is little to no relationship being created. The true value of social media is the interactive conversation, so keep that in mind.

Now that we've talked about what interaction consists of, let's talk about the *how* of interaction. This relates to things like the words you use to share information, the length of your post, and anything else that contributes to the tone and experience you create. When you interact on social media, the goal is to be out there doing so in a way that informs, attracts, and influences. Are your posts memorable? Humorous? Inspiring? Or do they fall flat, confuse people, or seem overly promotional? You can start to see how important it is to pay attention to not only what you are posting but how you are posting as well. Said in a humorous or clever way, a post might build your community's interest in reading and sharing your future posts. Said in the wrong way, a post can make you seem socially awkward, self-absorbed, mean spirited, or intrusive.

Also, when you interact on social media, you need to respect the culture of the platform. Although posting what you ate for dinner last night can work great on Facebook because it makes you seem human, on LinkedIn, it would seem out of place and unprofessional. On LinkedIn, Twitter, or Google+, if you post some interesting business-related links, it may be acceptable and provide value to your readers, whereas on Facebook it is likely to be seen as an irritant because the culture of Facebook is far more personal than professional.

Another way of saying this is that there is a place on social media for both professional interaction and personal interaction—it's just a matter of where. For example, LinkedIn is a great place for you to show your professional expertise by contributing thoughts to a group discussion or by posting a useful update on changes in your industry. Facebook is the right spot to show your personal side by posting a vacation photo or a favorite quote. The important thing to keep in mind is the psychology and culture of each platform—with their own unique language, unwritten rules, norms, and expectations—and then the general motivation for why people are using each platform. Suffice it to say that to really get SPICEY, you need to interact in ways that attract and influence your clients through professional and personal interaction that is customized for each platform. Social media's power multiplies exponentially when you use it to connect with others on multiple levels.

Choose Your Social Media Manager: You or Someone Else?

There is a great question that is frequently asked of me: "How do you feel about letting someone else manage or handle my social media?" Let me answer that with a question to you: "How do you feel about someone speaking for you to another person face-to-face?" Your answer probably would be, "I guess it would depend on the person." Exactly. I do believe it is best if you can do your own social media, especially when it comes to demonstrating your knowledge on LinkedIn discussions and personal interaction on Facebook. However, there may be places where others can help you with your social media, but again, there is an issue of the right, qualified person to do it. You do not want just anyone to represent you or your company. Here are my guidelines, in brief.

First, if you simply cannot do social media yourself, then it needs to be done by someone whom you completely trust with your business. If you cannot trust this person with your business, then he or she should not be considered. Second, it should be a person that you would trust to speak for you in person. If you would not allow this person to represent you with a current or future client, then he or she should not be representing you online.

Third, the person should be an employee rather than a contractor. I am not saying that you have to hire a social media person; I am saying that you more than likely have a current employee in whom you have complete confidence and whom you could consider for handling your social media. I have seen small companies that have successfully assigned social media duties to a member or two members of the staff in whom the owners have confidence, and they do very well. These folks are not allowed to handle the owners' personal social media, but they do handle their business pages.

Of course, if you are going to experience the full benefits of social media for business, the personal page and personal interactions are of extreme importance, and here I don't believe you can hire out. This is why you need to be organized, understand the platforms, and have a plan.

One final note on allowing others to do your social media for you: Even when you have the utmost trust in the people conducting it for you, you still need to monitor it to make sure that these people are following the predetermined standards you have provided them to help represent you well. This will also allow you to stay in the loop regarding the content that's being posted for those times that your social media followers refer back to it (e.g., "Loved your post on Topic X"!)

Commitment and Consistency

Next, when getting SPICEY, you will need to remember that for social media to work, you will need to be *committed* to it—stay with the strategy you set over the long-term, engaged in the right behaviors regardless of your attitude—not just start engaging and then fizzle out because you don't enjoy being on it, you get too busy, you are bored with it, or some other excuse. It is about using the social media platforms consistently over time, even if that means that you sometimes have to fake it till you make it (yes, your behavior can change your attitude). There is no value judgment here, just the reality of the situation: If you are only going to partially engage on social media, your efforts are going to have limited effectiveness. Like any marketing that you do, if you do not do it enough, it will have extremely limited effects, and if you do nothing on it, you can be fully assured you will get nothing out of it.

I say *commitment* because using social media is not necessarily about wanting or liking to do it. It has nothing to do with the way you feel; it is about the way you act and behave. It's much like staying in shape and exercising. Just like you have to show up at the gym (or the yoga studio or the bike trail) to experience the benefits of exercise, you have to show up on social media over and over again for there to be real success. When we are truly committed, we show up, rain or shine, good feelings or bad.

This is why it is important that you have a strategy and a plan in place for your social media. If you have your strategy and plan, you will know which social media platforms to use and why. You will have a roadmap for what to do there, which will make it easier to show up on social media consistently, each and every day. In contrast, if you don't have a strategy or plan, you are likely to aimlessly wander through the social media platforms, wasting time clicking links, hitting likes, randomly posting, and so on, without really knowing what the purpose is.

Here's my recommendation. When you are ready to take the social media plunge, plan to use it consistently for a minimum of ninety days. If you are going to evaluate any marketing plan to determine its effectiveness, typically you need to test it for three to six months. Social media is no different in this respect. However, I am going to add one caveat to this. Relationships are not developed in ninety days, with you then being able to walk away from them.

Relationships need to be nurtured and maintained over time. If you would like these relationships to last, you must stay committed to them. After all, these are real people whose perceptions will be formed by what you say and how you say it. If you are active and then all of a sudden disappear, what does that say about your commitment to the relationships that you have built and cultivated on the different platforms? It is important that you do not underestimate the power and influence of the relationships that you make in the time you are on social media, especially the personal relationships with those who will be the biggest advocates for you and your business.

In sum, consistency and commitment lead to results on social media. There are some measurable results of this consistency, but in a general sense, I can say you are likely to see an increase in web traffic, which can be confirmed by checking your website analytics. You should also see either a boost or new entries in the first couple of pages of search engine results, especially if you are using Google+. Although it is a very rough measure, you can also check to see how many people have liked your Facebook business page, requested to be a connection on LinkedIn, added you to their Google+ circles, followed you on Twitter, and so on.

That being said, I can assure you that none of those benefits will be evident if you are not committed to and consistent with your social media. Commitment is something you must choose to do; you will have to make your time on social media a habit. It will come from the strategy of choosing the right platforms, making sure you have a simple plan to follow that works for you, and using your appropriate professional and personal influence on a consistent basis.

Building Your Social Media Interaction Over Time

Initially, you may not see much response to your social media interaction; this is because you are new and therefore an unknown social media personality. Like any new business, it will take some time for you to establish your credibility on these networks, so plan to stay with it. Think of it as your foundation building. You cannot just join a social media platform, start posting, and expect that people will immediately be enthralled with everything you have to say. You have to develop your voice, be seen, and create your social media professional presence first.

Once you have established your presence and what you say begins to generate interactions, pay attention to what others are responding to or not responding to so you can scrap what isn't working and replicate more of what is. This kind of experimentation takes time, as does establishing your persona online—more reasons why consistency and commitment are so important.

Experiment

You've got a strategy and a plan, you're out there interacting, and you're committed to being on social media consistently. How else do you get SPICEY? Give yourself permission to *experiment*.

Many times people will not use social media because they are afraid that they are going to do something wrong. I have already described the pitfalls and dangers of associating yourself with negative things or violating cultural norms. As long as you avoid those things that I have discussed throughout this book (also see the Social Media Do's and Don'ts callout box, which follows), you can let go of any worry and just do.

As I have previously alluded, there are still many unknowns about what is effective and not effective for social media; as a result, you will need to try different things. Be creative and try multiple tactics. One of the things I enjoy most about social media is being able to use it as a sort of research laboratory. I am constantly trying new things—different pictures, short posts, long posts, quotes, humor, links, and so on—to see who responds and in what way.

I also experiment with posting at different times of day. In this way, I have discovered, for instance, that the majority of the people that I interact with read either early in the morning or after dinner. A smaller group seems to interact over lunch. I also have discovered that when I post on the weekends, I get much more interaction. These things are important, and I would never have discovered them had I not experimented and paid close attention to what was happening as a result of what I was doing.

I have also experimented with using different kinds of tones with my posts, whether lighthearted, edgy, intellectual, fun-loving, or something else. In the process, I have found through comments I receive that I sometimes come across to others in my discussions as arrogant. I certainly do not want that as a badge. Confident, yes; arrogant, no. In such cases, I have had to look closely at how others seem to read and think about how I write and then make adjustments to future interactions. In other cases, I can see from the likes or comments that people have enjoyed my tone, sense of humor, or insights. Experimenting with social media has helped me to shape my behavior, and it has made me better at what I do with it and how I interact with others.

Ultimately, experimenting with social media requires that you take some risks as social media use is not an exact science and thus involves some trial and error. That being said, the more scientific you can be about experimenting with social media and learning from the results, the easier social media will become for you and the more effective it can be for your business. As a result, I encourage you to follow the principles and strategies offered in this book to help you follow a clear path toward success rather than just "throwing spaghetti on the wall" to see what sticks. And as with any good experimentation, do pay very close attention to the results. Write them down; compare them. It is the only way you can truly know if your hypothesis has been verified or not.

Social Media Do's and Don'ts

Social media offers a grown-up playground on which to share, communicate, ask, listen, and try new things. But beware—a few rules should be followed to make sure that you make friends, not enemies.

1. **No name-calling.** As Mama always said, if you don't have anything nice to say about someone, don't say anything at all. So resist the urge on social media to vent about someone who has made you angry or to criticize a group of people that you don't like or agree with. Not only is it hurtful, but you will make others wonder when you might turn on them. It certainly serves no useful purpose. On social media, do say nice things about others and treat people with respect so you can build trust; do not develop a reputation for stereotyping, gossiping, or criticizing.
2. **Avoid being political or religious.** You've seen the political posts before. Sometimes it's a harmless link to a political statement; other times it's an over-the-top rant. Either way, getting too political is not a good idea for business building. If you make a political statement, you are guaranteed to lose a significant chunk of your audience; if you make a religious statement, you may alientate every person who has a different faith. Even with sports teams, if you root for one of the three local college basketball teams, you will automatically alienate two groups in your potential audience. Does that build the kind of knowing, liking, and trusting you are aiming for? Avoid polarizing issues and you will be able to build relationships, not weaken them.

3. **Don't be promotional.** People are on Facebook to connect with friends, family, and folks they've lost touch with; less than 10% of the peope are interested in connecting with a brand or a business. People are on Twitter for interactions and to be retweeted; they are not there to read your advertisements. Even on LinkedIn, where it's okay to talk business, self-promoting comments are not welcome. So do not use these platforms as your personal billboard because that's not why people are there. Instead, find the best way to interact with users to transform them into clients, who will, in turn, bring their friends; on social media, that happens through relationships, not advertising.

You (Being Authentic)

This is the last word on being SPICEY when it comes to your social media efforts: Being SPICEY means being *you*—being authentic. Sincerely try to cultivate real relationships in a real way and aim to make a difference in the lives of people by giving them time, respect, and personal and professional help. Remember the know, like, and trust factor we discussed in Chapter 1? A huge part succeeding on social media is helping people learn to know, like, and trust you—simply through your authentic interactions there—so that they will later feel comfortable referring people to your business or doing business with you themselves.

If you are motivated to use people for financial gain, this will quickly be detected by the majority of social media users. What many businesspeople do not understand is that most social media users are very digital-relationship savvy. They can see right through your motivations, and they have ways of cutting you off, some you may never be aware of, whether they defriend you or simply hide your posts. So be authentic, and be genuine. Few things make people turn on you faster than giving them the impression that you are interested in them only because of the money they can bring to the table.

I am sensitive to this issue. I probably have not been more offended than when someone wants to friend me and interacts with me in a friendly way only to later tell me that they have an opportunity they want to share with me. When this happens to me, and it does, I think to myself, "How clever this person was for months having personal interactions only to have a motivation all along to want to sell something to me." I am sure there are some who have been sucked in by these tactics. In nearly every case when I responded with, "I am not interested," the social media friendship was lost, I was defriended, or the person moved on. That was neither authentic nor genuine; it was simply a long-term relationship ploy with the wrong motivation for using social media.

I have been very intentional about getting you to understand that these social media platforms are cultures, not billboards, mailers, e-mail marketing, and the like. These are places where people communicate, interact, learn, grow, and build relationships. If you want to get the most out of these platforms, try to understand each culture and become a genuine part of it. In the process, you will discover that people will come to trust you, the authentic you, who is truly interested in others.

If you follow the SPICEY regimen, I am confident you will have the ingredients and flavors needed to successfully influence your social media community and to enrich your ability to grow your business through your personal and professional interactions. With this ingredient list in hand, I'd next like to offer you some cooking instructions, practical directions for how you can manage your social media over the course of a single day.

Get to It: A Daily Plan for Social Media

Without a daily plan or checklist, you could easily spend all day surfing and sifting through social media: posting comments, reading links, responding to discussion threads, and more. With a plan, you will have some simple tasks you can complete each day to ensure you stay active and engaged without spending all of your time on social media. To help you get the most out of social media without it taking a huge chunk out of you, I am going to give you a sample way of doing social media in fifteen to forty-five minutes per day.

We are going to divide your social media time up into three segments—morning, lunch, and evening—which you can customize for your needs. For the social media junkie or the business owner who is super serious about engaging in social media, pay particular attention to the tasks at all three times of day. For the social media newbie or business owner who would like to try out the benefits of social media without dedicating too much time, think about following the checklist two times per day, which will give you a chance to post original content and then follow up later in the day. Yes, you can even cut it down to one time a day, but remember what I said earlier about the importance of interacting with others on social media, which is hard to do if you post something in the morning but don't check to see if you receive any comments or replies. And although some will argue that it's okay to comment and reply the following day, in the world of social media, most people have moved on by then. It's those who respond to us within minutes or hours that we tend to feel the most connected with. In the end, it is you who must determine when and how often to be on social media. Just remember that interaction and consistency are important. The more you put into social media, the more you are likely to receive back from it.

Social Media Daily Checklist

When you first get started on social media, following a checklist may help you manage the different platforms. Here is a peek into the mental checklist that I use every day. Feel free to customize it for you. Timer optional!

Morning

LinkedIn (four minutes)

- ☐ Check notifications.
- ☐ Endorse three people.
- ☐ Respond to a discussion if one of interest has come through an e-mail to you (e-mail option set up ahead of time).

Facebook (seven minutes)

- ☐ Check notifications on personal and business page.
- ☐ Select the ones that you feel you should or need to respond to.
- ☐ Respond to friend requests (if any, and make sure you know them, your friends know them, and/or they are not spam).
- ☐ Send greetings to all people who have a birthday.
- ☐ Interact with client lists that you have set up ahead of time (e.g., "like" some posts that you truly like or appreciate, comment on a few posts that interest you, and/or share one or two posts from others that you feel are worth sharing).

- ☐ If you have something to post, post it; if not, leave.

Twitter and Google+ (four minutes)

- ☐ Check messages and mentions (get notified via e-mail or text ahead of time; if someone has responded to something you have written, then respond).
- ☐ Grab a shortened URL link to post on Twitter with creative title.
- ☐ On Google+, create a post that asks a question, post a link, or simply respond by adding a +1 or comment to a post. If you posted on your business page on Facebook, cross-post it on your Google+ page.
- ☐ Schedule a tweet or two through a management program such as HootSuite or TweetDeck.

Lunch (recommended)

Facebook (three to five minutes)

- ☐ Check notifications, respond to any comments made on a post, check client lists.

Google+ (two to five minutes)

- ☐ Check on people in your colleague and client circles, look through posts, +1 a few if you like them, or make a comment.

Twitter (thirty seconds)

- ☐ Make sure tweets scheduled earlier actually posted.

Evening (optional)

(generally before bed but after dinner)

Facebook (seven to ten minutes)

- ☐ Respond to notifications, click client and friend lists: Like, comment, and share posts when necessary.

Twitter (three to five minutes)

- ☐ Post a link or retweet a link that you like.

Google+ (three to five minutes)

- ☐ Respond to notifications; +1 or comment on posts from different circles that you find interesting.

And that sums up one way to make sure you interact on several social media platforms in a given day. I didn't mention anything about pinning for Pinterest; that is because once you have Pinterest, you can put it right on your browser and if you see something you want to pin as you are browsing the Internet, you just click the *Pin It* button, put it on your selected board, and write a quick note (this will take two minutes, tops). Personally, I do not use Pinterest every day, only when I find something I believe is worth pinning.

What about YouTube? Honestly, YouTube takes longer. For me, that is going to be a well-planned, intentional portion of my day, because it does not fit into my normal schedule. I may search for a YouTube video that I have been alerted to that I may share, or I may upload a video that I have recently created, but that happens just once in a while. YouTube has an important place in helping to grow your business, but it need not be part of your everyday social media activities.

If you follow a plan and keep an eye on the clock, social media does not have to be a time hole. As a matter of fact, the more you use it and understand it, the faster you will get it done and the easier it will be for you.

I am the first to admit that if you are thinking about using all the social media platforms, the task can appear overwhelming. But don't worry: *You are not going to use all of the platforms!* You are going to get SPICEY and strategically pick the platforms where the majority of your potential clients are. Look, nearly 85% of the people on Twitter are not actively using it. Unless the majority of your potential clients are using Twitter, it may not be on your list; they may not be using Google+ or Pinterest, either. On the basis of your target market, you can choose to be on the platforms where your clients are.

When you strategize and plan in this way, you may even find that you spend a great deal less time than forty-five minutes a day on social media. Chances are, if you are controlling your social media in the way I am suggesting, you may be able to do all of this in just twenty minutes a day. It takes discipline and focus, but it can be done. People say they do not have time; well, when it comes to social media, you do. You can type on your phone while eating a sandwich, watching TV, waiting for your train or bus, warming up your car, or waiting for your coffee to brew. There is almost always a small bit of time you can take to hit your social media to-do list. Make it important, practice it regularly, and it will become part of your routine.

Try This!

Create a personalized social media checklist for you and your business. Use the checklist provided in this chapter for inspiration, and make adjustments as needed. Consider the following questions when customizing the plan to your needs:

1. What times of day will you interact on social media (morning, lunch, evening)?
2. Which social media platform or platforms will you interact on (LinkedIn only? LinkedIn and Facebook? YouTube or Pinterest as an add-on?)

Once you have created your social media checklist, print a copy and post it somewhere where you can see it or reference it every day. If someone else will be running your social media program, create the plan together.

In Sum: Stay SPICEY

Interacting on social media can be overwhelming, but it doesn't have to be. It all depends on whether you have done a good job of deciding which social media platform or platforms to focus on (**S**trategizing) and creating a customized **P**lan for implementing your social media activity on a daily basis. Over the long-term, be sure to **I**nteract **C**onsistently, **E**xperiment with your approach to see what works best for your audience, and finally, win devotees by being authentic and by being **Y**ou. With this SPICEY approach, you will have a clear path to getting the most out of social media for your business.

What's Next?

> The newest computer can merely compound...the oldest problem in the relations between human beings, and in the end the communicator will be confronted with the old problem, of what to say and how to say it.
>
> —Edward R. Murrow

My, how quickly things change! Who could have once imagined how social media would alter the way people get news and share news or how news would become so personal? Social media is now the place many go to catch breaking news; tune into cultural trends; get updates on the job changes of peers; see the latest in home décor, food, and design—the list goes on and on.

What's more, social media surrounds us and continues to grow in numbers of users of all ages, ethnicities, economic statuses, and industries. It is impossible to escape, not only touching our present reality but also shaping the professional and personal realities of our future. Some people are hoping that social media is nothing more than a fad that will just go away. There are even those who are searching for evidence that these platforms will simply cease to exist or that perhaps they will have less of an impact on society and business in the future.

I am here to tell you that social media is not going to go away. Further, you can expect that as a result of advances in technology, social media is likely to become an even greater influence on our daily lives. It is true that Facebook may not look like Facebook ten years from now, that Pinterest might turn into an e-commerce site, or that Google+ may become a dominant player, but one thing is for sure: The social media world is here to stay. If anything, it is only going to become more accessible as mobile technologies continue to develop.

While some are busy resisting social media altogether, others are willing to dip their toe in the water, while still others are jumping right in. Where are you on this spectrum? Are you in the same place you were at the start of this book, or have you started to see things differently? Maybe having done some of the *Try This!* exercises in this book or perhaps by simply spending more time on social media, you have begun to see where these platforms can help you make new connections, stay in better touch with potential clients, and build your credibility.* In case you are still on the fence regarding social media or if you would simply like one last refresher on social media's potential before completing this book, let's quickly recap the benefits of these diverse online platforms.

Remind Me: Why Social Media?

If you have read this book from start to finish, you may now agree with me that social media is more than a space for teens to chat or for grand-

---

* I would love to hear how this book has changed your outlook on social media and to learn about what you have found helpful, so feel free to drop me a line at jay@socialmediology.com.

mas to get family photo updates. Social media has a very real place in the American business landscape. As we have seen, that doesn't mean that we always need to act corporate while communicating on social media. In fact, that's discouraged on platforms like Facebook. Yet social media provides some extraordinary benefits for the small and growing business. Here are some of them in a nutshell:

- Social media can expand your personal and professional network. It opens up the number of people you can get connected to, whether potential clients for the future or those in a position to send you referrals.
- Social media can provide a quick, easy, and no- to low-cost means of branding yourself and your business online.
- Social media allows you to follow up with more business leads and clients in less time than you ever could by picking up the phone or sending personal e-mails.
- Social media allows you to connect to clients as a multifaceted business owner or leader, revealing the human you (Facebook); the professional you (LinkedIn); the savvy you (Twitter); and the living, breathing you in three dimensions (YouTube).

And the list of benefits goes on and on, including that social media allows you to showcase your credibility and thought leadership as well as to create relationships that lead to referrals. Have I made my case? By now, you know I'm an ardent advocate for the use of social media in business. Now it's your turn to decide whether any of these benefits—or others that you've discovered along the way—are compelling enough to get you to take your social media activity to the next level. Are you ready to take the plunge or simply to dive deeper?

Got Social Mediology?

Good. So you kept on reading—even you, the social media curmudgeon. Bravo! That tells me that you do see some potential for growing your business on social media or maybe that you've even begun to use it regularly or in new ways. Just remember as you continue your journey into the brave new world of social media that you must bring social mediology with you. You must have an understanding of the culture of your chosen platform or platforms and the motivations and behaviors of the people using it. You must also be aware of the ways in which those processes are similar or vary for each platform. To be successful in growing your business via social media, you need to tune into, respect, and adhere to the way people tend to use and interact on each of the different platforms. Once you have this understanding and respect, you will be ready to develop influence on social media. And that's where the goodies for your business come in.

It is my opinion that we underestimate just how powerful we can be when it comes to influencing others. Our ability to reinforce others for their behavior has tremendous influence. It is nearly impossible to calculate what effect a retweet, like, comment, share, favorite, repin, or +1 has on another's behavior, but our behavior does change when we receive them. It reminds me of when I introduce clients to social media: They post something, it receives ten or twenty likes and ten comments, and they get excited about social media and want that same experience again. They begin to see that people are paying attention and that they are connecting with each other.

Even social media curmudgeons may have trouble ignoring the positive feelings they experience as a result of receiving a relatively significant number of likes, comments, shares, and so on in response to something they posted. It is so reinforcing, in fact, that it stimulates the behavior and we find ourselves posting again.

Recall the study we talked about in Chapter 1? The same parts of the brain light up when people use social media as when they have sex. What's more, respondents in the same study would choose to talk about themselves on social media over receiving money. It's important for us as humans—and business owners—to recognize that people are attracted to social media because of the mental stimulation and emotional reinforcement they experience as a result of interacting within it. Thus, we have tremendous influence over others, and social media is a great place to exercise that influence. This potential can be used for good or evil. I am a proponent of doing good.

In the end, the only way to get through these issues of effectively working with social media is to view these platforms from the psychological perspective of the user. Social mediology reminds us that every piece of social media is really not about media but about how people behave, use, interact, and relate with others on these platforms. Unless we understand the motivations, the habits, and the behaviors displayed by users both individually and in groups within these platforms, we are only trying to leverage the platform rather than truly connecting with the most important element of these platforms: the people who use it.

It does not matter all that much how technologists change it, because it is the culture, not technology, that keeps these platforms alive and thriving. It does not matter how marketers say you should use it, because typically they do not make up the majority of your consumers and in reality they may even be the reason why most people leave the platform, because they are inundated with marketing messages that interfere with their user experience. The most important thing to understand in social media is the user and how to best relate to him or her. Remember and apply the key principles of social mediology, and you will be able to grow your business on these platforms for years to come.

Why We Need Social Mediology

It has been argued that social media is a microcosm of society. I disagree. We would never invite people to our home to put on a bathing suit, tell them all to come to the bathroom with us, and watch us take a picture. We would not scream at the top of our lungs in front of hundreds or thousands of people, telling them that we are lonely or that we are hungry.[1]

How many times have we read or heard in the news about some athlete or celebrity that posted something to some social media platform that was completely offensive, stupid, or wrong, only to try to delete it (a post, by the way, can never be completely deleted) and then either rationalize it, attempt to excuse it, insist it was "taken out of context," or occasionally admit they were wrong? Is it not obvious that had this person been in front of a camera or a face-to-face group that he or she (or we) would not have said or done many of the things that are posted? There is something quite unique about social media that does not seem to apply to real life. It is not a microcosm of society; it is a society unto itself.

If we are to understand social media fully, we need to understand the psychology and social psychology of the social media user individually and in groups. The fact is that the user is the real owner of these platforms; it is how users act, interact, behave, and relate on the platforms that will ultimately determine your success there. Follow a few of the principles I have outlined for you here, and I believe that you will find that social mediology for your business will be as successful for you as it has been for the people mentioned in this book, my clients, and myself.

The Future of Social Media

I have done my best to share with you the reality of social media today, but, as we all know, technology is always evolving. So let's see if we can take a quick glimpse into the future. One of the biggest changes we will see with social media will result from the movement to mobile technologies. You may have already found yourself using social media on your tablet or phone, and you may see others doing the same. In fact, research by Nielson shows that the amount of time people spent on their smartphones and tablets using social media increased by 76% between 2011 and 2012.[2]

Think about it this way. The desktop computer still exists, yet because of technology, we have less need for a desktop now that laptops have the same capabilities. Even laptops are becoming obsolete, as we have tablets that connect to cloud computing platforms, negating the need for hard drives.

And it keeps on going. Google now has released Google Glass, which allows people to access the Internet, connect with their social media, take pictures, and capture video through a pair of glasses. Watches, too, are currently being designed that allow you to keep up with your social media activities. Talk about mobile! Gadgets that we once thought could only be owned by a fictional character like James Bond are now a reality. We now have access to a universe of information at any moment, whether while waiting at the dentist's office, sitting in a meeting, walking down the street, or boarding an airplane.

It probably will come as no surprise that more than half of the people in the United States own some version of a smartphone, and 63% of those users access some form of social media via their smartphones.[3] It may not even shock you that 46% of smartphone users access social media multiple times per day. But it may rock your world to know that as of this writing, seventy-one million Americans check their social media profiles several times a day as compared with 2008, when only twelve million people were checking their social media profiles. What is more, four out of ten smartphone users describe themselves as habitual social networkers that check their profiles multiple times a day, and the numbers are increasing. All of this research indicates that social media is not a dying entity; it is, in fact, an ingrained part of our society. For better or for worse, our social media lives are now intertwined with nearly everything.

Snap a photo of your lunch and post it to Facebook. See a great talk and post the speaker's name on LinkedIn before you have even left the auditorium. Find a cool new piece of furniture and post it to Pinterest before you've exited the store. Yes, mobile makes social media more user friendly, more appealing, and more accessible, as we can do everything from our phones; soon enough, we may be accessing social media via our Google glasses or our smartwatches.

In the end, though, social media is not so much about the technology as it is about, well, being *social*. We as humans are naturally social and have a need for interaction. Research has been limited, and yet opinions have been many in regard to what social media's role is in our social interaction. With more than a billion people currently using the various social media platforms, I would argue that most people's use is not based on a fascination with technology but on the ability to in some way connect with other human beings.

This is not a new concept. People have been trying to connect since the start of time, whether it was to develop spoken language, written words, the printing press, the telegraph, or the telephone. And the transition wasn't always easy. I can only imagine when the first telephone was put in the local store or café how people rejected it or perhaps feared that they would get a shock from it. Now we take phones for granted. Social media is simply our newest way to connect. And today, the speed at which we are able to make a connection with others, anywhere in the world, is always increasing.

Will you and your business resist this wave of change or embrace it? Will you criticize and downplay it, or will you open the door and try it out for yourself? Will you consider, instead of being stubborn or afraid, getting SPICEY? When in doubt, don't forget our acronym: Strategize,

Plan, Interact, Commit, Experiment, and Be You. You can also work your way through the different *Try This!* exercises offered throughout the book to get yourself going. And if you remember nothing else, remember the principle of reciprocity—give to others on social media, and they will give back to you.

The Last Words, I Promise

It is my hope that you have learned something that you can apply to yourself and your business through social media that will make a tremendous difference. I want you to be successful when using it. I want you to experience the personal, professional, and financial rewards as a result of using social media in the right way. I understand that not everyone is going to like social media or want to work with it. I hope I have given you at least some motivation to sink yourself into social media and create, cultivate, and maintain relationships.

Every principle I have mentioned in this book, I have been able to demonstrate myself or with my clients. However, remember that social media is not magic and cannot work for us if we don't work with it. In short, social media is most effective with commitment and consistency. It is impossible to have effective results from any social media if you are not committed to learning it, applying the principles, being a real part of it, and doing all of this on a consistent basis.

If you are going to jump into social media personally and professionally and you have some strong emotional disenchantment with the idea of social media, you will need to put those feelings aside and be committed to using these platforms in the right way. Just as important, these platforms have to be used consistently. True, you do not have to use some platforms, like LinkedIn, every day. However, I can honestly tell you that a half-in, half-out user of social media never gets much benefit. That user meets with frustration instead.

Social media works not because of the platform; it works because people are committed to the relationships with the people on the platform.

A better way to say this is, stay committed to your friends, followers, and connections, and they will more likely stay committed to you. When you commit to people, to the real human beings on the platform, you are giving you and your business every single opportunity to receive the greatest benefits from the interactions you have there. As Edward R. Murrow noted forty years ago, it is "the oldest problem in the relations between human beings" that social media exposes. If you want people to be committed to your business, then you must be committed to a relationship with them.

So never forget that these are relational platforms with real people. They have lives. They have emotions. They have wins; they have losses. Now we get to see them on the front page. You can make a monumental positive impact on these fellow friends, followers, and colleagues. It never ceases to amaze me how sometimes a few words in a comment, post, or tweet can change a person's outlook or inspire them to move in another direction. At the time, I think what I said was insignificant, only to find out later in a private e-mail that my words helped or encouraged someone, changed an attitude, or pushed them to keep going. That is the real power of this thing we call social media. It can be an amazing experience for both the reader and the writer.

I have often been asked, "What should I say?" or "How should I say it?" The best advice I can give you is, "Be human." As long as you remain genuine, you will never have to worry about the what or the how, because you are now a real part of your social media connections' lives as they are a part of yours. If you understand that your business is based on real people who have real emotions and real lives, you will find that social media can be one of the most human places to grow personally and professionally.

To your success!

Jay Izso, Internet Doctor

NOTES

CHAPTER 1: Why Are We Here?

1. This concept is further defined at http://www.socialmediology.com.
2. IBM, "Black Friday Report 2012: IBM Digital Analytics Benchmark," http://www-01.ibm.com/software/marketing-solutions/benchmark-reports/benchmark-2012-black-friday.pdf.
3. When I refer to *traditional marketing,* I am referring to buying paid advertisements, or even purchasing promoted posts that show up on the side of the page of the middle of a timeline or news feed. I am also referring to the traditional idea of blatantly using these platforms as a form of a billboard or banner advertisement where you are attempting to directly persuade people to do business with you.
4. My definitions of *customer, consumer,* and *client* are not marketing based; they are behavior based. You more than likely will not find these definitions in a business or marketing dictionary, but, on the basis of behavior, you will quickly understand the distinction.
5. Chase Larson, "Mark Zuckerberg speaks at BYU, calls Facebook 'as much psychology and sociology as it is technology,'" *Deseret News,* March 25, 2011, http://www.deseretnews.com/article/700121651/Mark-Zuckerberg-speaks-at-BYU-calls-Facebook-as-much-psychology-and-sociology-as-it-is-technology.html?pg=1.
6. Kennon M. Sheldon, Neetu Abad, and Christian Hirsch, "A Two-Process View of Facebook Use and Relatedness Need-Satisfaction: Disconnection Drives Use, and Connection Rewards It," *Journal of Personality and Social Psychology 100*, no. 4 (2011): 766–75.
7. Diana I. Tamir and Jason P. Mitchell, "Disclosing Information About the Self Is Intrinsically Rewarding," *Proceedings of the National Academy of Sciences 109*, no. 21 (2012): 8038-43.

CHAPTER 2: Debunking the Social Media Myths

1. N. M. Incite and Nielsen Holdings N. V., *State of the Media: The Social Media Report* (report), http://www.nielsen.com/content/dam/corporate/us/en/reports-downloads/2012-Reports/The-Social-Media-Report-2012.pdf.
2. Scientist Isaac Asimov may have been the rare exception among us, with his predictions that we would "read passages of books" on screen. Alexis Kleinman, "Isaac Asimov's Predictions for 2014 From 50 Years Ago Are Eerily Accurate," *The Huffington Post*, January 2, 2014, http://www.huffingtonpost.com/2014/01/02/isaac-asimov-2014_n_4530785.html
3. Maeve Duggan and Aaron Smith, *Social Media Update 2013* (report), http://pewinternet.org/Reports/2013/Social-Media-Update.aspx.
4. Chris Lake, "STUDY: Noise, Promotion and Spam Will Reduce Your Twitter Followers," *Econsultancy*, May 23, 2012, http://econsultancy.com/us/blog/9968-study-noise-promotion-and-spam-will-reduce-your-twitter-followers.
5. ExactTarget, *Subscribers, Fans, and Followers: The Social Break-up* (Report #8), http://www.exacttarget.com/resources/SFF8.pdf.
6. Jim Edwards, "These Are the Biggest Advertisers on Facebook," *Business Insider*, November 28, 2013, http://www.businessinsider.com/top-advertisers-on-facebook-2013-11.
7. Luxury Institute, *Luxury Institute Wealth Survey: Social Networking Habits and Practices of the Wealthy*, http://www.scribd.com/doc/38313551/Luxury-Institute-Wealth-Survey-Social-Networking-Habits-and-Practices.
8. Robert Frank, "One Third of Millionaires Use Social Media," *The Wealth Report* (blog), June 16, 2011, http://blogs.wsj.com/wealth/2011/06/16/one-third-of-millionaires-use-social-media/?cb=logged0.1981750475242734#.

9. Cheryl Conner, "How Hashtags Attract Wealthy Customers," *Forbes*, July 24, 2013, http://www.forbes.com/sites/cherylsnappconner/2013/07/24/how-hashtags-attract-wealthy-customers/.
10. Kathryn Zickuhr and Mary Madden, *Older Adults and Internet Use* (report), http://pewinternet.org/~/media//Files/Reports/2012/PIP_Older_adults_and_internet_use.pdf.

CHAPTER 3: Social Mediology 101: Using Psychology to Master Social Media

1. Salesforce.com, "The Facebook Ads Benchmark Report," 2013, http://www.salesforcemarketingcloud.com/wp-content/uploads/2013/06/The-Facebook-Ads-Benchmark-Report.pdf?b9be0c.
2. The *click-through rate* is defined as the percentage of people who were exposed to your ad (viewed a page where your ad was featured) who actually clicked on it, presumably to view it, although they may have just as easily clicked on it by accident. Of course, once they click on your ad, they may or may not reach out to your business.
3. David Towers, "PPC Accounts for Just 6% of Total Search Clicks [infographic]," *Econsultancy*, August 23, 2012, http://econsultancy.com/us/blog/10586-ppc-accounts-for-just-6-of-total-search-clicks-infographic.
4. Ann Michaels, "Facebook Profile: The Eyes Have It," *Social Media Management Blog* (blog), http://www.socialmediamanagement.net/blog/tag/eye-tracking-study-facebook/.
5. Dennis T. Regan, "Effects of a Favor and Liking on Compliance," *Journal of Experimental Social Psychology* 7, no. 6 (1971): 627–39.
6. R. B. Zajonc, "Attitudinal Effects of Mere Exposure," *Journal of Personality and Social Psychology 9* (1968): 1–27.
7. It must be said too that paid social media ads, if frequent enough, may lead to the customer developing a preference for you, but bear in mind

that these ads cost money, whereas my suggested approach is free, and that many users have stopped noticing these ads because of habituation or they have simply blocked them with third-party applications.

8. Philip Graves, *Consumer.ology: The Market Research Myth, the Truth about Consumers, and the Psychology of Shopping* (London: Nicholas Brealey Publishing, 2010), p. 7.
9. David McRaney, *You Are Not So Smart: Why You Have Too Many Friends on Facebook, Why Your Memory is Mostly Fiction, and 46 Other Ways You're Deluding Yourself* (New York: Dutton, 2012), Kindle edition, Kindle Location 62.

CHAPTER 4: Putting LinkedIn to Work for Your Business

1. Steve W. Martin, "Top Salespeople Use LinkedIn to Sell More," *HBR Blog Network* (blog), April 5, 2013, http://blogs.hbr.org/cs/2013/04/top_salespeople_use_linked.html.
2. Emily Maltby, "Small Firms Say LinkedIn Works, Twitter Doesn't," *The Wall Street Journal*, January 31, 2013, http://online.wsj.com/article/SB10001424127887323926104578273683427129660.html?mod=ITP_marketplace_3#project%3DVISTAGE_2_CHARTS12%26articleTabs%3Darticle.
3. Enlign represents profitable, privately held companies for sale with gross annual revenues in excess of $1 million (http://www.enlign.com).
4. "LinkedIn.com" (rankings), Quantcast, accessed February 9, 2014, http://www.quantcast.com/linkedin.com#!demo&anchor=age-gender-container.
5. Dave McCandless, "Chicks Rule? Gender Balance on Social Networking Sites," *Information Is Beautiful* (infographic based on data from Google Ad Planner), May 2012, http://www.informationisbeautiful.net/visualizations/chicks-rule/.
6. Marcus Tullius Cicero, *169 Famous Quotes by Cicero (Marcus Tullius Cicero)*, http://www.worldofquotes.com/author/cicero+(marcus+tullius+cicero)/1/index.html.

7. Weber Shandwick and KRC Research, *Buy It, Try It, Rate It: Study of Consumer Electronics Purchase Decisions in the Engagement Era* (report), http://www.webershandwick.com/uploads/news/files/ReviewsSurveyReportFINAL.pdf.
8. "Skill Endorsements—Overview: What Are Skill Endorsements and What Are Their Benefits?" LinkedIn Help Center, last reviewed January 20, 2014, http://help.linkedin.com/app/answers/detail/a_id/31888/kw/endorsements.

CHAPTER 5: Facebook: Friends that Know You, Like You, and Trust You and Your Business

1. "About Facebook Statistics," Facebook, https://www.facebook.com/pages/Facebook-statistics/119768528069029?fref=ts.
2. "Facebook.com" (estimate), Quantcast, accessed May 5, 2013, http://www.quantcast.com/facebook.com.
3. Dave McCandless, "Chicks Rule? Gender Balance on Social Networking Sites," *Information Is Beautiful* (infographic based on data from Google Ad Planner), May 2012, http://www.informationisbeautiful.net/visualizations/chicks-rule/.
4. Dan Zarrella, *The Science of Marketing: When to Tweet, What to Post, How to Blog, and Other Proven Strategies* (New York: Wiley, 2013), Kindle edition, Kindle Locations 947-949.
5. Aaron Smith, *Why Americans Use Social Media* (report), http://www.pewinternet.org/Reports/2011/Why-Americans-Use-Social-Media.aspx.
6. Robert B. Cialdini, *Influence: The Psychology of Persuasion,* rev. ed. (New York: HarperBusiness, 2007).
7. Naomi K. Grant, Leandre R. Fabrigar, and Heidi Lim, "Exploring the Efficacy of Compliments as a Tactic for Securing Compliance," *Basic and Applied Social Psychology 32*, no. 3 (2010): 226-33.
8. Brandon Van Der Heide, Jonathan D. D'Angelo, and Erin M. Schumaker, "The Effects of Verbal Versus Photographic Self-

Presentation on Impression Formation in Facebook," *Journal of Communication 62*(2012): 98–116.

9. Dan Zarrella, "How to Get More Likes, Comments and Shares on Facebook," *Dan Zarrella, The Social Media Scientist* (blog), http://danzarrella.com/infographic-how-to-get-more-likes-comments-and-shares-on-facebook.html#.
10. Dan Zarrella, *The Science of Marketing: When to Tweet, What to Post, How to Blog, and Other Proven Strategies* (New York: Wiley, 2013), Kindle edition, Kindle Location 991.
11. Ibid, Kindle Locations 1005-1006.
12. Sara. "Like Us!" *Market Research: The Latest Social Media & Market Research News* (blog), September 24, 2012, http://blog.lab42.com/like-us.
13. Jack W. Brehm, *A Theory of Psychological Reactance,* (New York: Academic Press, Inc., 1966).
14. Jack W. Brehm, *Response to Loss of Freedom: A Theory of Pyschological Reactance,* (Morristown, NJ: General Learning Press, 1972).
15. "Facebook Page Terms," Facebook, last revised December 18, 2003, https://www.facebook.com/page_guidelines.php.
16. David Cohen, "INFOGRAPHIC: Facebook Timeline Contests, Promotions Make Engagement Rates Soar," *AllFacebook: The Unofficial Facebook Blog* (blog), October 25, 2013, http://allfacebook.com/infographic-krds_b126288.
17. Solomon E. Asch, "Effects of Group Pressure on the Modification and Distortion of Judgments," in *Groups, Leadership and Men,* ed. H. Guetzkow (Pittsburgh, PA: Carnegie Press, 1951), 177–90.Solomon E. Asch, "Opinions and Social Pressure," *Scientific American,* November 1951, 31–5.

    Solomon E. Asch, "Studies of Independence and Conformity: A Minority of One Against a Unanimous Majority," *Psychological Monographs 70,* no. 9 (1956): 1–70.
18. Dan Zarrella, *The Science of Marketing: When to Tweet, What to Post, How to Blog, and Other Proven Strategies* (New York: Wiley, 2013), Kindle edition, Kindle Locations 1127-1128.

19. Hyojung Park and Hyunmin Lee, "Show Us You Are Real: The Effect of Human-Versus-Organizational Presence on Online Relationship Building through Social Networking Sites," *Cyberpsychology, Behavior, and Social Networking 16*, no. 4 (2013): 265–71.

CHAPTER 6: Twitter: To Tweet or Not to Tweet, That is the Question

1. Jay Izso, "Will the Real Twitter (Followers) Please Stand Up?" *Internet Doctor* (blog), June 26, 2013, http://blog.internetdr.com/will-the-real-twitter-followers-please-stand-up/.
2. Y. Koh and Suzanne Vranica, "Twitter Advertisers Say Service Needs More Users," *The Wall Street Journal,* October 5, 2013, http://online.wsj.com/news/articles/SB10001424052702303492504579115753167390832.
3. Hayley Tsukayama, "Twitter Turns 7: Users Send over 400 Million Tweets per Day," *The Washington Post,* March 21, 2013, http://articles.washingtonpost.com/2013-03-21/business/37889387_1_tweets-jack-dorsey-twitter.
4. Johanna Brenner, *Pew Internet: Social Networking (Full Detail)* (commentary), accessed May 22, 2013, http://pewinternet.org/Commentary/2012/March/Pew-Internet-Social-Networking-full-detail.aspx.
5. Shel Israel, *Twitterville: How Businesses Can Thrive in the New Global Neighborhoods* (New York: Penguin Group, 2009).
6. These statistics were retrieved via the very helpful Twitter tracking tool at http://twitaholic.com/.
7. P. W. Ballantine and B. Martin, "Forming Parasocial Relationships in Online Communities," *Advances in Consumer Research 32,* no. 1 (2005).
8. "Stats & Rankings for Beyoncé Knowles," Twitaholic, accessed May 22, 2013, http://twitaholic.com/Beyonce/.

9. Liz Gannes, "Jack Dorsey: Twitter's Not Really Social," *All Things,* January 22, 2012, http://allthingsd.com/20120122/jack-dorsey-twitters-not-really-social/.
10. "Twitter.com" (rankings), Quantcast, http://www.quantcast.com/twitter.com.
11. Dave McCandless, "Chicks Rule? Gender Balance on Social Networking Sites," *Information Is Beautiful* (infographic based on data from Google Ad Planner), May 2012, http://www.informationisbeautiful.net/visualizations/chicks-rule/.
12. "Twitter.com" (rankings), Quantcast, http://www.quantcast.com/twitter.com#!demo&anchor=panel-EDUCATION.
13. Maeve Duggan and Joanna Brenner, *The Demographics of Social Media Users—2012* (report), http://www.pewinternet.org/Reports/2013/Social-media-users.aspx.
14. Mary Madden, Amanda Lenhart, Sandra Cortesi, Urs Gasser, Maeve Duggan, Aaron Smith, and Meredith Beaton, *Teens, Social Media, and Privacy* (report), http://www.pewinternet.org/Reports/2013/Teens-Social-Media-And-Privacy.aspx.
15. Search conducted on May 5, 2013.
16. Dan Zarrella, *The Science of Marketing: When to Tweet, What to Post, How to Blog, and Other Proven Strategies* (New York: Wiley, 2013), Kindle edition, Kindle Locations 667–679.16.
17. Dan Zarrella, "Tweets Between 100 and 115 Characters are More Likely to be ReTweeted" *Dan Zarrella, The Social Media Scientist* (blog), http://danzarrella.com/new-data-tweets-between-100-and-115-characters-are-more-likely-to-be-retweeted.html#
18. Dan Zarrella, *The Science of Marketing: When to Tweet, What to Post, How to Blog, and Other Proven Strategies* (New York: Wiley, 2013), Kindle edition, Kindle Locations 889-890.
19. Ibid, Figure 4.10, "Phrase Please Retweet Gets Four Times More Retweets," Kindle Locations 770-772.
20. Ibid, Kindle Location 766.

CHAPTER 7: Exploring Other Frontiers: Google+, Pinterest, and YouTube

1. Brett, "Google+ In Depth," *Global Web Index Blog* (blog), January 28, 2013, http://www.globalwebindex.net/google-in-depth/.
2. Thomas Watkins, "Suddenly, Google Plus Is Outpacing Twitter to Become the World's Second Largest Social Network," *Business Insider*, May 1, 2013, http://www.businessinsider.com/google-plus-is-outpacing-twitter-2013-5.
3. http://www.plusdemographics.com/country_report.php Retrieved June 4, 2013.
4. As mentioned in Chapter 4, Mike Lovas passed away before the publication of this book. I am grateful to Mike, who read this passage of text before his passing, for giving me the opportunity to include the Psychological Marketing Network on Google+.
5. Thomas Watkins, "Suddenly, Google Plus Is Outpacing Twitter to Become the World's Second Largest Social Network," *Business Insider*, May 1, 2013, http://www.businessinsider.com/google-plus-is-outpacing-twitter-2013-5.
6. John Suler, *Photographic Psychology: Image and Psyche* (Doylestown, PA: True Center Publishing, 2013), http://truecenterpublishing.com/photopsy/article_index.htm.
7. "Photo Psychology," *Wikipedia*, last modified May 31, 2010, http://en.wikipedia.org/wiki/Photo_psychology.
8. Jay Izso, "Men Are from LinkedIn, Women Are from Pinterest . . . Social Media Psychologically Speaking," *Jay Izso, Internet Doctor* (blog), May 28, 2013, http://blog.internetdr.com/men-are-from-linkedin-women-are-from-pinterest-social-media-psychologically-speaking-2/.
9. Maeve Duggan and Joanna Brenner, *The Demographics of Social Media Users—2012* (report), http://www.pewinternet.org/Reports/2013/Social-media-users.aspx.

10. Cooper Smith, "Social Media Demographics: The Surprising Identity of Each Social Network," *Business Insider,* October 18, 2013, http://www.businessinsider.com/a-primer-on-social-media-demographics-2013-9.
11. Erin Ledbetter, "Pinterest Demographic Data: The Marketers Guide to People Who Pin," *Ignite Social Media* (blog), January 24, 2012, http://www.ignitesocialmedia.com/social-networks/pinterest-demographic-data/.
12. http://www.repinly.com/stats.aspx. Retrieved June 11, 2013.
13. Ibid.
14. "YouTube.com" (rankings), Quantcast, accessed June 15, 2013, https://www.quantcast.com/youtube.com.
15. YouTube Official Blog, "Here's to Eight Great Years," May 19, 2013, http://youtube-global.blogspot.com/2013/05/heres-to-eight-years.html. Retrieved June 15, 2013.
16. Nicole McDermott, "Why We're Obsessed with Reality TV," *Greatist,* July 11, 2012, http://greatist.com/happiness/why-were-obsessed-reality-tv.

CHAPTER 8: Social Media: ROI or ROLie?

1. Philip Graves, *Consumer.ology: The Market Research Myth, the Truth about Consumers, and the Psychology of Shopping* (London: Nicholas Brealey Publishing, 2010), Kindle edition, Kindle Locations 601–605.
2. Vasily Klucharev, Ale Smidts, and Guillén Fernández, "Brain Mechanisms of Persuasion: How 'Expert Power' Modulates Memory and Attitudes," *Social Cognitive and Affective Neuroscience 3,* no. 4 (2008): 353–66. doi:10.1093/scan/nsn022.
3. Nielson, *Consumer Trust in Online, Social and Mobile Advertising Grows* (newswire), April 10, 2012, http://www.nielsen.com/us/en/newswire/2012/consumer-trust-in-online-social-and-mobile-advertising-grows.html.

4. Michael Trusov, Randolph E. Bucklin, and Koen H. Pauwels, *Effects of Word-of-Mouth versus Traditional Marketing: Findings from an Internet Social Networking Site* (Robert H. Smith School Research Paper No. RHS 06-065), http://papers.ssrn.com/sol3/papers.cfm?abstract_id=1129351.
5. Barbara Cater, "The Importance of Social Bonds for Communication and Trust in Marketing Relationships in Professional Services," *Management: Journal of Contemporary Management Issues 13*, no. 1 (2008), http://www.questia.com/read/1P3-1969493161.
6. William Arruda, "Get to Page One in Google and Showcase Your Brand," *Forbes,* October 29, 2013, http://www.forbes.com/sites/williamarruda/2013/10/29/get-to-page-1-in-google-and-showcase-your-brand.

CHAPTER 10: What's Next?

1. This has also been referred to as the *online disinhibition effect* in John Suler, "Online Disinhibition Effect," *Cyberpsychology and Behavior* 7, no. 3, 2004.
2. N. M. Incite and Nielsen Holdings N. V., *State of the Media: The Social Media Report* (report), http://www.nielsen.com/content/dam/corporate/us/en/reports-downloads/2012-Reports/The-Social-Media-Report-2012.pdf.
3. A recent survey by Arbitron Inc. and Edison Research on how people are using digital technology has revealed key information on where we are headed in regard to how we access and use social media.

INDEX

A

B

C

D

E

F

G

H

I

K

L

M

N

O

P

R

S

T

Acknowledgments

I am grateful to the team of people who helped to bring this book to life, some of whom directly influenced the production of the book through their hands-on help and some of whom, through their encouragement and support, provided me the motivation to get started, keep going, and finish.

The first person I need to acknowledge is Maggie Lichtenberg, my Book Publishing Coach at Publishing-Options.com, for always offering her tremendous wealth of book marketing experience and vast knowledge. She has guided me through the entire process, helping me find the right people to add to my team and always sharing sound and sage advice to make sure the book has optimal chances for success.

I would also like to thank Suzanne Murray, my editor from StyleMatters. In addition to being a great developmental and copy editor, Suzanne has the patience of a saint. She has not only been my editor, but because of this experience has become my friend. She has made me lists and calendars to help stay on track, and I am eternally grateful for her professional skills, knowledge, and experience as well as her friendship.

I would like to offer a special thank you to Kathi Dunn of Dunn & Associates for creating the cover of *Got Social Mediology?* She had an amazing vision for the project, has been graciously flexible, and is a fantastic designer to work with. Thank you, Kathi!

A debt of gratitude also goes to Alex Charfen, CEO of the Charfen Institute, who told me after speaking at one of his conferences, "You knocked it out of the park!" and then followed that with, "But you will not speak for me again until you write a book." It was the exact impetus I needed to really get this project moving forward. Thank you, Alex!

I would also like to thank friend and colleague Jeff Snell, who is owner of Enlign Business Brokers. Always witty and wise, Jeff has kept me accountable and has encouraged me along the way. I am grateful to Jeff as well for suggesting that we adjust the "talking bubbles" on the front cover from 2-D to 3-D. This was just the design change we needed to bring everything together.

I am both thankful and grateful to my mom and dad. First, they gave me life, which is pretty darn cool; then, they taught me lessons, some of which I learned not from the things they told me, but by watching them in my youth as they interacted with people. Three beliefs I know I have been given from my parents are that there is no such person that is a stranger, always treat people in the right way, and have a sense of humor.

Thank you to my Facebook friends, too, some of whom I have met face to face and many whom I have not. As I have posted about this journey, you have always remained faithful, encouraged me, and made me smile, sometimes even laugh. Regardless of what time of day it was, you always cheered me on during the journey.

I would also like to give a hearty acknowledgment to Philip Graves, author of the book *Consumer.ology*. I have never met Philip face to face, but as a result of social media (specifically LinkedIn), we have moved along the continuum of "know, like, and trust." Philip is not only a colleague, but I also consider him a friend. I look forward to the day when I can shake his hand and buy him his favorite beverage.

Thank you to Stefanie Lazer, for independently editing the book when not on the job as a manuscript editor in the Journals Department of the American Psychological Association. I was so grateful for Stefanie's no-nonsense review, which challenged me on different points of the manuscript and helped me move the book to the place it needed to be. Thank you!

I would also like to offer warm gratitude to Patrick Lilly, owner of the Patrick Lilly Real Estate team in New York City. He is not only a top-tier real estate professional; he is also a top-tier person, whose generosity and kindness toward Linda and me has been amazing. Patrick has given me opportunity after opportunity to get my message out to others, and I am both thankful and grateful for his support and belief in both this project and myself.

I need to also acknowledge Michael Lovas, who tragically passed away in October of 2013. Michael, whom I met through social media, is yet another person whom I never met face to face. Nonetheless, through our phone calls, emails, and social media interactions, we became friends. Michael gratefully contributed to parts of this book and gave me some valuable psychological insights. He will be missed by all of us who are a part of the Psychological Marketing Network on LinkedIn.

I have mentioned her before, but I will mention her again and that is my lovely, talented, and amazing wife, Linda. She is an incredible businessperson, who owns and runs her real estate company Linda Craft and Team, Realtors, in Raleigh. Among all her duties that she performs seven days a week, she has taken time to encourage me, have true faith in the project, and help me see the possibilities. She is more than a wife or a life partner; she is my best friend, at times my most honest critic, but by far my most ardent supporter. This book did not happen without her...and I am forever grateful.

I know that there are so many others I could thank. Please forgive me for not calling you out by name, as it is difficult to include everyone. The truth is that I could probably write a complete book on all the people who have been instrumental in creating *Got Social Mediology?* Please know that I am grateful and thankful to you all for keeping me accountable and for all of your encouragement!

Resources

Getting Started with Social Media

- GCF Learn Free: Social Media (http://www.gcflearnfree.org/socialmedia)
- Social Media Examiner: Getting Started With Social Media: A Resource Guide (http://www.socialmediaexaminer.com/getting-started)

Psychology and Business Books

- *Buyology* by Martin Lindstrom (http://www.martinlindstrom.com/books-by-martin-lindstrom)
- *Consumer.ology* by Philip Graves (http://philipgraves.net/portfolio/consumer-ology)
- *Influence: The Psychology of Persuasion* by Dr. Robert B. Cialdini (http://www.influenceatwork.com/store)

Social Media Books

- *Twitterville: How Businesses Can Thrive in New Global Neighborhoods* by Shel Israel
- *The Science of Marketing: When to Tweet, What to Post, How to Blog, and Other Proven Strategies* by Dan Zarrella (http://danzarrella.com/books)

Journals

- *Cyberpsychology, Behavior, and Social Networking* (http://www.liebertpub.com/overview/cyberpsychology-behavior-brand-social-networking/10)

- *Journal of Consumer Psychology* (http://www.journals.elsevier.com/journal-of-consumer-psychology)
- *Journal of Consumer Research* (http://www.ejcr.org)

Websites and Blogs

- Jay Izso's Blog (http://blog.internetdr.com/) and Website (www.internetdr.com)
- Chris Brogan's Blog (http://www.chrisbrogan.com)
- *Forbes*, Social Media (http://www.forbes.com/social-media)
- Mashable (http://mashable.com)
- Psychological Marketing Network (https://www.linkedin.com/groups/Psychological-Marketing-Network-2271201/about)
- Social Bakers (http://www.socialbakers.com)
- The Social Media Hat (http://www.thesocialmediahat.com)
- Social Media Today (http://socialmediatoday.com)

About the Author

Jay Izso, the Internet Doctor, is a psychological business consultant, social mediologist, speaker, and writer who helps entrepreneurs and small businesses reduce their marketing budget and achieve higher ROI by understanding the psychology of their consumer on social media and beyond. He has a Master's of Science in Experimental Psychology and has taught psychology for more than twenty years, including at Washington State University and North Carolina State University. When he's not busy consulting, engaging on social media, writing, teaching, or speaking, Jay enjoys life as a wine geek, musician, sports fan, and movie buff. He lives in Raleigh, North Carolina, with his wife, Linda Craft, and their two dogs, Katie and Bandit.